The Promise of
Youth Anti-citizenship

The Promise of Youth Anti-citizenship

Race and Revolt in Education

KEVIN L. CLAY AND
KEVIN LAWRENCE HENRY JR.
Editors

UNIVERSITY OF MINNESOTA PRESS
MINNEAPOLIS • LONDON

Copyright 2024 by the Regents of the University of Minnesota

All rights reserved. No part of this publication may be reproduced, stored in a retrieval system, or transmitted, in any form or by any means, electronic, mechanical, photocopying, recording, or otherwise, without the prior written permission of the publisher.

Published by the University of Minnesota Press
111 Third Avenue South, Suite 290
Minneapolis, MN 55401-2520
http://www.upress.umn.edu

ISBN 978-1-5179-1246-8 (hc)
ISBN 978-1-5179-1247-5 (pb)

Library of Congress record available at https://lccn.loc.gov/2023056422

Printed on acid-free paper

The University of Minnesota is an equal-opportunity educator and employer.

Dedicated to my grandparents, Ainsley and Gloria Ashby and Dr. Jether and Clarence Clay, along with all of my other ancestors from Mississippi, to Barbados, to West Africa. I also dedicate it to two wonderful brothers whom I loved dearly: Duval Lowe and Nathan Hannon.

—KEVIN L. CLAY

To my grandmother, Gertrude H. Edwards, and my mother, Rockell E. Henry, whose love and sacrifice keep and propel me. To the people of New Orleans, who are my "South" Star, guiding me toward freedom, joy, and home. To Devon Wade and Elmer Henry Jr., whose force and light continue to illuminate my path. To my father, Kevin L. Henry Sr., intercessor and inspiration, may your indelible legacy continue.

—KEVIN LAWRENCE HENRY JR.

Contents

Acknowledgments   ix

Introduction. Predatory Inclusion in American Democracy: Youth and the Imperative of Anti-citizenship
KEVIN L. CLAY   1

PART I. AND THE CHILDREN WILL LEAD THEM: YOUTH FUGITIVITY AS ANTI-CITIZENSHIP PEDAGOGY

1. Black Youth Refusing: Drapetomania and Neoliberal Education in Post-Katrina New Orleans
KEVIN LAWRENCE HENRY JR.   25

2. Radicalizing Black Child Play, Conspiring in the Familiar Zones
ARIANA DENISE BRAZIER   45

3. Radical Black Joy Is Citizenship
DAMARIS C. DUNN   67

PART II. SEEING THE INVISIBLE: ON YOUTH ANTI-CITIZENSHIP AND THE STRUGGLE FOR THE (UNDER)COMMONS

4. Coloniality and Antiblack Racism in Black Adolescent Girls' Lived Experiences
KARLYN ADAMS-WIGGINS   85

5. Queering the Citizen? Exposing the Myths of Racial Capital Fantasies
DIANA GAMEZ AND DAMIEN M. SOJOYNER — 109

6. Black ~~Youth Organizing~~ for the Destruction of Schooling, the Citizen, and the World
MICHAEL DAVIS — 133

7. We Have Nothing Left to Prove, Yet a Whole New World to Accomplish
CHRISTOPHER R. ROGERS — 163

PART III. "WHO DO YOU LOVE, ARE YOU FOR SURE?" REJECTING CITIZENSHIP'S ASSIMILATIONS

8. Reclaiming the "Mexican Problem": Chicano Youth, Agency, and the Rearticulation of Citizenship
RACHEL F. GÓMEZ AND JULIO CAMMAROTA — 175

9. Unsettling the "Good Citizen": How Narratives of Palestinian Liberation Threatened a Liberal School
LUMA HASAN — 197

10. Enacting Identities of Resistance in Suburban Schools: Latinx Youth and the Possibilities of Anti-citizenship
GABRIEL RODRIGUEZ — 221

Contributors — 241

Index — 243

Acknowledgments

I am deeply indebted to those writers, historians, researchers, orators, activists, and organizers whose words have helped me to gain greater clarity about the world and my place in it, and whose public lives exemplify the kind service to humanity that I strive to emulate. There are too many to name.

Thank you to the chapter contributors for these wonderful and powerful narratives. I am deeply humbled that you each allowed me to harness these words in this collection. Thank you to the young people I've grown with and watched grow in my capacity as a teacher and youth worker, whose dynamism has inspired anything of value in my writing here. The Keimarks, Jasmines, Queens, Shaunas, Jasons, and Eriks of the world—I have more love for you than words can describe. I am always striving to be better at all of this because of what you saw in me that I didn't/don't always see in myself.

A special thank you to my adviser and friend Beth C. Rubin, friend and mentor Rick Ayers, and my friend and intellectual compatriot Ashley Woodson, who served as critical thought partners in this work and whose encouragement and insight were instrumental in informing the development of this volume at the initial stages. Thank you to Bianca Baldridge, Erika Bullock, David C. Turner, Deirdre Dougherty, Karlyn Adams-Wiggins, David Stovall, Freeden Blume Oeur, Chelsea Higgs Wise, and the anonymous reviewers for their words of wisdom, encouragement, and incisive feedback along the way. Thank you to Kevin L. Henry, my coeditor, for stepping up and stepping in for me when I needed support.

Thank you to Renée Roundy, who worked diligently and tirelessly to collate and format this manuscript.

The most important people in my life are my wife, Brittany, and my children, Miles Langston and Hampton Levi. Without my wife and my children, I have no inspiration for this writing beyond the satisfaction of excoriating the empire that I was born into. My parents, Michael and Valerie, my brother and sister, Mike and Khenya, and my in-laws, Darryl and Cecilia, have all been incredibly supportive of me and my work and our family. They have shown me incredible love and caring throughout this life. Thank you.

Lastly, I thank God. Thank you for revealing yourself to me in ways that break from the cultural orthodoxy of Western empire that shroud your true nature of justice, communalism, and love.

—Kevin L. Clay

Perhaps by now it is well established that ideas can come from unexpected places. So too may love. And it is love that keeps me and has kept me afloat and buoyed when ideas and words have escaped me.

To my family—blood and chosen—your love is a force without which I would not be. You all help to give purpose, inspiration, and meaning to my life and my work. To my ancestors, whose blood, strength, and memories lace my being; to my mother, Rockell Henry, my rock, who sacrificed so much in order that I might have; to my father, Kevin Henry Sr., who taught me how to listen to the stories people are trying to tell; to Sybil Huntley; to my sibling-child, Megan; to the Brown, Henry, Sigur, Gex, Smith, Grandison, Davis and Hailey, Pettifoot and Knapper, Howze, DeCuire, Thomas, and Hitchens families—thank you for all of your love, support, and encouragement. To Ryan, thank you for creating a home for me and showing me the contours of love. To the originals, Neil, Kayla, and Devan, thank you for being my Ais since day one, whose support is "second-to-none" and whose friendship exceeds time and space. To Gary, Myron, Kendall, Kuri, Denise, Dell, Theron, Megan, Marlon, David, Aaron, Tevin, Dazmine, RJ, Desiree, DeMarcus, Kadian, Zachary, and Adi—thank you for being intercessors of joy and radical care. I love you all and thank you for loving me.

Acknowledgments xi

I will always remain grateful to my teachers and mentors, especially those who saw my highest potential and made sure I saw it as well: Gloria Ladson-Billings, Carl Grant, Maisha Winn, Adrienne Dixson, Jamel K. Donnor, Colleen Capper, Marvin Lynn, Michael Dantley, Julia Koza, Michael Cunningham, Nghana Lewis, Rosanne Adderley, Mimi Schippers, Kate Drabinski, Constant Serrette, Abbie Fazande, Robert Riley, William Robinson, Larisa Otillio Levin, and Rose Murray.

To my UW colleagues—especially Mollie McQuillan, Brian Burt, Christopher Saldaña, Ain Grooms, Anjalé Welton, Rachelle Winkle-Wagner, Xueli Wang, Erika Bullock, and Rich Halverson—thank you for always indulging my ideas, supporting my work, and being constant light. To Terrance Green, Shameka Powell, Jennifer McCarthy Foubert, Ivory Berry, Cecilia Suarez, Montrischa Williams, Chezare Warren, Dana Maria K. Baldwin, Laura Chávez-Moreno, Bianca Baldridge, La Marr Bruce, and fahima ife—you all have taught me the meaning of study, of friendship, and of tenderness within the academy.

To my students, thank you for your patience and pushing. You all inspire me daily to do the necessary intellectual and justice-focused work. Mark White, thank you for always holding it down.

To my coeditor, Kevin Clay, thank you for the opportunity to be in community with you and for the opportunity to see this to fruition; and to those who contributed so mightily to this volume, thank you for your brilliance, for bearing witness, and for your commitment to study, struggle, and love.

Finally, thank you to the Most High, whose radical, unapologetic love "sees me," keeps me, and moves me . . . may I forever know the joys of being used by you.

—KEVIN LAWRENCE HENRY JR.

INTRODUCTION

Predatory Inclusion in American Democracy

Youth and the Imperative of Anti-citizenship

KEVIN L. CLAY

Black youth and other youth of color (particularly poor youth) have been predatorily included in American democracy, (often) bearing the title of "citizen" (e.g., "undocumented citizen") but experiencing a civic existence that has normalized (and required) their suffering to preserve conditions of exploitation that are beneficial for both the state and capital. In her 2019 book *Race for Profit: How Banks and the Real Estate Industry Undermined Black Homeownership*, Keeanga-Yamahtta Taylor uses the term *predatory inclusion* to describe conditions set forth by a series of federal policies throughout the late 1960s and 1970s ostensibly intended to stimulate greater access to quality housing for Black Americans. Aside from their motivation to exit what were for many cramped, structurally compromised, rat-infested, and overall dreadful rental conditions, Taylor notes that poor Black urban dwellers' desire for homeownership was fundamentally attached to a more universal notion of "homeownership [as] a pathway to political, cultural, and economic citizenship in the United States."[1]

Predatory inclusion describes how HUD/FHA (Housing and Urban Development and Federal Housing Administration) incentivized terms for the real-estate, insurance, and banking industries for the sale of decaying single-family urban residences to interested and desperate Black homebuyers by offering guarantees to fully reimburse mortgage lenders in the event that urban rent-to-owners defaulted on payments and went into foreclosure (as this coalition of private industry predicted and hoped for). Along with superficial oversight and enforcement of antidiscrimination and civil rights law, these practices incubated conditions for the real-estate industry and lenders (including Black lenders) to conspire in ways that led to Black folks living in the worst, most dilapidated housing under financing terms that were more expensive (e.g., higher interest rate loans) and that punitively targeted them for foreclosure compared to their white suburban-living counterparts. It also describes the disingenuous position of the federal government in the postredlining housing market to extend Black "citizens" the same opportunity for fair and quality housing that it had guaranteed white Americans for decades under the FHA and GI Bill. Creating a "risk-free" and oversight-free environment for banking and real estate in contexts where Black residents were presumed to be inherently risky investments, the FHA disincentivized the private sector's commitment to providing fair ownership terms or homes of quality condition to Black residents because if residents defaulted on their payments for their overpriced homes (as many did), the federal government would cover the cost, while Black residents suffered foreclosure. Taylor concludes, "The concept of predatory inclusion . . . captures the failure of racial liberalism and its premise that inclusion into American democracy through the vehicles of citizenship, law, and free market capitalism could finally produce equality for its Black citizens."[2]

Taylor's remarks serve as a rebuttal against the common assertion that those who have been pushed to the margins by a state invested in racial capitalism can be made whole through congenial civic apparatuses designed by the very same state. It is this common sense of citizenship and its incumbent theory of change that I push back against in my offering of anti-citizenship as a lens through which to view youth positionality and emancipatory struggle in so-called American democracy. Youth embody anti-citizenship both in the ways that they experience pervasive antagonisms across domains of social, political, and economic life and in their deviations from what has been typically regarded as "good citizenship." I argue that, far from being a problem that demands correction, such deviations offer hope and promise for this generation. I regard these youth as enacting anti-citizenship when threatening the maintenance of a social

Introduction 3

order that functionally harms them and their communities and when participating in radical reimaginations and rearticulations of a society and world in which they can be legitimate citizens. The legitimacy of citizenship is premised on the assumption that the state is a judicious promoter of social welfare. While social contract theory suggests there is an unspoken agreement between the state and citizens who consent to be governed in order to promote the welfare of all, pervasive and enduring patterns of social suffering in society illuminate that such an agreement, if it even exists, is reserved for whites, wealthy, and propertied individuals, leaving those who fall outside of this scope to confront a state that is increasingly hostile to their presence and uses violence to hold them down.[3] To this end, Charles W. Mills suggests that what masquerades as the social contract is in fact a racial contract—a contract he implores us to analyze if we are to expose harmfully reproductive social arrangements. He says:

> The point of analyzing the nonideal contract is not to ratify it but to use it to explain and expose the inequities of the actual non-ideal polity and to help us to see through the theories and moral justifications offered in defense of them.[4]

Heeding Mills, this volume's discussion of the anti-citizen and anti-citizenship reveal that notions of U.S. citizenship imbuing images of proverbial melting pots and narratives of linear social progress belie a society that has never existed for Black, Latino, and other youth of color, particularly those who are undocumented, experience poverty, or live in communities under constant police repression.

Therefore, part of this volume's work is to expose the fragility and, perhaps, meaninglessness of nominal designations of citizenship status in the United States for youth who struggle against the weight of U.S. empire's persecutions.[5] In this way, anti-citizenship reflects an ascribed status—one that youth are often keenly aware of and respond to in ways that may at times further illuminate this status. Unpacking these responses is the other part of this volume's work—that is, understanding how youth themselves negotiate and exercise anti-citizenship. For

Introduction

foreign-born noncitizen youth—so-called illegal aliens and stateless youth—the absence of nominal status thus becomes a justification for the stripping of basic rights so that the state and its for-profit agents might inflict violence and violate their human rights with impunity.[6] Yet even noncitizen youths participate in political subversion, resist oppression, and challenge us to reexamine the very notion of democratic subjectivity.[7]

This book is, first, an effort to critically reexamine the foundational rights, freedoms, and protections that belie "democratic citizenship" for many youths. Second, it will grapple with and explicate the various ways in which youth themselves negotiate and exercise anti-citizenship as a politics of resistance, subversion, and refusal within communities, compulsory institutions, and social organizations. Several recent critical ethnographies have heightened our collective understanding of the complexities many youths living or incarcerated in the United States experience navigating the social world within and against their designations of citizenship.[8] With this collection, the editors of this volume hope to both raise and answer the question "What can youth anti-citizenship teach us about the projects of liberation and abolition?"

Citizenship and Schooling

In *Citizenship and Social Class,* British sociologist T. H. Marshall offers a classic theory of citizenship premised on civil, political, and social rights—a theory that places citizenship under the microscope of social class divisions. Evaluating citizenship according to the heuristic established by Marshall, contemporaries like Evelyn Nakano Glenn force us to distinguish between formal citizenship and substantive citizenship, arguing that formal "rights" are a poor threshold for citizenship.[9] It is how people experience justice, equality of due process, the right to exercise political power, and the right to equitable access to public educational goods at the local level that reveal inherent and predictable differences in substantive citizenship, along social class lines. Though historians and philosophers have waxed romantically about U.S. educational reform's preoccupation with citizenship and democracy at the end of Reconstruction, schooling has never been a pathway for either formal or substantive civic inclusion for nonwhite children.[10]

Introduction 5

Citizenship is a central preoccupation of contemporary educational theory and research, addressed through multiple disciplinary and theoretical perspectives. The National Council for the Social Studies states that "a primary goal of public education is to prepare students to be engaged and effective citizens," defining an "effective citizen" as "one who has the knowledge, skills, and attitudes required to assume the 'office of citizen' in our democratic republic."[11] Positioned by theorists and practitioners alike as deeply connected to the mission of schooling in a democratic society, "philosophers, historians, and political scientists have long debated which conceptions of citizenship would best advance democracy."[12]

The core purpose of the first public schools founded by Horace Mann in Massachusetts in 1837 was to inculcate "Protestant-republican" ideology—nonsectarian Christian moral values and citizenship knowledge for participating in bourgeois democracy.[13] As the model spread to other states, schools were free, locally funded and governed, and open to all white children. As education became more urbanized in the late nineteenth century, conflict over access to education and the purposes of education were common. The structure of schooling was dominated more and more by business theorists, creating the factory-model school. Citizenship preparation came to be identified as preparation of youth for passive roles in the workplace, defined by the class and race of the student.

The history of U.S. schooling has made it clear that these institutions were not meant for communities who were colonized, enslaved, or subject to genocide. This included Black people, Indigenous people, and immigrants from Asia and Latin America. Many of the stories of marginalization concern the struggle to gain access to U.S. schools. But there is a long history of resistance and rejection of the homogenizing project of school envisioned by Horace Mann.

For instance, in 1895 nineteen Hopi men were imprisoned in Alcatraz for resisting the U.S. government's demand that they send their children to public boarding schools.[14] So urgent was the project of homogenizing youth citizenship behavior that the rejection of schooling was an offense punishable by prison. Further critique of the core project of U.S. schools was evident in Carter G. Woodson's *The Mis-education of the Negro* (1933). He exposed how schools structured inequality: "The same educational process which inspires and stimulates the oppressor with the thought that he is everything and has accomplished everything worthwhile depresses and crushes at the same time the spark or genius of the Negro by making him feel that his race does not amount to much and never will measure up to the standards of other peoples."[15] And, in contrast to such a smothering view of education, he proposed that "real education means to inspire people to live more abundantly, to learn to begin with life as they find it and make it better."[16] William H. Watkins traces how education for Black subservience was established by white educators, driven by the same ideological framing of civilizing the so-called savages as seen in the project of Richard Henry Pratt at the Carlisle Indian School.[17]

Educational anthropology focusing on the ways that social reproductive processes were instantiated in daily practice provided a new lens onto youth resistance to participation in schooling. Paul Willis's ethnography of working-class youth in an industrial town in England, for example, explained his young male participants' resistant behavior not as failure but as an expression of agency, of their self-preparation for the working-class jobs ahead of them, for activism in unions and survival strategies.[18] Jay Gillen, through his work in Baltimore with Bob Moses's Algebra Project, explores how schools introduce technologies for the production of accepted social purposes, so-called citizenship development. But, he argues, the social and political purposes of school are contested by Black students.[19] What is regarded by school authorities as problematic is actually an exercise in resistance, in developing an alternate vision of society.

Given the ways coloniality and capitalism organize U.S. society, particularly in schooling, it is no surprise that the project of citizenship (development) is a site of contention and struggle. While T. H. Marshall was much more optimistic about this disjuncture between social class and citizenship resolving itself, scholars like Glenn and the authors in this collection look at the struggles being waged by the most civically maligned young folks in American schools and community-based organizations for their optimism. Those with outsider status—the oppressed, colonized, imprisoned—have sometimes struggled to get into the larger polity. Other times they have chosen to reject it, to build an undercommons that sustains their cultural heritage, material needs, and political struggle.

Introduction

ANTI-CITIZENSHIP

Where citizenship in the U.S. context is commonly defined by legal status within the nation and typical notions of "the good citizen" invoke characteristics of civility, patriotism, and lawfulness, behaviors like volunteerism and electoral participation and, above all, faith in the U.S. Constitution and systems of government to be responsive to the concerns of one's self, family, and community, the anti-citizen and anti-citizenship cast doubt on the legitimacy of all of this. "The good citizen," conceived in Western capitalism, also submits to *Homo economicus,* neoliberal, moral strivings, while the anti-citizen, cast outside of the official economy and society, sets out and strives to build a meaningful life against the establishment.

Prior conceptions of anti-citizenship. Several researchers—many of whom write under the disciplinary umbrellas of organizational and social psychology—introduce formulations of the anti-citizen in scholarly work that often speak to a lacking—morally, civically, and behaviorally—in the constitution of such individuals who occupy spaces within society or professional organizations.[20] Framings of the anti-citizen and anti-citizenship have also evolved under the disciplinary umbrellas of history and cultural studies. David Matless, for example, explores formulations of the (good) citizen and anti-citizen in the geospatial regulatory politics of English countryside leisure during and after World War II.[21] Read by lawmakers as a distinction in morality, the anti-citizen (or cockney) was positioned as an uncouth "urban" rule-breaker disrupting the tranquility of the countryside (e.g., playing loud, "negroid" jazz music), while the citizen demonstrated appropriate middle-class stylizations (e.g., discreet, civil, clean). Matless notes how these depictions drove land-use policy and planning in ways that sought to deny anti-citizens access to public spaces, writing:

> Plans for popular citizenship reach out to the citizen yet also exclude, promoting landscape as public cultural space through rules of conduct which exclude certain members of the public. This was a moral geography posing the question, what kind of public space for what kind of public?[22]

8   Introduction

Common across scholarly theorizations of the anti-citizen is a consensus that certain (mis)behaviors enacted by the individual relegate her to a status of anti-citizen; in other words, these behaviors transform someone who was previously a citizen in good standing into an anti-citizen.

These anti-citizenship behaviors also disrupt the well-oiled, business-as-usual functioning of the organization or society and perhaps might even corrupt others, with the potential, if taken up en masse, to unravel the very fabric that holds together the organizational or societal status quo. For instance, Scott A. Myers discusses what he calls "student anti-citizenship classroom behavior," describing "intentional" acts of defiance in which a student engages to disrupt a classroom:

> Instructors and students have expectations for how students should not communicate in the classroom, namely because these messages and behaviors can be destructive or disruptive to the classroom environment.... *Student anti-citizenship classroom behavior* . . . we consider to be the verbal and nonverbal communication behaviors in which students intentionally engage for a specific reason, regardless of whether it is articulated to their instructors or their classmates, that disrupt the flow or function of the learning environment.[23]

Myers goes on to offer a typology of student anti-citizenship classroom behavior: participatory (or contributing to classroom discussions in a disruptive manner, including "arguing with instructors" or "dominating class discussion" or "not participating"), technological (i.e., using devices for nonclass purposes), physical (i.e., students moving their bodies in ways that "distract" other students like "leaving class early" or "fidgeting or acting restless"), and etiquette (i.e., violating "classroom norms" and "basic courteous behavior" like "eating in class" or showing up smelling of "alcohol or smoke"). Observing similar conduct in their ethnographic works, scholars like Douglas E. Foley and Paul Willis note that such behaviors among working-class and poor youth, which typically positioned them as failures, were in fact acts of political agency, as classroom disruptions and resistance formed the basis of their rejection of capitalist culture.[24]

Introduction 9

The robust nature of Myers's typology suggests that there are very few ways for any student to completely avoid descending into anti-citizen status, yet it is highly unlikely that educators view or treat all their students and their violations as equally "disruptive and destructive."[25] In fact, research on school discipline consistently finds that despite racial parity in violating classroom norms, students of color are overwhelmingly disproportionately meted out formal punishments like suspension and expulsion.[26] When considered against the disproportionality phenomenon or the many other ways that race factors significantly into classroom level disparities, it is hard to conceive that the anti-citizen is the sole architect of his own alienation.[27]

Anti-citizenship in this volume. This volume seeks to shed light on the ways in which social and institutional structures relegate individuals to the status of anti-citizen. Indeed, this work contends that anti-citizenship is an ascribed status of racial capitalism both maintained and enforced by the very state under which they have nominally been declared citizens. In this way, those who have been relegated to anti-citizens were never in good standing with the state, despite often endlessly working to conform to the conventions of Western respectability and neoliberal moral strivings.[28] Indeed, the irony of citizenship for these youth is reflected in their being compelled to verbally pledge faith in and allegiance to the United States by the use of police force and under the threat of legal penalty.[29] Strangely, the ("undocumented") noncitizen faces the same coercion, despite being denied even symbolic access to the rights nominal status affords.[30]

Unlike Myers's and others' pejorative theorizations of the anti-citizen, I argue that a disruptive and, indeed, destructive approach is the only way for those who have been relegated to the status of anti-citizen to destabilize and expose the arrangements of the nonideal polity.[31] The intentional acts of subversion exercised by the anti-citizen so agitate the legitimized citizen because they force the legitimized citizen to bear witness to the oppression that has been normalized and institutionalized in zero-sum favor of his class. This volume seeks to further explore how anti-citizenship functions in relation to freedom, self-determination, and social gestalt—and against imperialism, orientalism, racism, anti-Blackness, sexism, capitalism, and neoliberalism—to undermine the reproduction of social and economic arrangements.[32] It must also be said that while such an orientation can create the space from which liberation projects might spring forth, individual, aesthetic-performative acts of counterculture can be co-opted and mislead radical energies back into white-supremacist, capitalist reproduction and away from the work of calculated and collective struggle. And although the anti-citizen will never be in good standing with the reactionary establishment, it has been permissible and effective for some members of the maligned class to be absorbed into the ruling class or capitalist class to legitimize the veneer of democracy and meritocracy that conceals the reproduction of social arrangements.

For this reason, anti-citizen(ship) should not be understood as an individual status defined solely by phenotypic race or any other identity marker, nor should it be regarded as a fixed political subjectivity; rather, it should be treated as a collective condition of subaltern struggle, revealed through evolving and embodied antagonistic relationships to the state and through acts of subversion, departure, and resistance intent to waylay exploitation, white supremacy, and other forms of oppression. As forms of oppression inevitably evolve to conceal their true nature, so too one would expect the space occupied by and the forms of dissidence engaged by anti-citizens to evolve coincidently. Although it is the position of the editors not to circumscribe the theorization of anti-citizenship within a set of typologies, this volume's formulation of anti-citizenship draws on critical theory and radical histories of material struggle to conceptualize anti-citizenship as a subaltern form of agency and collective practice.[33] Such theorizations often do the necessary work of exposing the fragile, reactionary, liberal, and, ultimately, socially reproductive nature of what I am calling "good citizenship" while simultaneously illuminating the decidedly political, radical, and dissident nature of actions that point toward liberation and life. Domingo Morel's juxtaposition of the civic versus that which can be considered "political" is instructive here as a symbol of this distinction.[34] He writes that "'Civic' is a safe word. It

Introduction

suggests public action undertaken through approved venues and within the confines of long-standing public agendas. 'Political' is a more charged term."[35] The supposed virtue of the "good citizen" is his conformity to "civil" democratic processes of engagement within the scope of allowable discursive and ideological frameworks often reflected in the politics of respectability.[36] However, the political actions of the anti-citizen necessarily betray the order imposed under these frameworks.

Damien M. Sojoyner's "Black Radicals Make for Bad Citizens" is also instructive, as he describes the reactionary ways in which educational policy has historically worked to avert and immobilize Black revolutionary groundswell by preemptively foreclosing and actively disrupting Black proletarian opportunities to advance self-determination through grassroots organizing in schools.[37] Sojoyner describes coordinated state neutralization efforts in 1960s Los Angeles surrounding the issuance of the *Youth Problems and Needs Report* by the city's Welfare Planning Council. Authored by powerful members of the city elite, the report was an attempt to quell rising Black political militancy in the face of white mob violence, police repression, and structural poverty. The report spawned several forms of reactionary state efforts, one of them being a policy that moved cops into the classroom with police officers teaching what were billed as "civics education" classes.

Schools served as a common space for Black students to meet and organize, which made them a battleground. Sojoyner's review of archival curriculum documents reveals that lessons being taught in these classes overstated the legal authority of police to regulate the lives of people, framed the legal system and state as unbiased, and heavily implied that good citizenship was concomitant to unquestioning subservience to law enforcement. Efforts were even made to get students to incriminate themselves and their families through classwork activities that surveyed students on their own and their family's views of law enforcement and involvement in criminal activity: the "good citizen" in training.

Similarly, Robert L. Allen's account of antecedent events leading to the March on Washington corroborate that the project of good citizenship seeks to cannibalize radicalism. He writes:

Grassroots leaders talked about marching on Washington and shutting the city down until blacks were granted full equality. But this militant sentiment was quickly co-opted by the Kennedy Administration and the liberal coalition in the Democratic party. . . . Thus, the March on Washington, which drew over 250,000 participants, became a summer picnic held in honor of John Kennedy and his civil rights bill, which blacks were led to believe was the answer to their prayers.[38]

Actions taken underneath the banner of good citizenship masquerade civic virtue on the front end and destabilize transformational political action on the back end. In this way, the government, private and philanthropic sectors, and others whose interests it serves to preserve civil society's veneer of civility can safely advocate for the civic engagement of diverse coalitions without having to contend with the ramifications of what the political engagement of the anti-citizen might portend.

Anti-citizenship destabilizes liberal-democratic conceptions of good citizenship that suggest, for instance, that "Black communities would improve if" Black people voted in greater numbers, showed up to city council meetings to let their voices be heard, banded together to clean up a park or form a neighborhood watch, formed or embraced nonprofits to deliver direct services in areas where the government falls short, cooperated with law enforcement to root out criminals, or worked harder, practiced greater morality, and valued education. The logic follows that if these traits of supposed good citizens were exercised by a critical mass of marginalized communities, good civic institutions would reveal themselves (i.e., better schools, parks, policing, and a tangential influx of private capital) on par with the experience many white communities enjoy. Despite the fact that many Black communities have in the past and continue to place faith in these mechanisms of change, to no avail, this citizenship discourse problematically presupposes the benevolence of the current system.[39]

Other narratives of good citizenship that offer it as a mechanism of change embrace a view that relies on the need for only some (e.g., the "Talented Tenth") to rise into a higher economic status and placates expectations of a fundamental shift in structures that reproduce race and

Introduction 13

class.[40] It favors the creation of a Black middle class that is equivalent to the comprador bourgeoisie in traditional colonialism. The success stories that emerge are designed to keep the great mass of the oppressed in place and to expend the energy and passion of reformers on projects that fail to challenge the fundamental contradiction of colonial oppression. The promise and hope of youth anti-citizenship rests in its ability to expose the fallacy of this template—to illuminate lived disjunctures experienced by youths who, for good reason, have never been able to trust that behaving as a "good citizen" would ensure their own or their families' access to equal rights, safety, protection, and inclusion in so-called U.S. democracy.[41] Such an orientation suggests that the oppressed cannot wait to be allowed into small spaces in the political economy as it exists, but rather that they need to imagine and build new economics, new social relations, new political power, that would actually make it possible for these communities to survive and thrive—economically, culturally, and politically.

The promise and hope of youth anti-citizenship rests in the possibilities that spring forth when youth engage so-called taboo forms of agency and collective practice that undermine the functional reproduction of racial capitalism, anti-Blackness, and structural racism in their own lives and communities. And it gestures toward the possibility of meaningful solutions—viable economic projects, engaging community institutions, life that is secure and joyful—that can be worked out from below, through empowered communities. And finally, the promise and hope of youth anti-citizenship rests in actions that advance new renderings of social arrangements that restore honor and dignity to the most maligned.

Outline of the Book

This volume is divided into three parts, each with distinct yet overlapping epistemological goals that interpret anti-citizenship and use it as a frame of analysis to advance applied and theoretical understandings of youth positionality, political contestation, and liberatory ways forward. Chapters include historiographical works, extended reflections on field experiences, and research in schools, communities, community organizations, and youth programs. All chapters directly address one or more of the following three central questions: How are youth of color positioned as anti-citizens within particular community and organizational contexts? How do youths and educators exercise anti-citizenship as a politics of resistance, subversion, and refusal within communities, compulsory institutions, and social organizations? What does and what can youth anti-citizenship contribute to the project of subaltern liberation?

Part I, "And the Children Will Lead Them: Youth Fugitivity as Anti-citizenship Pedagogy," offers chapters that explore how school-aged youth and older youth carve out and create counterspaces within and against institutions that attempt to lock them into hegemonic destinies. In these spaces, youth anti-citizens upend the taken-for-granted arrangements they are presented through problematizing the existing social order and creating new spaces in which the pedagogies and practices of creativity, play, imagination, and inquiry serve as the ark of refuge for legitimate citizenship and liberation. Kevin Lawrence Henry Jr.'s chapter, "Black Youth Refusing: Drapetomania and Neoliberal Education in Post-Katrina New Orleans," opens Part I. Relying on the narratives of Black youth in post-Katrina New Orleans, his chapter links the resistances and refusals of Black youth within the charter school experiment to their enslaved ancestors who refused and resisted enslavement. He argues that the custodial powers of whiteness both then and now were concerned with the narrowing of Black humanity, freedom, and participation in democracy. Henry frames current Black youth resistance using the white fictive notion of "drapetomania," which was a purported mental condition that caused enslaved Africans to flee and resist their enslavers. As such, Black youth refusals of neoliberalism locate them as anti-citizens, who (re)imagine an otherwise world. His chapter concludes that such refusals and reimaginings disrupt the neoliberal social order and provide critical guidance on educational justice initiatives.

Ariana Denise Brazier's chapter, "Radicalizing Black Child Play, Conspiring in the Familiar Zones," theorizes how Black child play enacts a radical subjectivity within "the Black Ghetto." Using school- and community-based ethnographic fieldwork, Brazier identifies how familiar zones within the Black Ghetto manifest the horizontal worlds of sociality and agency between Black children and their larger communities. Within these zones, children "confuse the adult order" and bolster their own subsect of children's culture. These shifting performances and scripts between institutions and zones reinforce the sagacity and reveal a double consciousness that children possess as they maintain the boundaries of their familiar zones. Responding directly to the questions of how Black youth are positioned as anti-citizens, and how their anti-citizenship contributes to the project of subaltern liberation, Brazier argues that Black children learn how to resist the associated constraints and debilitation of hegemonic childhood and citizen scripts as they engage a form of cultural and social criticism and knowledge exchange within these zones, frequently masked as culturally informed play. Essentially, in these zones, Black children establish alternatives to their structurally unjust realities as they develop the skills necessary to demand and advocate through play.

Damaris C. Dunn's chapter, "Radical Black Joy Is Citizenship," closes Part I. This chapter centers Black girl anti-citizens who often lie furthest on the periphery. The author looks to historical iterations of Black joy in literature, art, and music as the goalpost for world-making as they wrestle with the precarity of Black girls' futures in the face of capitalism's death knell. Black girls are the architects of radical Black futures free from pain and suffering in a postabolitionist world where capitalism and the carceral state no longer exist. According to Black girls, radical Black joy is their birthright, a reimagined existence where they are full citizens of a society in which they routinely experience dignity, love, and care.

Chapters in Part II, "Seeing the Invisible: On Youth Anti-citizenship and the Struggle for the (Under)Commons," theorize anti-citizenship, giving voice to historical and contemporary narratives of youth that explicate the race/ism–capitalism nexus and the human–Black dichotomy. These authors ask us to grapple with notions of citizenship, race, and political economy to gain a deeper understanding of anti-citizenship and proffer ways liberation must move forward in light of their findings. In doing so, they reveal the dilemma of pursuing social gestalt as a project of restoring the commons (communalism) versus pursuing a posture of societal abjection and plotting its ruin. Opening Part II, "Coloniality and Antiblack Racism in Black Adolescent Girls' Lived Experiences,"

16   Introduction

finds Karlyn Adams-Wiggins arguing that it is necessary to understand the role of coloniality and antiblack racism in structuring Black youths' social environment. This chapter demonstrates this point through analysis of interviews with six Black middle-school girls in East Texas, revealing how girls experienced being positioned as Black and its relationship with constructions of anti-citizenship. Adams-Wiggins argues that the neoliberal iteration of capitalism and its refusal to recognize anything beyond the individual insists on individual-level explanations of racism as an exclusively interpersonal (and not economic) ill. Adams-Wiggins compels us to see that any press to upend the racial/colonial order must address capitalism, as she argues that antiblackness and coloniality originate within the capitalist mode of production.

Diana Gamez and Damien M. Sojoyner's chapter, "Queering the Citizen? Exposing the Myths of Racial Capital Fantasies," engages with anti-citizenship through their reflections on the impact of the 1980s Salvadorean migration into South Central Los Angeles, set in motion by the Reagan administration's invasion into El Salvador. This chapter troubles the very notion of citizenship at a moment when "pathways to citizenship" have become dominant narratives to ameliorate structural problems that are imbricated within the citizenship process itself. Drawing on the frameworks of "racial capitalism" and "queering of ethnicity," Gamez and Sojoyner demonstrate the pitfalls and limitations of citizenship and reveal natural fissures within the configuration of citizenship that have been made apparent by Salvadoran youth who refuse to abide by processes of civility. "Queering the Citizen" seeks to address the interlocked systems of power that work hand-in-hand with inclusion tropes that enact state violence.

In the penultimate chapter in Part II, "Black ~~Youth~~ Organizing for the Destruction of Schooling, the Citizen, and the World," Michael Davis utilizes Afropessimism to (re)think the ways in which the (non)ontological position of Blackness permanently denies Blackness "citizenship" and argues that Black (non)existence is always already "anti-citizen." To further examine and theorize anti-citizenship, this chapter draws on data from a qualitative study that examined the ways in which Black ~~youth organizers~~ in American schools resisted not only anti-Black school violence but the structure of schooling itself. Theoretically, this chapter offers insight

Introduction 17

in regard to how we might understand antischooling as a branch of anti-citizenship and what a project of antihumanity might consist of as we strive to "destroy the world" and get free in a worldly and human context that denies Black agentic capacity.

Christopher R. Rogers's timely and concise chapter, "We Have Nothing Left to Prove, Yet a Whole New World to Accomplish," offers a prescient conclusion to Part II as Rogers sits in dialogue with Black studies about its relationship to Black struggle. Acknowledging both the importance of critique and its limitations as a solitary site of struggle, he advocates for anti-citizenship within the multiplicity of what he calls "freedom experiments" that seek to disrupt, resist, escape, refuse, and transform the anti-Black world order.

Part III, "'Who Do You Love, Are You for Sure?' Rejecting Citizenship's Assimilations," includes chapters that explore the cultural politics of assimilation and integrationism for youth and educator anti-citizens. Each chapter forces us to examine the excruciating discomfort youth experience as they are compelled by schools and other state institutions into citizenship's assimilationist rituals and compulsory integration projects that seek to rehabilitate and proliferate the United States' global image of melting pot diversity. Through these chapters, authors reveal anti-citizens refusing their role in imperialist fantasies of harmonious colonization. Rachel F. Gómez and Julio Cammarota enter this conversation with "Reclaiming the 'Mexican Problem': Chicano Youth, Agency, and the Rearticulation of Citizenship," a chapter that historiographically traces the legislated violence of assimilationist U.S. policy formations and the colonial rhetorics attached to them that were aimed at subordinating and exploiting Chicano people. Examining the lineage of various institutional projects behind the "Mexican Problem" discourse that served to justify these policy measures, Gómez and Cammarota find that Chicano youth movements indeed have posed a problem for the white-supremacist system. Chicano youth have perpetually resisted cultural genocide and colonial educational policy to reclaim racial and ethnic identities against the imposed imperialist, colonial order.

Luma Hasan reflects on her experience as a critical educator in her chapter, "Unsettling the 'Good Citizen': How Narratives of Palestinian Liberation Threatened a Liberal School." Hasan recounts the many and various ways in which she and her students were compelled by school leaders to submit to the school's tokenizing diversity agenda and the reactionary hostility they encountered when their discursive and pedagogical offerings critiqued the U.S. structure and affirmed Palestinian liberation. Hasan offers a take on decolonizing classrooms as the way forward out of the reactionary liberal bind that schools impose.

Finally, in his chapter "Enacting Identities of Resistance in Suburban Schools: Latinx Youth and the Possibilities of Anti-citizenship," Gabriel Rodriguez examines how Latinx youth attending a majority white high school struggle with racial and ethnic identification. Rodriguez's chapter points to the complexities of identity formation within and against the structure of imposed whiteness and how Latinx youth construct oftentimes-competing understandings of racial and ethnic representation and authenticity, against which they evaluate their peers. Rodriguez's analysis situates these complicated identity struggles as survival strategies within the context of a white-supremacist schooling structure. He argues that schools must confront their own ethnocentric and deficit-based frameworks that hold Latinx students captive to a white gaze.

NOTES

1. Keeanga-Yamahtta Taylor, *Race for Profit: How Banks and the Real Estate Industry Undermined Black Homeownership* (Chapel Hill: University of North Carolina Press, 2019), 30.

2. Taylor, *Race for Profit*, 8.

3. Walter Benjamin, "Critique of Violence," in *Walter Benjamin: Selected Writings,* vol. 1, *1913–1926,* ed. Marcus Bullock and Michael W. Jennings, 236–52 (1921; Boston: Harvard University Press, 2004).

4. Charles W. Mills, *The Racial Contract* (Ithaca, N.Y.: Cornell University Press, 2014), 5.

5. Sally Bonet, *Meaningless Citizenship: Iraqi Refugees and the Welfare State* (Minneapolis: University of Minnesota Press, 2022).

6. Tendayi Bloom, "The Business of Noncitizenship," *Citizenship Studies* 19, no. 8 (2015): 892–906, https://doi.org/10.1080/13621025.2015.1110283; David Weissbrodt and Michael Divine, "Unequal Access to Human Rights: The Categories of Noncitizenship," *Citizenship Studies* 19, no. 8 (2015): 870–91, https://doi.org/10.1080/13621025.2015.1110282.

Introduction 19

7. Soo Ah Kwon, "Deporting Cambodian Refugees: Youth Activism, State Reform, and Imperial Statecraft," *positions: east asia cultures critique* 20, no. 3 (2012): 737–62.

8. Aimee Meredith Cox, *Shapeshifters: Black Girls and the Choreography of Citizenship* (Durham, N.C.: Duke University Press, 2015); Sabina E. Vaught, *Compulsory: Education and the Dispossession of Youth in a Prison School* (Minneapolis: University of Minnesota Press, 2017).

9. Evelyn Nakano Glenn, "Constructing Citizenship: Exclusion, Subordination, and Resistance," *American Sociological Review* 76, no. 1 (2011): 1–24.

10. Benjamin Justice, "Schooling as a White Good," *History of Education Quarterly* 63, no. 2 (2023): 154–78.

11. National Council for the Social Studies, *Expectations of Excellence: Curriculum Standards for Social Studies* (Washington, D.C.: National Council for the Social Studies, 1994), 3.

12. Joel Westheimer and Joseph Kahne, "What Kind of Citizen? The Politics of Educating for Democracy," *American Educational Research Journal* 41, no. 2 (2004): 238.

13. Joanne M. Marshall, "Common Schools Movement," *Education Publications* (2012): 67, http://lib.dr.iastate.edu/edu_pubs/67.

14. Matthew Sakiestewa Gilbert, *Education beyond the Mesas: Hopi Students at Sherman* (Lincoln: University of Nebraska Press, 2010).

15. Carter Godwin Woodson, *The Mis-education of the Negro* (Associated Publishers, 1933), xiii.

16. Woodson, *Mis-education of the Negro,* 29.

17. William H. Watkins, *The White Architects of Black Education: Ideology and Power in America, 1865–1954* (New York: Teachers College Press, 2001); Herbert M. Kliebard, *The Struggle for the American Curriculum, 1893–1958* (New York: Routledge, 2004); R. H. Pratt, "Proceedings of the National Conference of Charities and Corrections" (Denver, Colo., 1892), https://carlisleindian.dickinson.edu/sites/all/files/docs-resources/CIS-Resources_1892-PrattSpeech.pdf.

18. Paul Willis, *Learning to Labour: How Working-Class Kids Get Working-Class Jobs* (Farnborough, U.K.: Saxon House, 1977).

19. Jay Gillen, *Educating for Insurgency: The Roles of Young People in Schools of Poverty* (Oakland, Calif.: AK Press, 2014).

20. Scott A. Myers, "Exploring College Student Anti-citizenship Behavior: An Alternative Form of Classroom Misbehavior," National Communication Association, October 1, 2015, https://www.natcom.org/communication-currents/exploring-college-student-anti-citizenship-behavior-alternative-form; Scott A. Myers et al., "Assessing College Student Use of Anti-citizenship Classroom Behavior: Types, Reasons, and Association with Learning Outcomes," *Communication Teacher* 29, no. 4 (2015): 234–51; Craig L. Pearce and Robert A. Giacalone, "Teams

Behaving Badly: Factors Associated with Anti-citizenship Behavior in Teams," *Journal of Applied Social Psychology* 33, no. 1 (2003): 58–75; David Matless, "Moral Geographies of English Landscape," *Landscape Research* 22, no. 2 (1997): 141–55; Jonathan F. Cox and Henry P. Sims Jr., "Leadership and Team Citizenship Behavior: A Model and Measures," in *Advances in Interdisciplinary Studies of Work Teams*, vol. 3, *Team Leadership*, ed. M. M. Beyerlein, D. A. Johnson, and S. T. Beyerlein, 1–41 (Stamford, Conn.: JAI Press, 1996).

21. Matless, "Moral Geographies of English Landscape."

22. Matless, 143.

23. Myers, "Exploring College Student Anti-citizenship Behavior."

24. Douglas E. Foley, *Learning Capitalist Culture: Deep in the Heart of Tejas* (Philadelphia: University of Pennsylvania Press, 1990); Willis, *Learning to Labour.*

25. Myers, "Exploring College Student Anti-citizenship Behavior."

26. Russell J. Skiba et al., "Race Is Not Neutral: A National Investigation of African American and Latino Disproportionality in School Discipline," *School Psychology Review* 40, no. 1 (March 1, 2011): 85–107, https://doi.org/10.1080/0279 6015.2011.12087730.

27. Lindsay Fox, "Seeing Potential: The Effects of Student–Teacher Demographic Congruence on Teacher Expectations and Recommendations," *AERA Open* 2, no. 1 (2015), https://doi.org/10.1177/2332858415623758; Jane M. Gangi, "The Unbearable Whiteness of Literacy Instruction: Realizing the Implications of the Proficient Reader Research," *Multicultural Review* 17, no. 1 (2008): 30–35.

28. Evelyn Brooks Higginbotham, *Righteous Discontent: The Women's Movement in the Black Baptist Church, 1880–1920* (Cambridge, Mass.: Harvard University Press, 1993), 7; Robin D. G. Kelley, *Freedom Dreams: The Black Radical Imagination* (Boston: Beacon Press, 1997); Kevin L. Clay, "'Despite the Odds': Unpacking the Politics of Black Resilience Neoliberalism," *American Educational Research Journal* 56, no. 1 (2019): 75–110.

29. German Lopez, "A Florida Boy Was Arrested after Refusing to Cite the Pledge of Allegiance in Class," Vox, February 18, 2019, https://www.vox.com /policy-and-politics/2019/2/18/18229336/pledge-of-allegiance-arrest-florida -school.

30. Ana Ríos-Rojas and Mark Stern, "Do 'Undocumented Aliens' Dream of Neoliberal Sheep? Conditional DREAMing and Decolonial Imaginaries," *Equity & Excellence in Education* 51, no. 1 (2018): 92–106.

31. Myers, "Exploring College Student Anti-citizenship Behavior"; Mills, *Racial Contract.*

32. *Social gestalt* refers to the legitimate wholeness, restoration, and balance in human relationships to one another and to the natural world.

33. Robert L. Allen, *Black Awakening in Capitalist America: An Analytic History* (Trenton, N.J.: Africa World Press, 1992); Cathy J. Cohen, "Deviance as Resistance: A New Research Agenda for the Study of Black Politics," *Du Bois*

Review: Social Science Research on Race 1, no. 1 (2004): 27–45; Cedric J. Robinson, *Black Marxism: The Making of the Black Radical Tradition*, 3rd ed. (Chapel Hill: University of North Carolina Press, 2020); Reiland Rabaka, *Africana Critical Theory: Reconstructing the Black Radical Tradition, from W. E. B. Du Bois and C. L. R. James to Frantz Fanon and Amilcar Cabral* (Lanham, Md.: Lexington Books, 2009); Leigh Patel, "Pedagogies of Resistance and Survivance: Learning as Marronage," *Equity & Excellence in Education* 4 (2016): 397–401.

34. Domingo Morel, *Takeover: Race, Education, and American Democracy* (New York: Oxford University Press, 2018).

35. Morel, *Takeover*, 33.

36. Higginbotham, *Righteous Discontent*.

37. Damien M. Sojoyner, "Black Radicals Make for Bad Citizens: Undoing the Myth of the School to Prison Pipeline," *Berkeley Review of Education* 4, no. 2 (2013), https://doi.org/10.5070/B84110021.

38. Allen, *Black Awakening in Capitalist America*, 24.

39. Lester K. Spence, *Knocking the Hustle: Against the Neoliberal Turn in Black Politics* (Brooklyn, N.Y.: punctum books, 2015), 190.

40. W. E. B. Du Bois, *The Souls of Black Folk* (Chicago: A. C. McClurg, 1903).

41. Beth C. Rubin, "'There's Still Not Justice': Youth Civic Identity Development amid Distinct School and Community Contexts," *Teachers College Record* 109, no. 2 (2007): 449–81.

PART I

AND THE CHILDREN WILL LEAD THEM

Youth Fugitivity as
Anti-citizenship Pedagogy

CHAPTER 1

Black Youth Refusing

Drapetomania and Neoliberal Education in
Post-Katrina New Orleans

KEVIN LAWRENCE HENRY JR.

On July 5, 1852, abolitionist Frederick Douglass delivered what would become one of his most lauded and consequential speeches, "What, to the Slave, Is the Fourth of July?" On the heels of the seventy-sixth anniversary of the signing of the Declaration of Independence, Douglass brought into sharp relief the vicious reality and parasitic institution of American chattel slavery. Sidestepping the somnambulating zombiism often associated with the Fourth of July that almost always requires—both then and now—a hollow patriotism, uncritical of the brutal truths of U.S. empire, Douglass piercingly questioned what freedom and independence mean from the perspective of those whose lives are imperiled and shaped by human trafficking, subjection, and bondage. Douglass remarked:

> What, to the American slave, is your Fourth of July? I answer: a day that reveals to him more than all other days in the year, the gross injustice and cruelty to which he is the constant victim. To him your celebration is a sham; your boasted liberty, an unholy license; your national greatness, swelling vanity; your sounds of rejoicing are empty and heartless; your denunciations of tyrants, brass fronted impudence; your shouts of liberty and equality, hollow mockery; your prayers and hymns, your sermons and thanksgivings, with all your religious parade, and solemnity, are, to him mere bombast, fraud, deception, impiety, and hypocrisy—a thin veil to

cover up crimes which would disgrace a nation of savages. There is not a
nation on the earth guilty of practices, more shocking and bloody, than are
the people of these United States, at this very hour.[1]

Critically, Douglass lays bare the webbed fabrications that prevailed in
commonsensical thinking in the United States about the United States.
Central to Douglass's argument about the brazen contradictions of these
official, dominant narratives about the United States are the perspectives not of the kidnappers and beneficiaries of human trafficking who
enslaved Black people but rather the perspectives of the captives ensnared
in enslavement. This crucial departure locates truth from another gaze
and puts into question the very narratives of a nation.

What Frederick Douglass did is what other activists, scholars, and
people of color have often done: provide a counternarrative to the stories
of the dominant group. As critical race legal scholar Mari Matsuda reminds us: "Those who have experienced discrimination speak with a
special voice to which we should listen. Looking to the bottom—adopting
the perspective of those who have seen and felt the falsity of the liberal
promise—can assist critical scholars in the task of fathoming the phenomenology of law and defining the elements of justice."[2] This chapter
holds sacred the perspectives and lived realities of Black youth and understands that such realities are a necessary starting point for our thinking
about schooling and education policy, citizenship, and, most essential,
these young people's humanity.

In this chapter, I focus on the neoliberal reforms of post-Katrina New
Orleans. Neoliberalism is a world-making and world-taking project that
is, on face value, centrally invested in the upward accumulation of capital
and expansion of economic logics in almost every area in life. Yet, over-
laying and underwriting neoliberalism is a racial project that props up
its carnivorous reality. Neoliberalism aims to secure the primacy of the
individual and individual liberty over the community and communitarian
concerns; it privileges competition while simultaneously reworking the
role of the state to hollow, deregulate, and disinvest in various social services, institutions, and legacies of the welfare state; it aims to muzzle critique of structural and institutional inequity by, once again, suggesting a

rugged individualism; it marks certain people, places, and ideas as disposable. Neoliberal reforms often find parasitic expansion following disaster and catastrophe.[3]

In the wake of the political and environmental disaster of Hurricane Katrina, New Orleans education was restructured to expand and solidify neoliberalism in the form of charter schools. While charter schools were advertised to be a salvific balm for Black children in post-Katrina New Orleans, Black youth experienced intensified policing and an anti-Black educational ecosystem. By relying on the narratives of Black youth in post-Katrina New Orleans, this chapter links the resistances and refusals of Black youth within the charter school experiment to their enslaved ancestors who refused and resisted enslavement. I argue the custodial powers of whiteness both then and now were concerned with the narrowing of Black humanity, freedom, and participation in democracy. I use the white fictive notion of "drapetomania," which was a purported mental condition that caused enslaved Africans to flee and resist their enslavers, to frame current Black youth resistance within neoliberal educational enclosures. The resistances and refusals of Black youth are often criminalized or located on a spectrum of pathology within official narratives.[4] Yet the issue of what Black youth are in fact resisting is often left invisible or silenced and eclipsed by an often deficit-laden, decontextualized projection of their supposed misbehavior. Like their enslaved ancestors were not mad or afflicted or malefactors, yet were constructed as such, the refusal is transgressive, an act of self-assertion, and a critique of a system of oppression. As such, Black youth refusals of neoliberalism locate them as anti-citizens who (re)imagine an otherwise world. I argue such refusals and reimaginings disrupt the neoliberal social order and provide critical guidance on educational-justice initiatives.

Understanding the continuing legacy and afterlife of slavery, I begin this chapter by discussing drapetomania and other discourses during enslavement that spoke to what white enslavers and the scientific community understood as the maladaptive behavior of enslaved Africans. I then proceed to provide the policy context surrounding the neoliberal restructuring of New Orleans schools. Then I ground the perspectives of youth in New Orleans, who critiqued neoliberal charter schools and

28 KEVIN LAWRENCE HENRY JR.

imagined an otherwise world. Finally, I provide some additional reflections on these perspectives, situating them within a larger consideration of anti-citizenship and neoliberalism.

FLEEING FROM BONDAGE:
DRAPETOMANIA AND DYSAETHESIA AETHIOPICA

I want to set a type of intellectual grounding to frame this chapter. This grounding acknowledges that slavery and its afterlife affect current manifestations of Black life. This perspective is drawn from the insights of scholar Saidiya Hartman, who remarks:

> If slavery persists as an issue in the political life of black America, it is not because of an antiquarian obsession with bygone days or the burden of a too-long memory, but because black lives are still imperiled and devalued by a racial calculus and a political arithmetic that were entrenched centuries ago. This is the afterlife of slavery—skewed life chances, limited access to health and education, premature death, incarceration, and impoverishment.[5]

Hartman's insights provoke a lingering question of what ways slavocratic rule still haunts us. She critically points out that, within the field of education, the vestiges remain. Without rehashing what Gloria Ladson-Billings frames as the education debt, suffice it to say, issues abound and Black students feel the brunt of those burdens.[6] Schools have been ground zero in the reproduction of white supremacy and are clearly marked for the ideological work of whiteness that shows itself via hidden curriculum and grammars of subjection.[7] Jarvis Ray Givens, for instance, illuminates how white-supremacist education aims to misrecognize Black subjects as subhuman.[8] The ideological work of schools creating certain kinds of beings and citizens postemancipation is critical. Again, Hartman is instructive as she explains the shift in the formal power of the plantation to the mechanism of the school for governing Black people. In describing ideological curricular work, Hartman argues:

Black Youth Refusing   29

In freedman's handbooks, the displacement of the whip can be discerned in the emphasis on self-discipline and policing. The whip was not to be abandoned; rather, it was to be internalized. The emphasis on correct training, proper spirit, and bent backs illuminated the invasive forms of discipline idealized as the self-fashioning of the moral and rational subject.[9]

In Hartman's articulation, schools were central locations for continuing the work of disciplining Black people. So-called proper comportment, thinking, and being were all instilled within the schoolhouse. While being full-fledged citizens remained a spurious feat for formerly enslaved Africans due to the exclusionary residue of a white-supremacist civil society, schools were critical in the ideological work of attempting to fashion an ideal Black "citizen-being" that fit within the parameters of the white imaginary in a postbellum United States.

In the immediate aftermath of the Civil War, the afterlife of slavery and its manifestations in schools seemed most pronounced. Certainly, the period of enslavism that preceded emancipation was barbaric, yet even in the midst of such cruelty and restricted life chances, enslaved Africans would risk life and limb to dream, desire, and create educational spaces and lives that were not totally circumscribed by enslavism.[10] I want to acknowledge that enslaved Africans refused and resisted under the pronounced brutality of enslavement, and I want to link such refusals not only to Black freedom dreams and assertions of humanity but also to the scientific discourses of the day. Black resistance and freedom were incompatible with a democracy that built itself on Black obedience, dehumanization, and captivity. I would like us to consider how past narratives that pathologized enslaved Africans may very well lace some of the current logics and practices within charter schools generally and in post-Katrina New Orleans specifically.

The Unruly Negro

The 1851 issue of *DeBow's Review* published out of New Orleans presents an article entitled "Diseases and Peculiarities of the Negro Race." This article, written by physician Dr. Samuel Cartwright, illustrates the

30   KEVIN LAWRENCE HENRY JR.

anti-Black scientific racism that was central in the epistemological and
material project of whiteness. Cartwright terms the notion of "drapetomania" as the mental disorder that "causes negroes to run away." This
disease was one that pathologized Black freedom and the desires of life
outside the boundaries of servitude and objectification. Cartwright goes
even further in discussing the "disease of the [negro] mind" by suggesting that those Black people who did find freedom were struck with
another pathology that afflicted them: "dysaethesia aethiopica." This disease, according to Cartwright, inflicted both the mind and body and
could be clearly seen in free Black people, who were not under the control of white overseers. Cartwright uses Haiti as an example of how this
disease has run amok. For Cartwright, the disease shows itself in the
"mischief" of negros. As La Marr Jurelle Bruce remarks, the codification
of these illnesses aligns with "antiblack antebellum epistemology," adding that "it is no wonder, then, that antebellum medicine pathologized
[black freedom]. In that obscene epistemic order, black freedom was
crime, sin, liability, and sickness, too."[11]

While not explicitly stated, students' desires for freedom and even their
push for more emancipatory schooling is often pathologized and seen as
suspect. Student efforts to refuse the boundaries of market-based, neoliberal orders are drapetomaniacal. Turning the logics of white-supremacist
science on its head, what would it mean for us to embrace the resistance
and so-called peculiarities of our youth who refuse what they understand
as an unjust system? How might understanding the discursive whip of
white supremacy not as truth but as that which narrows Black humanity,
freedom, and participation in democracy shape our practices? How might
it be instructive to learn from those who have tried to free themselves from
bondage? Before addressing the refusals of Black youth, I want to move
to a discussion of the neoliberal restructuring of post-Katrina schools.

WHEN DISASTER STRIKES:
THE NEOLIBERAL RESTRUCTURING OF NEW ORLEANS

The increasing number of catastrophic natural disasters affecting mil-
lions of people on this globe has steadily intensified as climate change

has the greatest impact on the most vulnerable populations. Scholars have rightly observed that, while hurricanes may be no respecters of persons, often the governmental and policy responses to them tend to be reflective of the existing stratified social order. Moreover, those made vulnerable by structural racism and economic alienation experience the uneven and perhaps deadly realities of these large-scale systems of oppression. The inability to prepare and secure one's home, to evacuate, or to afford the additional costs of living once evacuated all contribute to and illuminate the flagrant disparities that mark the lives of so many Black people who are lodged and ping-ponged between rocks and hard places—or, said differently, the ever-present realities of white supremacy, vulgar capitalism, and its iterations of environmental racism and state-sanctioned abandonment.

The tragedy of Hurricane Katrina, which decimated the city of New Orleans in August 2005, made obvious the salience of race and class in the United States. As geographer Clyde Woods remarks, "The picture of twenty thousand slowly dying African Americans chanting 'we want help' outside of New Orleans's Convention Center was a blues moment. It disrupted the molecular structure of a wide array of carefully constructed social relations and narratives on race, class, progress, competency, and humanity."[12] Woods makes clear that Hurricane Katrina and the resulting political response indexed that there could be no "plausible deniability" regarding the reality of racism in the United States. Although Hurricane Katrina broadcasted for all to see the profound extent of Black suffering, there were also policy realities that washed upon the shore that aided in the restructuring of public education in the city. Such policy enactments, while not as visible and visceral as what was witnessed on television, speak to how education policy can also be a site of white supremacy. In critical race scholar David Gillborn's articulation, when evaluating policy, the basic questions of who or what drives the policy, who are the winners and losers of the policy, and what are the effects of the policy are central considerations for evaluation.[13] More to the point, when keeping those questions in mind, the face of race and racism may very well become more discernible. The policy context, which I will discuss in this section, makes clear how the policy shifts following Hurricane

Katrina laid the groundwork for the expansion of neoliberal educational reforms and had a racist impact. This context is central for understanding the larger content of this chapter.

To be clear, in the days and weeks prior to Hurricane Katrina's arrival, very few would claim that the New Orleans public school system was the model for educational success. Like many districts that serve predominantly Black, low- and no-income people, the district experienced the typical realities of white supremacy—white flight, disinvestment, and a city challenged by structural realities of oppression that left many Black residents without adequate homes, jobs, transportation, food, and health care. Despite these pernicious assaults on Black life, Black people in New Orleans are still here standing. Conjuring and creating, weaving and working toward an otherwise that grounds Black life, Black family, Black joy, Black community, and Black love. From pounding the pavement during a second line to aromatic laughs that linger in Mama's kitchen, to the motley-colored homes that hold our histories, Black people in New Orleans find a way.

Raynard Sanders, in his critical work on post-Katrina New Orleans, notes that although challenges prevailed in New Orleans, almost 80 percent of New Orleans public schools saw improvement on traditional measures of school performance.[14] Yet these improvements could not subdue the push for a privatized system. To be clear, conservatives have long held aspirations to dismantle public education. For instance, during the civil rights era, in an effort to dodge desegregation mandates, white supremacists created taxpayer-funded "segregation academies." As part of various "freedom of choice" plans constructed by elected officials, these equity-evading, justice-circumventing schools would offer white families vouchers. In doing so, public education was undermined and, in some instances, entire school districts were closed, as in the case of Prince Edward County, Virginia.[15] These efforts to privatize public systems out of the responsibility of equitably educating Black students casts serious doubt on the role of school-choice programs.

Some years prior to Hurricane Katrina, conservative legislators attempted to pass a voucher program in Louisiana. The bill was ultimately defeated; however, it did set in motion other efforts to restructure public education. One of the measures was the passage of Act 9 in 2003, which created the Louisiana Recovery School District (RSD). The RSD would serve as a central takeover district for schools legislatively contrived as failing based on metrics associated with the school performance scores.[16] The RSD and the school performance scores are central in the takeover of public schools in New Orleans in 2005. Critically, one must note that although neoliberalism as a political rationality and governing philosophy often eschews the role of the state and state bureaucracy, as a matter of course neoliberalism relies on the state to make manifest its ends. Said differently, the state lubricates neoliberal ideals and grants legitimacy and resources to actors and institutions who puncture the remaining vestiges of the Keynesian welfare state. As I have said elsewhere, these policies of the neoliberal state "are both fertilizer and instrument, condition and process."[17]

Following Hurricane Katrina, there were several key policy initiatives that made possible neoliberal charter reform. There were four components of the reform that helped to expand and solidify the neoliberal regime. First, one of the central mechanisms for the expansion of school choice was the infusion of nearly $20 million from the Department of Education under then Secretary of Education Margaret Spellings. These funds were exclusively for the creation of charter schools. No equivalency was provided for traditional public schools. This infusion of funds was central in the expansion of charter schools. Second, at the state level, existing charter school laws that required parental, faculty, and staff votes of approval before a school could be taken over and converted as a charter were suspended. This revoked important democratic decision-making from overwhelmingly Black communities. Third, there was the passage of Act 35, which reconstituted the definition of success and failure by altering the school performance scores. Act 35 raised the score from 60 to 87.4, which effectively constructed more schools as failing and needing to be turned around and included within the RSD's dossier of forthcoming charters.[18] This nearly 30-point increase essentially allowed more schools to be governed by the RSD. After Act 35, 107 schools were included in the RSD's portfolio, compared with their operation of only 5 schools prior to the passing of the act.[19] Finally, an overwhelming number of Black veteran educators were fired en masse, marking one of the largest displacements of Black educators since *Brown v. Board of Education*.[20]

In spite of, or perhaps because of, the decades of racialized educational disinvestment and larger race-based inequities that cocoon public schools, these Black educators strove for academic rigor and practiced culturally relevant ethics of care. Yet following Hurricane Katrina, these teachers were shamed and treated as disposable and subsequently replaced with white teachers affiliated with alternative programs such as Teach for America and TeachNOLA. The removal of Black educators not only changed the demographics of personnel within schools and instructional practices and cultures within classrooms but also hollowed out the teachers union, thereby dispossessing educators of their labor interests. Taken together, all of the aforementioned events illuminate how power was operating to foreclose demographic participation for Black communities in the remaking of the city, target a workforce of overwhelmingly Black women educators, and solidify the legitimacy of charter schools. Importantly, it is critical to note that these policy prescriptions took place while most Black people were displaced due to Hurricane Katrina. These realities laced the reform movement in such a way that foreshadowed what life could be like within schools for Black children.

REFUSING THE NEOLIBERAL TURN

And so I was trying to ask the question again, ask it anew, as if it had not been asked before, because the language of the historian was not telling me what I needed to know. Which is, what is it like in the interstitial spaces where you fall between everyone who has a name, a category, a sponsor, an agenda, spokespersons, people looking out for them—but you don't have anybody.[21]

In reflecting on one of her most germinal articles, literary theorist Hortense Spillers speaks to the dire need to reinterpret the past and to look askance at the narratives provided by dominant knowledge brokers. For Spillers, it was a break with convention and to look anew at violent, repetitious narratives and ways of knowing surrounding Black women,

Black men, and Black families. Spillers then and now is offering a reconsidering of conceptualizations of race, class, and gender and the violent systems of racial capitalism and patriarchy that inform and shape them. To question the "language of the historian" was to set as not only debatable but fundamentally problematic the official narratives of the academy and state that occluded and disappeared the trace and terror of white supremacy and its imprint on past and current iterations of Black life. Spillers instigates a line of questioning and way of thinking that refuses detached, so-called objectivist accounts that marshal deficit, oppressive logics that substantiate Black suffering and ontological debasement. Spillers's intellectual and political project lingers and is part of a larger constellation of Black thinkers engaged in Black study.

Spillers's thinking generates similar questions regarding post-Katrina New Orleans education and what life is like for Black children most specifically. What must be asked anew about post-Katrina New Orleans? What is not being told that we need to know? Who are those who might not "have anybody" in the academic discourse and what might they say about life that enunciates a truth that others may want silenced?

The general, taken-for-granted narratives of post-Katrina New Orleans tell a story of success. In some instances, this success was heralded before there was any empirical evidence to support that. More recently, scholars suggest that school closures positively affect children of New Orleans and that academic achievement has increased; this is debatable.[22] While necessary unpacking of those claims is needed, the scope of this chapter will not allow for such. The question that begs to be asked is: Success for whom? And how are we measuring success? And in what ways might this success move our students to what Carl A. Grant frames as a "flourishing life"?[23]

In this section, I want to focus on the critiques that Black youth offer within the neoliberal city of New Orleans. These range from refusing the logics of the charter system to those that critique larger issues of racism and gentrification. Importantly, as I suggested, these critiques are part of a long lineage of Black people seeking freedom. While often not valued by the prevailing, custodial powers of whiteness, these narratives index the project of Black freedom and mark these young people as anti-citizens within the neoliberal imaginary.

According to a report from the Louisiana Department of Education, during the 2013–2014 academic year, while African American children made up less than half (44 percent) of the student body population, they accounted for 63 percent of in-school suspensions, 67 percent of out of school suspensions, and 68 percent of expulsions.[24] Even more disturbing, in some New Orleans charters, over 25 percent of the student body was suspended at least once. In some charter schools, the numbers are even more appalling. For instance, during the 2012–2013 academic year, Carver Collegiate and Carver Preparatory suspended 69 percent and 61 percent of their student bodies respectively, while Sci Academy and Joseph S. Clark suspended 58 percent and 46 percent of the student bodies, respectively.[25] These numbers evidence the ways Louisiana schools and teachers are culpable in, as the NAACP Legal Defense and Educational Fund states, "remov[ing] children from mainstream educational environment[s] and funnel[ing] them into a one-way path toward prison."[26] It is no surprise that, according to a 2014 report by the United States Justice Department, Louisiana ranks highest among states in incarceration.[27] Yet, underneath these dismal statistics is the reality that criminality and pathology is always already inscribed on the Black body, already envisioned in the white American imaginary. Underneath these statistics, I would argue, is the residue of anti-Black logics, particularly that of drapetomania and dysaethesia aethiopica. The need to police, surveil, and punish Black students into submission reeks of a project to constrain Black freedom and indexes a subtle endeavor of constructing the idealized Black neoliberal citizen in the aftermath of Hurricane Katrina. This "citizen," of course, would be one who would submit to authority, who would not question the prevailing system or have a level of criticality, who would not imagine, desire, or demand an otherwise and justice-focused world.

I want to briefly focus on the accounts of a group of students who protested what they experienced as racist and undemocratic educational experiences at their charter school. I will also highlight the narratives of students associated with Rethink NOLA, an organization that supports youth mentoring and advocacy. As indicated on their website, Rethink has a simple philosophy that guides their work: "Young people deserve a voice in radically changing the systems in which they operate."[28]

Walking Out on a No-Choice Charter

On November 20, 2013, a group of students from Carver Collegiate and Carver Prep organized against what they deemed as unfair treatment in their schools. These two schools were operated by Collegiate Academies, a charter-management organization. The students held a walkout and protest and provided a list of demands to the Collegiate Academies board of directors and administrators. Some students were suspended, while others were pushed out for speaking their minds. I will quote, at length, some of the statements of students.[29]

We get disciplined for anything and everything. We get detentions or suspensions for not walking on the taped lines in the hallway, for slouching, for not raising our hands in a straight line. The teachers and administrators tell us this is because they are preparing us for college. But walking on tape doesn't prepare us for college. It trains us for the military or worse for jail. If college is going to be like Carver, we don't want to go to college.

We get suspended for trying to ask why we must do certain things—teachers consider this to be "disrespectful" and it is the most common reason we get suspended from school. Sometimes teachers take things as disrespect when they aren't meant to be disrespectful. Asking questions about why something is done a certain way shouldn't be considered as disrespect. We want to know why we have to do these things. We want answers, and suspending us for asking questions isn't an appropriate response.

We want a discipline policy that doesn't suspend kids for every little thing. Suspensions should only be used for very serious matter. We want a discipline policy that keeps kids in school, learning.

We don't have any say into school policies. We can't explain ourselves. We also get talked to like we are little kids, or sometimes like animals. We want our teachers to treat us with respect, and we want to have a say in the school policies.

The teachers don't connect with us or where we come from. There are no black teachers.

Some of the teachers are racially insensitive. None of the teachers are from New Orleans. They can't relate to us, our neighborhoods, or our community. They have no respect for our customs and culture, and simply want to make us more like them without understanding us and our background.

Critically, these young people pushed against the tired script embedded within a neoliberal charter school in New Orleans. In walking out of school and protesting, they provide a necessary critique of what they saw as central harms of their charter school. These students' perspectives can also be taken to illuminate the unspoken truths of a neoliberal democracy: the erasure and disposability of Black educators and workers, hollow diversity that does not value the culture and customs of Black people but merely consumes them and profits from them, the silencing and limiting of the power of Black people, and the carceral and punitive practices and logics that are bedrocks to neoliberalism. They provide witness to the anti-Black realities of school choice in post-Katrina New Orleans, and in doing so they also chart demands for an otherwise. They make clear their desire for a school that values their humanity and cultural ways of knowing and being. They want a school that is predicated on actual student learning and safety. They want local, Black educators tied to the land and history of New Orleans, not transplants often affiliated with alternative programs, such as Teach for America.

Rethinking the Shards of Democracy

Similarly, the students of Rethink NOLA provoke us to reconsider the taken-for-granted norms of neoliberal citizenship. In creating a series of zines by young people, Rethink NOLA is honoring the legacy of Black people who have used media as a counternarrative to the hegemonic logics of the day. As Joanna Brooks reminds us, Black print was a "counterpublic" that challenged the mainstream discourse. In discussing public print works of the eighteenth century, Brooks remarks, "a distinctly black tradition of publication . . . premised on principles of self-determination and structured by criticisms of white political and economic dominance" was central for Black people.[30]

Rethink NOLA's zine, *The People's Press,* provides incisive commentary on a host of issues affecting New Orleans. The cover of volume 3, "The Charter School Edition," has images of young Black students and the inscription "We are the experts of our own experiences." From the outset, these youth mark the centrality of their interpretive authority, challenging always-already statist epistemologies that muzzle their ways of seeing, knowing, and experiencing. They start by framing this issue around privatization, giving a straightforward definition of *privatization.* Importantly, they locate privatization as central to the harm they have experienced. They state, "Most of the trauma we have experienced in New Orleans since Hurricane Katrina is the result of privatization. And most of the trauma we're still experiencing since Hurricane Ida is because of privatization." With laser-like focus, these young people understand privatization as key to producing structural inequities that mark them, their families, and communities toward vulnerability. They further state:

> New Orleans is the first and only 100% charter district in the country. That means that our education has been privatized. Decisions are made based on the best interest of charters companies, and not based on the best interest of our students and our communities. We have been front row witnesses to the dismantling of our schools. We've been the victims of multiple school closures, passing off of schools to new charter operators, and school administrations that dismiss the needs and concerns of students and their parents.

For the students of Rethink NOLA, the charter experiment is one that further disenfranchises and harms Black and Brown communities. The students of Rethink understand one central aspect of the charter experiment in New Orleans is the rejecting and refusing of the desires of their communities. Not only must they experience the harm and uprooting of the charter system, but their interests and needs are seen as superfluous. Crucially, however, in making plain these concerns, these young people

Black Students as the
Anti-citizens of Neoliberalism

Quite simply, Black people have given meaning to democracy and have enlivened what it means to be a citizen. From voting rights to education, Black people as anti-citizens have occupied the contradictory position as actual vanguards of citizenship, turning the logic of white supremacy on its head. Although white perceptual, legalistic, medical, and educational discourse and practices have worked to cast Black people as anything but—as abnormal, as mad, or deviant, as in need of their governance—Black life, Black resistance, and Black intellect has cast such aspersions aside, charting a way forward that refuses statist epistemologies of violence. In doing so, Black people have worked as anti-citizens, confronting a state that rejects our humanity, while also charting otherwise worlds. The students whom I have discussed in this chapter have also entered this tradition, but, of course, not without consequence.

The removal of Black students from charter schools via suspension and expulsion and the muzzling or ignoring of Black educational desires illuminate how neoliberal charter schools in New Orleans uphold specific logics around what is seen as the ideal student. That ideal student, a neoliberal citizen in the making, is one who respects authority, accepts the violence of the state, is concerned with individualistic matters, and has no structural or critical analysis. Like their enslaved ancestors, who resisted and desired freedom, these students' supposed misbehavior and governance wants could be seen as pathological or unnecessary. In fact, as a consequence for their resistance, some students who protested were punished and removed. Yet these students' protest and refusals were ways they spoke back to and challenged the neoliberal orthodoxy of charter schools. Such practices of freedom took off the restricted notions of the ideal neoliberal citizen who accepts their lot based on the perspectives of white people who are in the process of remaking the city in their image and along their desires. The students who protested and wrote for

Rethink NOLA were anti-citizens of the neoliberal social order. Their radical dreaming is instructive and provides critical guidance on educational-justice initiatives. We must listen to and fight for the visions they have articulated. These students are both within and outside of the neoliberal imaginary. Within as they must daily contend with the tentacles of neoliberalism and its desired hold and anticipatory capture of them. But also these students are outside of it, exceeding the logics of the confines, documenting and refusing the racism of the state, even as the state erases its trace and hides its hand. These young people are part of a tradition of seeing what seems to not be present and in so doing are architects of an otherwise.

Notes

1. Frederick Douglass, "What to the Slave Is the Fourth of July?" EDSITE-ment!, accessed February 8, 2023, https://edsitement.neh.gov/student-activities/frederick-douglasss-what-slave-fourth-july#:~:text=What%2C%20to%20the%20American%20slave,he%20is%20the%20constant%20victim.

2. Mari Matsuda, "Looking to the Bottom: Critical Legal Studies and Reparations," *Harvard Civil Rights-Civil Liberties Law Review* 22 (1987): 324.

3. Kevin Henry, "The Price of Disaster: The Charter School Authorization Process in Post-Katrina New Orleans," *Educational Policy* 25, no. 2 (2021): 235–58; Naomi Klein, *The Shock Doctrine* (New York: Picador, 2007).

4. Matthew C. Fadus et al., "Unconscious Bias and the Diagnosis of Disruptive Behavior Disorders and ADHA in African American and Hispanic Youth," *Academic Psychiatry* 44 (2020): 95–102; Sabina E. Vaught, *Compulsory: Education and the Dispossession of Youth in a Prison School* (Minneapolis: University of Minnesota Press, 2017).

5. Saidiya Hartman, *Lose Your Mother: A Journey along the Atlantic Slave Route* (New York: Farrar, Strauss and Giroux, 2007), 6.

6. Gloria Ladson-Billings, "From the Achievement Gap to the Education Debt: Understanding Achievement in U.S. Schools," *Educational Researcher* 35, no. 7 (2006): 3–12.

7. Savannah Shange, *Progressive Dystopia: Abolition, Antiblackness, and Schooling in San Francisco* (Durham, N.C.: Duke University Press, 2019); William Watkins, *The White Architects of Black Education: Ideology and Power in America, 1865–1954* (New York: Teachers College Press, 2001); Jean Anyon, "Social Class and the Hidden Curriculum of Work," *Journal of Education* 162, no. 1 (1980): 67–92; Henry, "Price of Disaster"; Zeus Leonardo, *Race, Whiteness, and Education* (New York: Routledge, 2009).

8. Jarvis Ray Givens, "A Grammar for Black Education beyond Borders: Exploring Technologies of Schooling in the African Diaspora," *Race Ethnicity and Education* 19, no. 6 (2016): 1,288–302.

9. Saidiya Hartman, *Scenes of Subjection: Terror, Slavery, and Self-Making in Nineteenth-Century America* (Oxford: Oxford University Press, 1997), 140.

10. James Anderson, *The Education of Blacks in the South, 1860–1935* (Chapel Hill: University of North Carolina Press, 2010).

11. La Marr Jurelle Bruce, "Mad Is a Place; or, The Slave Ship Tows the Ship of Fools," *American Quarterly* 69, no. 2 (2017): 305.

12. Clyde Woods, "Do You Know What It Means to Miss New Orleans? Katrina, Trap Economics, and the Rebirth of the Blues," *American Quarterly* 57, no. 4 (2005): 1,005.

13. David Gillborn, "Education Policy as an Act of White Supremacy: Whiteness, Critical Race Theory, and Education Reform," *Journal of Education Policy* 20, no. 4 (2005): 485–505.

14. Raynard Sanders, *The Coup D'état of the New Orleans Public Schools: Money, Power, and the Illegal Takeover of a Public School System* (New York: Peter Lang, 2018).

15. Wilbur B. Brookover, "Education in Prince Edward County, Virginia, 1953–1993," *Journal of Negro Education* 62, no. 2 (1993): 149–61.

16. Beth Sondel, "Raising Citizens or Raising Test Scores? Teach for America, 'No Excuses' Charters, and the Development of the Neoliberal Citizen," *Theory & Research in Social Education* 43, no. 3 (2015): 289–313.

17. Henry, "Price of Disaster," 244.

18. Daniella Cook and Adrienne Dixson, "Writing Critical Race Theory and Method: A Composite Counterstory on the Experiences of Black Teachers in New Orleans Post-Katrina," *International Journal of Qualitative Studies in Education* 26, no. 10 (2013): 1,238–58; Kevin Henry, "Heretical Discourses in Post-Katrina Charter School Applications," *American Educational Research Journal* 56, no. 6 (2019): 2,609–42; Henry, "Price of Disaster."

19. Kevin Henry, "Discursive Violence and Economic Retrenchment: Chartering the Sacrifice of Black Educators in Post-Katrina New Orleans," in *The Charter School Solution: Distinguishing Fact from Rhetoric* (New York: Routledge, 2016), 80–98.

20. Henry, "Discursive Violence and Economic Retrenchment."

21. Hortense Spillers et al., "'Whatcha Gonna Do?' Revisiting 'Mama's Baby, Papa's Maybe: An American Grammar Book': A Conversation with Hortense Spillers, Saidiya Hartman, Farah Jasmine Griffin, Shelly Eversley, and Jennifer Morgan," *Women's Studies Quarterly* 35, no. 1–2 (2007): 308.

22. Whitney Bross, Douglas N. Harris, and Lihan Liu, *The Effects of Performance-Based School Closure and Charter Takeover on Student Performance* (New Orleans: Education Research Alliance for New Orleans, Tulane University,

2016); Douglas N. Harris and Matthew F. Larsen, *The Effects of the New Orleans Post-Katrina Market-Based School Reforms on Medium-Term Student Outcomes* (New Orleans: Education Research Alliance for New Orleans, Tulane University, 2018).

23. Carl A. Grant, "Cultivating Flourishing Lives: A Robust Social Justice Vision of Education," *American Educational Research Journal* 49, no. 5 (2012): 910–34.

24. Danielle Dreilinger, "Strict Collegiate Academies Charters Are Working to Eliminate Suspensions," NOLA, October 8, 2014, http://www.nola.com/educa tion/index.ssf/2014/10/strict_collegiate_academies_ch.html.

25. Dreilinger, "Strict Collegiate Academies Charters."

26. NAACP Legal Defense and Educational Fund, *Dismantling the School-to-Prison Pipeline* (New York: NAACP Legal Defense and Educational Fund, 2015), 2.

27. E. Ann Carson, "Prisoners in 2013," *Bureau of Justice Statistics,* September 30, 2014, https://bjs.ojp.gov/content/pub/pdf/p13.pdf.

28. Rethink, https://therethinkers.org.

29. Carver Collegiate and Carver Prep students' letter to Collegiate Academies board and administration, available at http://media.nola.com/education_ impact/other/Carver%20Students%20Demand%20Letter%20(2).pdf.

30. Joanna Brooks, "The Early American Public Sphere and the Emergence of a Black Print Counterpublic," *William and Mary Quarterly* 62, no. 1 (2005): 68.

CHAPTER 2

Radicalizing Black Child Play, Conspiring in the Familiar Zones

ARIANA DENISE BRAZIER

W alking past the long rows of bookshelves and the locked offices on either side of the main entryway, excited whispers rose amid the clashing music and gleeful shouts of approximately fifteen or more Black girls from second to fifth grade. The whispers were emanating from the wedged corner of the T-shaped media center. In the absence of an after-school counselor or administrator, a huddled group of five or six girls were plotting as they peered into the screen of one student's cell phone. "WE FIGHT OUR OWN BATTLES!" was all that was legible before the moment was interrupted and students were instructed to prepare for dismissal.

Watching them take the situation into their hands by engaging each other as recourse to some perceived transgression, I wondered if the girls had forsaken bureaucratic (read: adult) systems of redress—or, more likely, if they had been forsaken by those same systems. What was observable in their brief interactions was how the girls identified and seized a moment of adult mismanagement to exchange information that ignited a collective galvanizing, a series of lateral power negotiations, and obvious playfulness evidenced by their furtive grins. Moments such as this one, I argue, resist normative conventions of "childhood," and the associated identities of "student" and "citizen," that are based in white middle-class heteronormative ideals of obedience and deference to institutions as well as the policies and individuals who undergird them.

While I would never learn what the transgression was or the ultimate outcome of the girls' rebuttal, as these were my last moments at the school before returning to my university, this glimpse into the social terrain of Black childhood, specifically situated within the Black Ghetto, is emblematic of the exploration initiated by this chapter.[1] The Black Ghetto can be conceptualized as both a phenomenon delineated by the domination of external institutions that incite neighborhood disorder and a geographically and socioeconomically defined space of social death where Black children are positioned as anti-citizens liable to political, social, and physical violence.[2] This chapter theorizes how Black child play enacts a radical subjectivity—anti-citizenry—within the Black Ghetto. Such violence is exacerbated by dichotomies attached to their intersectional identities: Black children are positioned as simultaneously invisible and hypervisible;[3] criminal and innocent;[4] adultified and infantilized;[5] hypersexualized and desexualized;[6] threatening and passive, etc. These dichotomies are exacerbated in the context of Black poverty that sociopolitically justifies militarized police states that terrorize Black children and their families.

Located in a predominately Black neighborhood within a majority Black city in the southeast United States, Blaze Rods Elementary School and Fun Middle School are situated in the most concentrated area of chronic poverty in the state of Georgia.[7] Located a few blocks from a federal penitentiary and a few miles from a landfill, each Blaze Rods student is considered "economically disadvantaged" and nearly all are Black. Using school-based ethnographic fieldwork from my years-long engagement with the second- to sixth-grade students at Blaze Rods and Fun, I identify how familiar zones within the Black Ghetto manifest the horizontal worlds of sociality and agency between Black children and their larger communities. Familiar zones can be conceptualized as relatively unregulated spaces established and utilized by youth to nurture social networks, hide misbehavior, and maintain the impression of obedience.[8] Within familiar zones, children establish their own cooperative learning spaces as they play with language, practice, perform, and switch between different identities necessary for survival on the streets and inside institutions.

Radicalizing Black Child Play 47

I believe that I was allowed occasional entry into students' familiar zones because I inhabited a sort of liminal identity as a researcher—students frequently treated me as a member of their demographic as I was the same size, they were unsure of my age, and while I spent a significant amount of time with their teachers, I did not discipline them and consistently participated in recess and after-school care with them, and occasionally attended neighborhood functions with their families. Responding directly to the questions of how Black youth are positioned as anti-citizens, and how their anti-citizenship contributes to the project of subaltern liberation, I argue that Black children learn how to resist the associated constraints and debilitation of hegemonic childhood and citizen scripts as they engage a form of cultural and social criticism and knowledge exchange within these zones; this criticism and exchange of knowledge is frequently masked as culturally informed play. Essentially, in these zones, Black children establish alternatives to their structurally unjust realities as they develop the skills necessary to demand and advocate through play. This practice aligns with my conceptualization of anti-citizenship as an identity that responds to the meaninglessness of the status of citizenship by focusing inward on the constructive, socioemotional, and exploratory possibilities of their immediate community as opposed to prioritizing a fight against the state for human recognition.

Centering students' play practices and community narratives, I exhibit how play prepares them for the socioemotional as well as the historico-geographical experiences that these children must learn to navigate in order to operate within, resist, and deconstruct the hierarchical institutions that seek to surveil and confine them. These communal learning experiences promote and refine a relational culture that equips children with the knowledge and skills necessary to thrive as fully human. Their play unconsciously highlights their community's lived experiences and constructs an embodied praxis that can reframe and reject oppressive social constructions, ultimately resulting in liberatory possibilities for their entire community.

As a means to understand how play becomes an actively disruptive, negotiated, intergenerational, and co-conspiratorial praxis, as well as how

Black children apply daily the knowledge that is bequeathed to them and generated collaboratively, this chapter is divided into two major sections: the first consists of a definitional breakdown of anti-citizenship and the function familiar zones and play have in the cultivation of a culturally informed politics of resistance, subversion, and refusal. Then, I offer a series of ethnographic vignettes that provide insight into the seemingly minute, daily disruptions that students are actuating through playful dialogue within the obscurity of familiar zones. These peer-facilitated interactions and exchanges threaten the maintenance of institutional social order as they censure authority figures, teach each other, break down (sub)cultural knowledge, and organize themselves for their own joy and well-being.

Concepts and Connections

Anti-citizenship

I define the words *anti* and *citizen* separately to elucidate how they function collectively: while *anti* is traditionally a prefix and a noun, I understand the word as a catalytic when conjoined with certain nouns; thus, *anti* is less about merely being oppositional and more about creating new ways of being. First, *anti* connotes both an undoing and a movement. While distinct, the undoing of an authoritarian regime that operates via external and internalized policing and the movement toward subaltern liberation are deeply entangled and difficult to separate.

Second, *citizen* denotes a subjectivity, an allegiance to a government or regime that, within the United States, has historically espoused a discourse of individual freedom while legally authorizing the physical and spiritual murder of its own constituency.[9] The category of "citizenship," then, is an arbitrary means of bestowing legitimacy upon certain groups of people at the expense of the liberties entitled to all people. Essentially, everyone suffers under this notion of citizenship.

By situating the two terms together, I argue that *anti-citizenship* for Black people, Black children specifically, has become a defense of their self-pursuance. Against the edicts of the state that filter down into the policies and codes of conduct of educative and social institutions, Black children are exploring and imagining certain human liberties that can generate radical rearticulations of society.

Forsaking the traditional focus on a claim to legal rights, these children are creating spaces in which they can experience the liberties associated with gainful risks (the risk involved in challenging seemingly unbounded [adult] authority, in rebuking distortions of facts, and in deviating from standard, conformist practice). These experiences can expose the violence of micro-level arrangements with the state via community-based institutions such as schools and propel Black children toward an existence that honors the ways they choose to possess and retain the full capacities and potencies of their own Black child bodies.

Anti-citizenship is an action-based identity that Black children co-construct through self-facilitated play and dialogue.

Familiar Zones

In her ethnographic work with adolescent mothers who have become wards of the state, Lauren J. Silver coins the concept of "familiar zones" to explain how "case managers and mothers coped adaptively, creatively carving out spaces where the youth could live somewhat self-determined lives" as they navigated restrictive organizational policies and state surveillance; however, because these familiar zones were hidden or obscured, "abuse and violence went undetected by authority."[10]

Familiar zones are situated in opposition to "formal zones," which are constructed by officials who engage in "techniques that include procedural protocols, paperwork, record keeping, outcome measures, and audits." These techniques form the administrative processes that "produce a formal, objective reality that necessarily ignores contradictory, messy aspects of social life."[11] The administrative activities that construct the formal zones compose the average school day as teachers and students are expected to complete the instruction and meet the outcome measures necessary for standardized test prep. Aligning with state-sanctioned standards of academic "success," classroom-based instruction is increasingly becoming void of opportunities to respond to the "contradictory, messy" aspects of their students' personal and communal livelihoods, even against the desires of some of the most well-meaning educators.

Silver argues that familiar zones are sustained by the social distances created by spatial relations and institutional hierarchies.[12] Her argument is evidenced by the formation of the familiar zones I engaged at Blaze Rods. The zones I revisit in this chapter existed in the Blaze Rods media center during and after school as students transitioned between activities or awaited their guardians for pickup, as well as at the cafeteria tables after school while students awaited further instruction from staff or administrators. Neither school faculty nor after-school staff always sat with students during their lunch or dinner times or remained with them in the media center, and so students permitted themselves and each other some leniency in their behavior and emotional expressions. Sometimes, they invited or encouraged brazenness or insolence in each other in these spaces.

The conditions that undergirded the necessity for students to hide their dialogue, inquiries, and expressiveness in familiar zones included the "culture of fear and blame" that pervades our educational system, respectability politics, and white middle-class notions of childhood morality, as well as high-stakes testing that accompanies racist discourses on the "achievement gaps" that justify racialized play deprivation and the criminalization of Black joy in schools.[13] The students were utilizing familiar zones to meet social, safety, and economic needs.

Within my research sites, familiar zones refer to the peer-governed, unregulated spaces in which Black children and youth use their personal agency to form, discover, and exchange strategies to endure amid the rigidity of state demands, elder hierarchies, and the aforementioned tensions associated with their intersectional identities. Within these zones, children "confuse the adult order" and "create for themselves considerable room for movement within the limits imposed upon them by adult society. This deflection of adult perception is crucial for both the maintenance and continuation of the child's culture and for the growth of the concept of the self for the individual child."[14] These zones exist on the periphery of or obscurely within casual adult-governed spaces and formal bureaucratic institutions; for example, students' interactions and conversation topics shifted when we were playing on the trampoline, whispering at the kitchen table, laughing at the lunch table, climbing on the playground, waiting in the car, sitting on the sidelines or in the cut at recess, as opposed to in the classroom or in the living room with their guardians present. These shifting performances and scripts reinforce the sagacity that children possess as they maintain the boundaries of their familiar zones.

Because their play forms can be especially empirical, Black children speculate, discover, and innovate methods of disrupting the violent institutional agendas that seek to deprive them of the socioemotional, developmental, intellectual, and collective agency that play makes possible for all children. Black children living in poverty create their own survival practices that then become mechanisms of collective thriving transferred across generations through play and customs of care existing in familiar zones. Customs of care are the practice in which younger children are under the supervision of older children.[15] Through the play that occurs in these often-concealed zones, they learn, exchange, and create ways to signify and make meaning in spaces that deny them the freedom of personal signification.

The conversations that were had among the students in various familiar zones were reflective of students' attempts to dictate and negotiate their own learning experiences as these experiences informed and responded to the sociopolitical aspects and context that publicly defined their community.

While notions of citizenship are hyperfocused on individual obligations to the country via the discourse on a citizen's civic duty, the governmental negligence that normalizes the dire conditions of the Black Ghetto remains undiscussed in their classrooms and broader media. Within the familiar zones, children can learn the "process of mediating the space between who they are and how they are seen, and between their theoretical rights as citizens and the reality of their exclusion from full recognition as citizens."[16] This process of negotiation occurs on a micro-level within their schools as students are expected to perform the scripts required of a good pupil—passive, unquestioning subjecthood accepting the histories and content imparted to them as objective truths; at the same time, they are seen as "out of control," "troubled," "ghetto," or "ratchet" kids in need of intervention and discipline because of the "culture of poverty" in which they have been raised.

The youth with whom I interacted identified biases, understood the expectations, and grasped the repercussions. Hence, familiar zones offered the guise of safety as they could essentially talk the shit they could not in front of adults, investigate the content not covered in their formal learning spaces, and play the intimate body-to-body games that broke from the policies of individualism and isolation that defined their school day.[17] Students could explore risks and their natural consequences, thereby providing them experience in self-initiated or peer-facilitated forms of conflict resolution. Together, they learned to negotiate the constrained forms of power they had access to as they playfully controlled, subverted, and reimagined rules of and scripts for behavior and determined their own standards of belonging and identity.

Play and Racial Identity

Play is critical for the healthy growth of every person. Through play, young children learn conflict resolution and basic ethical standards, communicate traumas and achievements, evolve their vestibular system and strengthen core muscles, and establish spatial and social awareness. Play initiates a child's early understanding of politics and consumerism as they are invited in or excluded from group activities because of identity politics and corresponding ideas of citizenship or belonging that precede their existence in a space. In this way, play can trigger a child's earliest understandings of race and sociality; these experiences become the source of consciousness for Black children that they are indefinitely involved in a power structure of which they are not the authors.

Broadly, play builds strong interpersonal connections by organizing them around a central task or goal that necessitates cooperation, collaboration, strategy, and communication. In striving toward a shared objective, people are bonded by struggle and through laughter.[18] Play, then, can teach people to notice when others are treated unfairly, as well as how best to adapt to changing circumstances and individual needs. Children can learn how play has divided people and how play has brought people together. In the stories shared, they also learn how play created ways to survive, celebrate, love, and laugh. Stories and play are important for organizing communities because it gives a common ground on which people can see each other equally. Play is one way that children use their bodies to learn about and teach others.

A culturally specific form of familial and communal engagement, certain forms of play are passed down across generations as the games are shaped by the players' resources and the environment; the process of learning these play forms frequently becomes a means for storytelling and personal development.[19] Specific kinds of play can tell us not only about the beauty of a culture, about relationships across families and communities, but also about the violence and injustices that have been done to communities.[20] Through play, many Black and Brown children around the world reveal to institutions, adults, and each other how racism and poverty are a part of their daily lives.[21] For Black children in the United States, racism is literally denying them their right to play and, in far too many cases, their right to live.[22]

Racialized realities reinforce the significance of familiar zones that allow Black children the space to explore their Blackness while situating themselves in customs of care. This practice of care and the experiences that transpire away from direct adult supervision launch play-based mentor relationships that initiate a process of language learning that prepares the younger children to receive and construct a specific social identity. In play, Black children enact a radical subjectivity that becomes critical engagement. Immersed in customs of care and literacy traditions "defined by words, linguistic diversities, texts, engagements, multiple identities, and acts of performance within and across various sociopolitical contexts," Black children encourage and challenge each other to develop, practice, and enjoy the embodiment of racially counterhegemonic childhood scripts.[23]

The play that occurs within these spaces constitutes an "educational 'project'" far greater than "schooling itself, but rather the creation of social identities, the maintenance of power relations, and the reorganization of the relationship between a capitalist economic formation, the state and its citizen-subjects."[24] Through play, children reorganize themselves in accordance with social networks in which power is typically not distributed according to the governmental hierarchies of race or socioeconomic status. Play transfers cultural memory and equips Black children with the knowledge and skills that enable them to navigate anti-Black institutions and resist oppression. In this way, play creates the early foundation for their personal and collective identities.

ETHNOGRAPHIC MOMENTS

At the beginning of the 2018–2019 academic year for Blaze Rods and Fun Middle School students, I would typically spend most of my day in the media center, where I participated in literacy-based activities with students and dialogued with various teachers and parents. When after-school began, I would spend my days split between the activities scheduled for the third- to fifth-grade girls and the media center, where a few Fun Middle School students would entertain themselves while their younger siblings attended after-school and they awaited their parents for pickup. This was my routine for the first month of the 2019–2020 academic year as well; by then, students knew exactly where and when to find me, as well as with whom they might find me. Accordingly, the moments recollected below took place in one of the two locations with a reoccurring group of students.

Checking Authority

Throughout the summer of 2018, I established a singular relationship with Julio and C.J., seventh- and sixth-grade students at Fun Middle School who are also graduates of Blaze Rods and two of ten related siblings. Julio and C.J. spent their after-school hours in the Blaze Rods media center while their younger siblings attended after-school care. A few weeks into the school year, Julio developed a keen interest in my research and decided he would provide me with the notes he felt I should have if I was going to document his play practices and his perspective on childhood accurately.

One day, after checking to make sure I was taking notes, Julio informed me that he likes Takis, hot fries, and all the hot stuff. He shared this before explaining that teachers do not let students eat in class. When I asked why, he responded tersely:

A grown-up don't think like a kid.

In one sentence, Julio revealed a consciousness of the social distance between his status as a kid and that of adulthood. While he felt like the prohibition on snacks in the classroom was unjustified, Julio did not identify a logical reason as to why adults think so differently. He offered the difference as a statement of fact. Kids are involved in the construction of neither the institutions they are required to attend nor the social contract that positions them under the control of an adult. In many cases, adults not thinking like kids is the problem. The disparity in thinking leaves room for the operationalization of violent assumptions about the needs, desires, and capabilities of the students.

Moreover, in a school cluster where more than 90 percent of the students qualify for free lunch, the prohibition on snacks throughout the school day seems counterproductive. Rarely do schools operate from a rights-based framework that situates students' rights to a quality education and basic human needs at the center of their pedagogy and policy. Rather, pedagogy and codes of conduct reflect neoliberal perceptions of human need that is ageist, sexist, and racist. The perception is that children need discipline (read: punishment), poor Black children even more so; childhood sensibilities and pleasures must be repressed, poor Black children and girls even more so; children need deprivation and structure to prepare for a civically engaged adulthood, poor Black children even more so. As the target of this neoliberal discourse, students can develop a fatalistic attitude toward their daily realities within their school system and broader society. I believe Julio gestured toward the seeming irrationality in some of the decision-making processes and the corresponding meaninglessness in the grown-ups' omnipotent authority. He did not outwardly challenge the authority, but he peeped the contradictions.

Another commentary on adult irrationality occurred while I was sitting at the cafeteria table after school with Ariah and Zuri (in 2019), two girls in the third- to fifth-grade girls group. I must have asked them how their day went because my field notes from the subsequent discussion include frustrated commentary from Ariah and angrily handwritten notes from Zuri about the unfair treatment they had received from their teachers. Ariah shared, "Teachers play favorites. . . . She be mean to me 'cause she know I don't like her. . . . She be talkin' to me like she's my mama."

56 ARIANA DENISE BRAZIER

In the same conversation, but referring to a different faculty member, Zuri, with a wide grin and loud, expressive neck roll, declared that the "teacher done lost her mind!" I asked, "The teacher done lost her mind?" before writing these exact words on the page. Zuri snatched the notebook (which she had doodled in many times before) and wrote the following as a smile formed across her face:

> Why Because my big-chin teacher Ms. . . . don't lost her mind she drop me in the lower reading group because she told me to slow down.

The teacher had tried to make her slow the pace at which she was reading her assignment, and Zuri was irate about the teacher's decision to place her in a less advanced reading group. She, like Julio, suggested the teacher was acting irrationally. Yet, Zuri was left feeling somewhat powerless, as she could not affect the teacher's decision to change her reading group. Playfully, Zuri began joaning her teacher as a form of release, and this play provoked laughter and eventually redirected the conversation to her favorite books and reading habits.[25]

Ariah and Zuri express genuine exasperation as they straight-up reject the treatment they received from their teachers. As two of the most advanced readers and committed students in the school, they were aware that an injustice had occurred as the teachers had made assumptions about their character and capacities. And, in Zuri's situation, the teacher had impeded her academic growth. Within the familiar zone they initiated, and in the privacy of our dialogue—only their little sisters were present and attentive—both Ariah and Zuri refused to accept their place and passively trust the discretion of their teachers. By talking (a little) reckless—well, reckless for a child, especially a Black girl child—they ignored the white heteropatriarchal cultural norms and respectability politics that would tamper their anger and gaslight them into questioning their own inclinations toward self-preservation.

The experiences they recollected are a part of the socializing processes that seek to fracture the spirits of Black children to ensure passive obedience to authority and paternalistic institutions that nonconsensually situate themselves in locus parentis. Thus, ensuring the longevity of the "educational survival complex, in which students are left learning to merely survive, learning how schools mimic the world they live in, thus making schools a training site for a life of exhaustion."[26] Whether intentional or not, teachers of all races have been indoctrinated into the same system of anti-Black thinking and have been acculturated into a society that consistently negates child-generated insight and feedback, especially within hyperstructured, unilateral spaces like classrooms.

Together, Julio, Ariah, and Zuri highlight the seemingly minor injustices or transgressions that actually reveal deep flaws in the system as each student calls out interactions reinforced by policies that are not providing for their well-being. All three students exhibited a distrust and a sense of self-righteousness that reinforced a trust they harbored in their own intuition. Absent an adult authority, the students took a risk and spoke freely in the media center and at the cafeteria table in the presence of their siblings and peers. Their dialogues served not only to demonstrate the depths of their own subjectivity and social consciousness within the school system but also to equip their younger siblings with the skills for navigating the system. The loud voices, wide grins, and playful undertones in their interactions with each other as they shared their perception of the adult–kid binary informed me that while they cannot fight the system (or the adults who represent it), they did not accept the order either. Rather, they were just playing along.

Exchanging Knowledge

On another day (in 2018), in the media center after school with Julio, C.J., and Ocho Jinks, another sixth-grade student at Fun Middle School who also graduated from Blaze Rods, the three boys were excitedly recounting the most interesting part of their day, which involved a fight that broke out between a parent and someone else's child just as they were exiting the school bus to enter Blaze Rods. They students narrated the portion of the fight they could witness before shifting into a speculative conversation about the police, language, and grown-ups:

JULIO: We call the cops "twelve." . . . I think they call the police "twelve" because twelve police stations in Georgia.

OCHO JINKS: I think they call it "twelve" because there are twelve zones. . . .
We in zone twelve.

C.J.: We call "lyin" "cappin" and the teachers get on our nerves.

. . .

JULIO: [Ima write about] how grown-ups live.

ME: How do they live?

JULIO: For instance, they tell us to clean up the house, but it's they house.

. . .

JULIO: Since the grown-ups made you, they tell you what to do.

JULIO: Mama got a response to every question but the answer.

There is much speculation about the origin of the moniker "twelve" for the cops. But what is most intriguing about the conversation between the boys is how they confidently theorize with each other and demonstrate their participation within a larger community as they claim ownership over each of these popular terms. None of these terms, to my knowledge, were created by this set of kids. The boys freely exchanged knowledge that will become the social and cultural capital that enables their access into other familiar zones while exhibiting the efficacy of the customs of care in which they have been brought up or that they themselves have sustained as the older siblings in their respective families.

While researchers, educators, and adults in general, who have subscribed to white cultural instructional styles, are conditioned to denigrate peer-facilitated, cooperative learning experiences, Black children have the capacity to create and establish the rules of engagement and, therefore, dictate their own learning processes. For Black children, these rules are often not standardized either—they are improvised. The influence of customs of care exhibited in Black linguistic expression and critical literacy practices confirm countless studies that have emphasized the immense value of intergenerational and culturally responsive learning.

Their linguistic and dialogic play becomes the basis for the coded cracks and critiques they make on and of each other, authority figures, and various institutions. Here, again, Julio critiqued grown-up rationalities and authority as he stated, "They tell us to clean up the house, but it's they house." He was emphasizing how he was born into a power

Radicalizing Black Child Play

structure that preceded him. With his comment, "Since grown-ups made you . . . ," he began to offer some reason for their authority, but even in his conclusion, "they tell you what to do," there remains some skepticism as their telling is not always, or often, justified, logical, or consensual. Julio provoked an analytical examination of identity, considering how parents and guardians feel obligated to form a "successful identity" in their children, which rests on increasingly productive contributions to society. Schools assume the same responsibility. In both cases, neither the school nor the parents begin their respective processes of identity formation with the students; instead, they mobilize the assumption that the child is incapable of fashioning their own socially acceptable or successful identity.

Julio's final comment about his mama made me laugh. His mama is a fierce community advocate. Julio held a different perspective as someone who was "made" by her. Since their mamas and the grown-ups have responses but not answers, children turn to each other, thus subverting the conventional top-down movement of knowledge. In doing so, they can take ownership over the ideas and practices generated in these spaces, as well as practice and explore content and questions that may otherwise be silenced by grown-ups because the topics or language breach respectable notions of childhood or further distance them from the projection of childhood innocence that their home community imposes upon their children.

A relevant example of students critically engaging each other and challenging commonly accepted precepts taught about adults by adults happened when I was sitting around a table in a classroom during an after-school breakout session one afternoon with the third- to fifth-grade girls (in 2019). As we were discussing the social order in the neighborhood, one student began to share a story about the police coming to her door:

STUDENT 1: The police knocked on our door . . .
ME: Were you scared?
(Student 1 nods silently with wide eyes.)
STUDENT 1: All our hearts dropped.
ME: I don't like the police.

STUDENT 2: I like the police. They save lives.

ARIAH: Police don't save people. They take people to jail.

Though the fear in this child as she recollected the moment was visible, one student felt the need to interject her opinion of the police. In response, Ariah swiftly and confidently rejected not only the student's positive opinion but also the most popular teaching that U.S. citizens are offered: police are heroes because they save lives. Ariah, however, assertively explained the fallacy in this claim: "Police don't save people." Rather, by taking people to jail, the police interrupt and end many lives at once through the brutality of hypersurveillance, stop and frisk, civil forfeiture, coercion, and physical violence.

The circulation of social capital, knowledge of survival in the hood (i.e., street codes), and socioemotional consciousness was swirling all around us in what started as a serious and playful dialogue about the neighborhood. Schools seek to instill a supposedly healthy trust in authority within their students, yet within these zones students are learning the process of discernment. Engaging in conversations such as this one, students establish either trust or distrust in grown-ups, institutions, and their peers as they learn to recognize untruths and omissions in common teachings. Children, then, equipped with new knowledge, decisively develop an oppositional disposition toward the institutions and individuals who continually disseminate untruths.

Within familiar zones, children are having more critically engaged conversations than they are in most traditional learning spaces. Too frequently, children "are seen everywhere . . . without being perceived, recognized or engaged on their own terms as actors or social claim makers."[27] Nevertheless, here they were, constructing their own politics of anti-citizenship against the state; a politic that is both rooted in lived experience and reflective of local community ethics.

Organizing Collectively

On two (of many) remarkable, and almost imperceptible, occasions, I witnessed Blaze Rods students respond to an impulse to move against the bodily isolation enforced by the U.S. educational system by channeling "the embodied knowledge" that "in many cases, provide[s] the information that keeps them alive."[28] The first occasion (in 2018) was after school, awaiting direction from after-school administrators or counselors, the fourth-grade girls initiated a game of telephone among themselves. Similarly, during the school day the next year (in 2019), while half of the third-grade class waited for their turn on the laptops to take their Accelerated Reader tests, about six girls begin playing double-double tap-tap (a handclapping game) in pairs. They initiated this interaction, almost without words, the second the teacher left the room. When the teacher returned, she angrily yelled at the girls, "You know better!," and sent one girl to the back of the table to sit alone.

The isolation and individualism of traditional classroom spaces and all forms of standardized testing do not serve the best interest of these students who have been raised by and within concentric circles of community and kinship. These white-based cultural norms, enforced by policies and codes of conduct, serve to reinforce an institutional perception of order and control that obstructs and punishes children for their Black joy. This mandate for control is not unlike the governmental enforcement of law and order that leads to the criminalization of Black folks' peaceful protests and mass gatherings.

Through play, dominant social perceptions that lead people to believe that dialogic experiences about identities can only occur in certain places and formats are reframed as certain games confront perceptions of personal agency, as children are challenged to comprehend how their identities are laterally aligned (the fate of one is connected to the fate of all) instead of hierarchically (one person's actions being more influential or important than others). Hence, play can and should be understood as a tool for grassroots community organizing, as exemplified in the two aforementioned instances in which Black girls organized themselves for a moment of joy—even under the threat of being publicly chastised by the teachers and staff.

Accordingly, the playful dialogue and games engaged by Blaze Rods and Fun Middle School students recollected in this chapter are antineoliberal in nature, and thus a demonstration of their anti-citizenship, as they rely on each other for access to embodied knowledge, skills, and expression—all of which catalyze the production and exchange of social capital rooted in a local culture. Momentarily escaping the adult control and surveillance that composes their school day, students demonstrate the potency of cooperative play that responds to oppression and cultivates subversive practices of personal and collective agency. As Aimee Meredith Cox explains, "Protesting and playing are interconnected practices used . . . in very well planned and overt ways as well as in ways that appear unconscious and spontaneous." She uses "play . . . to refer to the joy in working collectively to confront the most subtle and difficult to define aspects of institutionalized injustice and everyday instances in which Black girls find themselves dismissed and/or violated."[29]

If educators, researchers, and adults, generally, broaden our understanding of play to encompass diverse forms and embodiments and critical engagement, we can allow the space necessary for the revelation of children's consciousness. We can learn how children challenge and affirm themselves and each other, thus building stronger communities that endure amid formidable conditions. Play provides a safe foundation for Black children to see, affirm, and cultivate each other as they identify shared needs, cultivate a social consciousness, and invent solutions.

Inside these familiar zones and customs of care, play is the prevailing pedagogy and organizing method. The older children (consciously and unconsciously) experiment with their instructional styles as they provide cooperative learning experiences for the younger children and challenge them to take risks while under their protection.

Play is disruptive because it interrupts violent acculturating processes that seek to distance children from the nonwhite cultures in which they have been raised. The prevailing white-supremacist culture that permeates the U.S. school system compels students toward individualism and competition, preparing them for the workforce that will sustain neoliberal capitalism. By inviting children into Black joy-filled body-to-body movement and peer-facilitated dialogue, play disrupts social conditioning by realigning children with their community. Thereby ensuring they will not confront the state alone—rather, they will confront it with their kin and comrades.

As pedagogy, play, particularly within familiar zones, invites risky dialogue, inquiry, and innovation. In taking these risks, children not only learn the limitlessness of their own minds and bodies, they also learn how their relationships make space and provide for them. Essentially, they learn a form of self-reliance and sufficiency that elevates their entire community. This moves the community against the state, as the state needs Black folks' reliance and struggle to maintain the illusion of scarcity and Black pathology, which justify systems of mass deprivation and state-sanctioned murder.

In forging a space replete with codes and strategies to center their own questions and vent their own grievances, children are subverting the myth that they are passive recipients of the knowledge bequeathed to them by their authority figures. They subvert, while preserving aspects of their well-being, identity, and struggle that are otherwise neglected and forgotten by the adults that dictate their lives.

Familiar zones are necessary sites of study for those seeking to identify and understand the strategies youth themselves create and employ to negotiate and exercise anti-citizenship. Youth anti-citizenship can teach us the value in shirking the fight against the state (from time to time) to focus on the internal work of building constructive relationships of accountability and fostering a culture of learning that honors risks and challenges resigned acceptance of divisive capitalist ideologies.

In examining how youth actuate their anti-citizenship, we—adults— can witness the ways we criminalize and distance them from their earliest liberatory experiences and practices. Liberation is a project that necessitates continuous critical inquiry, collaboration, and risk-taking. It is at the risk of confronting and reimagining our conditions that new, nonhierarchical alliances can be formed and mobilized. Moreover, from the youth we are learning that the project of liberation must be universally accessible and that we are all equipped with grassroots pedagogical and organizing tools, as we all have experienced some form of play. If joy is the reason, we should continually return to and uphold the potency of play as the tool that generated our earliest experiences of joy; therefore, play is a tool for accessing those embodied memories and experiences of freedom again and again.

Notes

1. My ethnographic research spanned the summer months of May to August in 2018 and 2019.

2. Mitchell Duneier, *Ghetto: The Invention of a Place, the History of an Idea* (New York: Farrar, Straus and Giroux, 2016), 225.

3. Aimee Meredith Cox, *Shapeshifters: Black Girls and the Choreography of Citizenship* (Durham, N.C.: Duke University Press, 2015).

4. Kathryn Bond Stockton, *The Queer Child, or Growing Sideways in the Twentieth Century* (Durham, N.C.: Duke University Press, 2009).

5. Rebecca Epstein, Jamilia Blake, and Thalia González, "Girlhood Interrupted: The Erasure of Black Girls' Childhood," *SSRN Electronic Journal* (June 27, 2017): https://doi.org/10.2139/ssrn.3000695.

6. Monique W. Morris, *Pushout: The Criminalization of Black Girls in Schools* (New York: New Press, 2016).

7. The school and students discussed in this chapter have been anonymized. Individual names and respective school names were created by the students themselves, except for Ariah and Zuri, with whom I was unable to follow up. Additionally, Blaze Rods Elementary is one of two schools that feed into Fun Middle School.

8. Lauren J. Silver, *System Kids: Adolescent Mothers and the Politics of Regulation* (Chapel Hill: University of North Carolina Press, 2015).

9. Bettina L. Love, *We Want to Do More Than Survive: Abolitionist Teaching and the Pursuit of Educational Freedom* (Boston: Beacon Press, 2019).

10. Silver, *System Kids*, 58.

11. Scott quoted in Silver, 54.

12. Silver, 54.

13. Silver, 54.

14. Allison James, "Confections, Concoctions, and Conceptions," in *The Children's Culture Reader,* ed. Henry Jenkins (New York: New York University Press, 1998), 395.

15. Erika Bocknek and Janice Hale, "Applying a Cultural Prism to the Study of Play Behavior of Black Children," in *Negro Educational Review* 67, no. 1–4 (2016): 90.

16. Cox, *Shapeshifters*, 258.

17. It is noteworthy that these familiar zones are not always morally ethical or nonviolent, as within these spaces children also learn to fight physically, joaning can become bullying, and false information can be shared.

18. ATL Parent Like a Boss, Inc. (@atlparentlikeaboss), "Race/Culture Connections," Instagram post, December 3, 2020, https://www.instagram.com/p/CIV2UKUHgQX/?igshid=11qezey52lzcv.

19. ATL Parent Like a Boss, Inc. (@atlparentlikeaboss), "Relationship Connections," Instagram post, December 1, 2020, https://www.instagram.com/p/CIQsxMinhrv/?igshid=gotaafzfsp2g.

Radicalizing Black Child Play   65

20. Some handclapping and rhythmic movements teach us about what was kept from Black people in slavery and how people who were enslaved responded to this deprivation creatively. So, while play is producing and illustrating the joy of a specific group, it is also informing us about the history of our country and how this history connects us to people around the world.

21. For some examples, see Paul Amar, "The Street, the Sponge, and the Ultra: Queer Logics of Children's Rebellion and Political Infantilization," *GLQ: A Journal of Lesbian and Gay Studies* 22, no. 4 (2016): 569–604; the [Black] "Doll Test" by Drs. Kenneth and Mamie Clark; Cox, *Shapeshifters*; Monique W. Morris, *Sing a Rhythm, Dance a Blues: Liberatory Education for Black and Brown Girls* (New York: New Press, 2022); Kyra Danielle Gaunt, *The Games Black Girls Play: Learning the Ropes from Double-Dutch to Hip-Hop* (New York: New York University Press, 2006).

22. See Article 31 of the U.N. Convention on the Rights of the Child for more on children's right to leisure and play. The United States has yet to ratify the convention. U.N. General Assembly, Resolution 44/25, Convention on the Rights of the Child, A/44/736 (November 17, 1989), available at United Nations Digital Library, https://digitallibrary.un.org/record/80502?ln=en.

23. Valerie Kinloch, *Harlem on Our Minds: Place, Race, and the Literacies of Urban Youth* (New York: Teachers College Press, 2010), 176.

24. Katharyne Mitchell, "Educating the National Citizen in Neoliberal Times: From the Multicultural Self to the Strategic Cosmopolitan," *Transactions of the Institute of British Geographers* 28, no. 4 (December 2003): 390, https://doi.org/10.1111/j.0020-2754.2003.00100.x.

25. Joaning is a reference, cited from Kyra Danielle Gaunt, meaning "oral and competitive verbal art" that "usually involves overt or covert, direct and indirect 'serious, clever conflict talk,' 'aggressive witty performance talk'; and 'nonferrous contest talk,' in everyday conversation, or in oral performance narrative traditions like playing the Dozens." Gaunt, *Games Black Girls Play*, 131.

26. Love, *We Want to Do More Than Survive*, 27.

27. Amar, "Street, the Sponge, and the Ultra," 579.

28. Cox, *Shapeshifters*, 195.

29. Cox, 141.

CHAPTER 3

Radical Black Joy Is Citizenship

DAMARIS C. DUNN

Black girl joy is TikTok hair tutorials, large pastel green bubbles for buns, a spray bottle, olive oil Eco gel, Megan Thee Stallion/ Beyoncé/Jhené Aiko songs bumping in the background, full dimpled cheeks, and warm brown eyes. *Radical* Black girl joy is a deliberate condition of the spirit and a dogged persistence that holds two truths. One truth is that "past is not yet past" and that as Black subjects, we live in the afterlife of slavery.[1] According to Saidiya Hartman, the afterlife of slavery includes "skewed life chances, limited access to health and education, premature death, incarceration, and impoverishment."[2] The other truth of Radical Black joy is expressed through the work of world-making. Radical Black joy is both a fugitive praxis and a destination. It conjures up visions of life, love, and freedom on the other side of abolition. As a fugitive praxis, Radical Black joy is a demonstration of what life can and should be like beyond the confines of life under capitalism's death knell, a future where Black girls lay their edges, bump the music of their choice, create TikTok videos, and walk in liberation. After we have abolished institutions like the foster-care system and the carceral state that specialize in death-dealing, Radical Black joy will be the principle of freedom by which we construct a new world. Ma'Khia Bryant's premature death cut her world-making short, but her persistence to create and invite other Black girls into her world-making via her TikTok hair tutorials are an extension of an abolitionist politic that refuses carcerality and the conditions that make carcerality possible, while actively dreaming the world anew— one where Radical Black joy is not subversive but a rite for Black girls.

Hence, in the eleven seconds it took for officer Nicholas Reardon to fire and murder Ma'Khia Bryant without de-escalation, the promises of "citizenship" set forth by the Fourteenth Amendment were snatched. Ma'Khia was deprived not only of her due process and protection under the law but her right to Radical Black joy. In 1921, fifty-three years after the Fourteenth Amendment was passed, historian Carter G. Woodson declared that "citizenship in this country for the Negro is fiction."[3] Resting on Woodson's words, citizenship in the twenty-first century is still unfathomable for Black subjects living in the afterlife of slavery.[4] In the afterlife of slavery, Black girls' bodies are not their own. They are policed and surveilled: dragged from desks for refusing to give up their phones, strip-searched for being too "giddy," subjected to scrutiny for the way their hair grows out of their heads, and reprimanded for their clothing.[5] In this sense, Black girls' bodies are reduced to flesh as things to be controlled.[6] According to educator and activist Connie Wun, "The spectacle of punishing Black bodies is ingrained in the 'dreams and desires' of the US racial society and its citizens."[7] Put another way, Black pain and suffering are inherent to America's project of citizenship.

But who gets to be a citizen? Surely not the poor Black girls in East Harlem, the South Bronx, Ferguson, Baltimore, and Baton Rouge who are victimized in and out of school by the state and the conditions it has engineered in their communities. According to scholar-activist Monique W. Morris, "Black girls remain the only group of girls to experience negative outcomes at every point along the full discipline continuum, from suspension, corporal punishment, and expulsion to arrest and referral to law enforcement."[8] Ma'Khia's death is merely a microcosm of how anti-Blackness functions in and out of schools. As a result, the precarity that Black girls face at the hands of the state pushes them to the periphery of the citizenship project, casting them as something other than citizens. Black girls are consistently denied citizenship; therefore, they can be read as anti-citizens. The characterization of Black girls as anti-citizens conveys their lived and embodied experiences, as being reduced to things to be controlled rather than human beings worthy of joy (radical or otherwise) and love. In this way, anti-citizenship casts Black girls as a "[sub] genre of being human."[9] By offering Radical Black joy as a liberatory praxis, I envision a lifetime where Black girls are fully citizens.

In an effort to center Black girls as anti-citizens who are constantly operating under the pretenses of state-sanctioned violence, I employ BlackCrit to attend to "the specificity of Blackness" in and out of educational spaces.[10] Michael J. Dumas and kihana miraya ross conceptualize the key components of BlackCrit theory, which assert: anti-Blackness is endemic; "Blackness exists in tension with neoliberal-multicultural imagination"; space for Black liberatory fantasy is necessary and collective; and we must resist a white revisionist history in which there is an erasure of white violence. Dumas and ross's BlackCrit helps us to consider how we might begin to imagine Radical Black joy as a tool of postabolitionary world-making in which Black girls can exist as authentic citizens. To the extent that it is possible for educators to be co-conspirators in this work, I interview education expert and abolitionist Bettina Love about Get Free: Hip Hop Civics Education as a vehicle through which to facilitate Radical Black joy. In the next section, I examine the precarious state of Black girlhood in schools to situate Black girls as anti-citizens in the afterlife of slavery. I see Radical Black joy as a site of authentic citizenship and reflect on the postabolitionary world-making project that it takes up.

BLACK GIRLS AS ANTI-CITIZENS

The Black community is widely perceived as a homogeneous group with similar interests, but Black girls have distinct experiences both in and out of school. While childhood for Black boys and girls appears both "socially unimagined and unimaginable," Black boys have gained greater public attention within education, affording them a clearer path to citizenship.[11] In their work, Dumas and ross encourage scholars who take up Black-Crit theory to recognize and attend to the multitude of ways that Black subjects' experiences differ—put differently, BlackCrit is not essentialist. Specifically, as it relates to Black girl anti-citizens, educators must be vigilant of this fact and take into account the many ways that Black girls know and be. Given the precariousness of their intersectional identities, as anti-citizens, Black girls remain subject to death-dealing inside and outside of schools. In addition, they also experience what legal scholar Patricia Williams calls "spirit-murdering" in their classrooms.[12] Take, for instance, Rutherford County, Tennessee, where four Black girls were forcibly removed from school by law enforcement and Judge Donna Scott Davenport for not breaking up a fight among their peers; charged with a crime that does not exist, "a sixth grader, two fourth graders and a third grader were arrested."[13] As anti-citizens, these four Black girls were introduced to the carceral state as early as third grade.

According to abolitionist Mariame Kaba, the false equivalency of Blackness and criminality is endemic in the United States.[14] Dumas and ross put it this way: "Anti-blackness constructs Black subjects, and positions them in and against law, policy, and every day (civic) life."[15] For Black girl anti-citizens who are a part of the subgenre of what it means to be human, they have experienced and continue to experience how law, policy, and everyday life are constructed by anti-Blackness and continue to engulf them in the afterlife of slavery. The African American Policy Forum began the #SayHerName campaign in 2014 to acknowledge that Black women and girls "get killed by police too."[16] According to the campaign, "Black girls as young as 7" have died at the hands of state-sanctioned violence and are rarely, if ever, acknowledged.[17] In schools more specifically, Black girls remain both hypervisible and invisible, according to educational researchers. The endemic nature of anti-Blackness, racism, and white supremacy in society are often mirrored in schools where Black girls are less likely to receive the care, love, and grace that is often afforded to white girls.[18]

While Black girls make up 15 percent of school-aged children, they are overrepresented in school discipline data.[19] In a 2014 study conducted at Georgetown Law's Center on Poverty and Inequality, Black girls were said to have experienced "adultification."[20] Adultification is the perception that Black girls are "less innocent and more adult-like than white girls of the same age."[21] In the same study, in which 325 participants were surveyed, 62 percent of participants identified as white women and 79 percent of all of the white people in the study held a degree beyond high school.[22] This study not only offers a small glimpse into the hearts and minds of white women but also is a snapshot of the more than 80 percent of white women who occupy the teaching force. These same teachers typically operate as an arm of the state—a carceral appendage—that facilitates the policing and imprisonment of Black girls caught in the school–prison nexus.[23] Put differently, the materiality of today's Black girl anti-citizens in the afterlife of slavery is consistent with the sociohistorical realties of the Black women and girls that came before them. With that said, greater attention to abolitionary teaching that attends to anti-Black racism in and beyond schools is required to equip Black girls with the capacity to advance liberation. In an earlier study, Mary Pattillo-McCoy found that, regardless of socioeconomic status, Black girls were more vulnerable to inadequate education and crime.[24] Because education is a predictor for how Black girls will fare in society, the consistent increase in Black girls' discipline and punishment is alarming.

Reimagining a future for Black girls where they are legitimate citizens in a postabolitionary world is crucial to undoing the carcerality that Black girls face in and out of schools. With the intent to radically upend the existing structures, we must center the lived and embodied experiences of the Black girls who are furthest on the periphery. Mother of the civil rights movement Ella Baker describes the need for a radical change, one that fully supports abolition of the systems and structures that uphold anti-Blackness, white supremacy, and racism. Joy James quotes Baker, who says this:

> In order for us as poor oppressed people to become a part of a society that is meaningful, the system under which we now exist has to be radically changed. . . . I use the term radical in its original meaning—getting down to and understanding the root cause. It means facing a system that does not lend itself to your needs and devising means by which you change the system.[25]

That is, in order to have meaningful change, there must be a full overhaul of the system. Baker was deeply invested in a world-making project as well as an ideological framework that influenced how we think about abolitionist politics. As she grew tired of liberalism, she began to criticize it. In the article "A Radical Doctrine: Abolitionist Education in Hard Times," scholars marshal Baker's position on radical change for a radical doctrine in education; the authors argue that radical joy, radical trust, and freedom dreaming are crucial to the project of abolition in schools.[26]

An impediment to an abolitionist politic, or "revolutionary" politic as Black feminist scholar Joy James describes, is liberalism. Examining Black feminism more closely, she says, "Differentiating between liberalism and radicalism—or even more so 'radical' and 'revolutionary'—to theorize Black feminist liberation politics is extremely difficult but essential."[27] In order to theorize a Radical Black girl joy for the Black girl who is faced with unmet needs and constantly being patrolled in her school, I take up Ella Baker's and Joy James's charge for a more radical approach to upending structures. In the same fashion, I theorize Radical Black joy as a postabolitionary construct that is informed by Black girl anti-citizenship. Following Radical Black joy, I engage in a dialogue about the Get Free: Hip Hop Civics curriculum as one site for Radical Black joy.

Radical Black Joy

Black studies scholars have examined Black literature, art, and music to theorize Black joy as a preoccupation of Black life and a site of resistance for Black subjects. In order to situate Radical Black joy as a postabolitionary project, I begin with Black studies scholars who attend to Black joy in their work. Katie G. Cannon, James H. Cone, Audre Lorde, and Alice Walker provide useful articulations of Black joy. Radical Black joy extends Dumas and ross's conceptualization of "Black liberatory fantasy."[28] For Radical Black joy to be possible, the conditions of poor and oppressed people must be abolished, and Black subjects must be seen as full citizens who marshal their joy as a means of creating a new world. Radical Black joy is what happens when the afterlife of slavery has ceased. Dumas and ross cite Frantz Fanon as an advocate for "Black liberatory fantasy" and a complete tearing-down of the state. Fanon puts it this way: "The work of the colonized is to imagine every possible method for annihilating the colonist."[29] As such, abolition is the work that will bring Black girl citizens a Radical Black joy.

Black liberation scholar Katie G. Cannon's close examination of the life of Zora Neale Hurston provides one articulation of Black joy by way of Hurston's mother. As a child, Hurston was encouraged to "jump at de sun" so that she would not "turn out to be a mealy-mouthed rag doll."[30]

I interpret her mother's words as not letting anyone steal your joy and saying what you mean and meaning what you say. Hurston also took her mother's words to heart, as she was very adamant about the "wholeness of Black life"; she was not interested in the fragmented stories of Black people.[31] According to Cannon, Hurston refuted "assumptions of genetic racism . . . in the face of oppressive slander of White supremacy," and she used "presentational methods to document the culture, history, imagination, and fantasies of Black people."[32] Jumping at the sun was not only an affirmation but an encouraging word to stay steadfast in her pursuit despite white and Black critics. In Hurston's writing, to be Black was not simply to be oppressed or to preoccupy oneself with whiteness but to be resilient despite it. By doing the work of centering Blackness and being, Hurston saw Black interiority as a strength and not a crutch, thus to "jump at de sun" was to be intentional in holding on to the joy that is Blackness.

To "jump at de sun" in spite of white supremacy, racism, and anti-Blackness could be seen by Audre Lorde as tapping into the power of the erotic. Lorde insists that the erotic is often reserved and misnamed by men in an effort to control women's innermost feelings and selves, yet she challenges women to tap into this deep feeling to fulfill their passions and work. Lorde insists that tapping into our innermost feeling is to reawaken our potential for joy, which is the deeply held awareness and consciousness that empowers us. She declares, "The sharing of joy, whether physical, emotional, psychic, or intellectual, forms a bridge between the sharers which can be a basis for understanding much of what is not shared between them, and lessens the threat of their difference."[33] In other words, joy is the life force that connects the collective "we."

Putting Audre Lorde in conversation with Black liberation theologist James H. Cone, it is clear that Black joy is collective in nature. Cone writes that "despite . . . pain and terror . . . blacks did not let lynching completely squeeze the joy out of their lives."[34] In an effort to capture Black joy, Cone insists that joy fueled place- and space-making that could be found in the Black church and the juke joint. For Cone, the Black church and blues music were sites of a shared fate by which Black people resisted, communed, and exercised their joy. Cone writes that "at

74 DAMARIS C. DUNN

the juke, blacks could talk back to the 'The Man.'"[35] He describes blues music as a disposition of an "existential affirmation of joy in the midst of extreme suffering."[36] Put differently, the blues was a site of both resistance and belonging whereby Black people tended to their pain and cultivated spaces of joy.

The joy that Cone centers in his writing is in response to lynching, pain, and suffering. Similarly, Alice Walker's protagonist Tashi is walking to be hung in *Possessing the Secret of Joy*, and she is met by her family with a sign that states that "RESISTANCE IS THE SECRET OF JOY!"[37] Not only is Tashi described as having a deep feeling of satisfaction in her resistance to Olinka culture, but she is set free. Tashi is resisting cultural norms, her dogged persistence to do so leads to the murder of M'Lissa, an Olinkan woman who performs female genital mutilation. Not only does Tashi kill M'Lissa, but she takes back her joy as she smiles walking to her execution. For Tashi, joy comes in mourning the death of her sister and taking control of her life. Like Lorde's joy, there is a deep-felt sense, and like Cone's joy, Tashi's joy is in response to cultural norms that are dehumanizing.

In essence, previous theorizations of Black joy exist in response to pain and suffering. Walker's joy as resistance is emblematic of how Black joy manifests in Black literary tradition, art, and music; for Black people, joy is a deeply felt sense of belonging and an innermost feeling that has traditionally been theorized as a response to pain and suffering. Attention to Black joy and its role in sustaining Black subjects helps us to critically engage how we might marshal Black joy as a vehicle for world-making beyond pain and suffering. I propose Radical Black joy as a fugitive praxis conceived in intentionality—a tool for living out in the present the lives we will lead in the future when we have eliminated the conditions that hold us down. Radical Black joy is citizen futurity; it is fleeting, but we escape to it while we endure poverty, police violence, white supremacy, and incarceration, in order to weave together a tapestry, a vision, for what our collective lives must look like on the other side of abolition. Radical Black joy on this side of revolution prefigures our collective future in the wake of capitalism's demise. Dismantling capitalism and carcerality will not only afford Black girls full citizenship, it will also make way for construction of a world that is worthy of them. In the next section, I offer the Get Free: Hip Hop Civics curriculum as a vehicle for promoting Radical Black joy.

HIP-HOP AS A SITE OF WORLD-MAKING?

Long time hip-hop scholar Tricia Rose asserts that "hip-hop emerged as a source for youth of alternative identity formation and social status in a community whose older institutions had been all but demolished."[38] Crafting alternative spaces within the demolition, Black and Brown subjects created sites of Black joy, much like the juke joints that Cone describes in *The Cross and the Lynching Tree*. Though different from the conditions that lynching created for Black men, women, and children in the South, hip-hop was the blues of the late 1970s and early 1980s and responded to the state's engineered conditions and its attack on Black and Brown subjects. Fifty years later, the art form has developed a complex personhood that has evolved into a multibillion-dollar industry driven by capitalism and heteropatriarchy.[39] Also an appendage of the state, the hip-hop that "started out in the heart" is problematic and causes pause for many.[40] The hip-hop that was once a site for young Black and Brown subjects' world-making has become an extension of the arm of capitalism and can be read alongside Black resilience neoliberalism.[41] Scholar Kevin L. Clay puts it this way: "[Black Resilience Neoliberalism] locates empowerment in individuated and collective, current and historical, efforts of Black folks to 'overcome' structural racism in civil society and its formal institutions to achieve mainstream success."[42] Radical Black joy does not align with Black resilience neoliberalism, but Black joy in the context in which it has been used in relation to hip-hop could be read this way. The rhetoric that forwards this notion that poor Black and Brown subjects created an art form that has catapulted into a multibillion-dollar industry is a true statement, but at whose expense and whose ability to truly reap the benefits of Black joy? In essence, hip-hop is a perfect example of Black resilience neoliberalism, pointing to the few that have made it out of the hood at the expense of glorifying and furthering capitalism and heteropatriarchy.

76   DAMARIS C. DUNN

And yet, today's hip-hop still has revolutionary potential. Hip-hop, for some Black folks, serves as the background music for our lives. Scholar Katherine McKittrick reminds us that music is a method for Black subjects. McKittrick cites Dionne Brand on music; she asserts that Black music "leaves you open, and up in the air and that is the space that some of us need, an opening to another life tangled up in this one but opening."[43] Put differently, Black music is a portal, one that allows for us to see ourselves as Black subjects, in and outside of the materiality of Black life. While Black subjects occupy the afterlife of slavery, music for some is a way out.

Because hip-hop is central to our epistemic and ontological presuppositions, I discuss Bettina Love's Get Free: Hip Hop Civics curriculum as a vehicle for Radical Black joy. As one of the most esteemed researchers in the field of education, Love was the Nasir Jones Fellow in 2016 at the W. E. B. Du Bois Research Institute at Harvard University, where she created the curriculum. In addition to her work at Harvard, Love is the William F. Russell Professor at Teachers College, Columbia University, cofounder of the Abolitionist Teaching Network, and author of *We Want to Do More Than Survive: Abolitionist Teaching and the Pursuit of Educational Freedom* and *Punished for Dreaming: How School Reform Harms Black Children and How We Heal*.[44] Her love of Black people and freedom dreams for Black children in schools is unmatched. In this interview, we discuss the Get Free: Hip Hop Civics Education curriculum. Love explains why she saw a need for it, why she chose hip-hop and civics, and who the intended audience is for the curriculum. Get Free is an online resource that has a plethora of materials with which educators who are invested in Black joy can engage.

DAMARIS C. DUNN [DD]: So, you received the title of Nasir Jones Fellow in 2016 at the W. E. B. Dubois Research Institute at Harvard. How did you arrive at Get Free: Hip Hop Civics Ed Curriculum?

BETTINA LOVE [BL]: So, you know, when I looked at the field of hip-hop education, I saw that there were a lot of people talking about English and there were a lot of folks talking about science, but nobody was really talking about social studies and civics. And the one thing that I really could not stand was when people would say, "We want students to be global citizens of the world." Like, yeah, that's true, but shouldn't they know their hood? Shouldn't they know their neighborhood? And nothing is as hyperlocal as hip-hop. Hip-hop is hyperlocal, like what's poppin' in New Orleans, might not be poppin' in Queens, what's poppin' in Brooklyn might not be poppin' in Queens, what's popping in Queens might not be popping in Rochester. Hip-hop is hyperlocal, the language. If you listen to Outkast, if you are not from Atlanta, not just Georgia, but from Atlanta, you do not know what they are saying.

DD: Mmhmm.

BL: I was thinking to myself how hip-hop tells these stories and how hip-hop is civics. When we think about civics, we think about voting and participating in elections, but hip-hop is so much more than that, and civics is so much more than that, so I wanted to try to think about how do you combine the ideas of civics, and then with so much activism taking place in 2016, and so many young activists, they are young, they are hip-hop heads, hip-hop culture is driving them. And so I just started putting hip-hop civics and activism together and thought it would be a dope way to talk about curriculum for civics but also to understand that hip-hop is civics. When we think about what civics is, it's speaking back to the establishment, informing ourselves about what is going on in our community, thinking very deeply about how oppression works, and getting ourselves out of oppression, hip-hop gives a roadmap to that. And so hip-hop is civics education.

DD: So, when you were coming up with all of this, who did you have in mind? Who was this curriculum for?

BL: Seventh and eighth graders, really, you know, middle schoolers was really where I was thinking, maybe elementary, but really just middle schoolers. I think oftentimes when we think about history, you know, we just tell them, "Oh, these people were so old." They were, you know, church folk, we just don't give them a real beautiful history of these folks. And so, you know, for middle schoolers to really get a history of Black young people who are doing this work, so they can see themselves, like you don't have to be ninety-five to be an activist, you don't have to be fifty to be an activist, these folks are twenty and eighteen and fifteen years old, trying to change the world.

DD: So, how important was Black joy in creating the Get Free curriculum?

BL: You know, Black joy was really central because I wanted students to see themselves. I wanted them to feel empowered. I wanted them to see that you could do this work and be young and be joyful and have youthfulness and be silly and love and be young. You know, I think sometimes, you know, joy for me is also like youthfulness. And just to be youthful, and that's why I went around the country interviewing young activists, you know, this was seven years ago, like Charlene Carruthers is twenty-four years old. Philip Agnew was twenty-six years old. You know, I went around the country trying to interview these young activists getting their stories. Leon Ford was twenty-three years old. I wanted them to be young, I wanted them to be youthful, I wanted them to see how much joy it brought them to do the work in their communities. You got to see the joy. I just didn't want them to talk about pain and trauma, but I wanted them to talk about their journey and their struggles and hear that music. And I think also, you know, hip-hop is youthful, hip-hop is joy. You know, it moves us in a particular type of way, and it registers in our body in a particular type of way that's joy. And so, you know, hip-hop, also always being seen as hard and tough, no, it's joy! You know, I hate when people say, like, you know, hip-hop was started, you know, as revolutionary music. No, it wasn't. No, it wasn't. It was for young, Black, Brown, Puerto Rican kids who were like, "Let's have fun. Let's tear shit up. Let's dance." They were not political, it became political, and it became that, but it's always been youth culture.

DD: So how do you see this curriculum having an impact on Black girls?

BL: You know, I really wanted, for me it was not Black girls, it was queer kids. That's where I saw the curriculum trying to make the most impact, because I wanted that queer section, I wanted queer kids. And I wanted, like, Black girls to see Charlene Carruthers, who was a queer Black woman, I wanted them to see L, who's a queer Black woman, so it was like Black girls yes, but also queer Black girls, right? I wanted them to

Radical Black Joy Is Citizenship

see themselves, because I think, I think oftentimes, sometimes, not all the time, we say, "Black girls." But we don't think about, like, the path of queer Black girls. The path of queer Black girls is different so, like, you know, I always, I always joke around and I, you know, I'll never say it publicly, but like Black Girls Rock. I love Black Girls Rock, but there are no Black girls like me in Black Girls Rock. It's very, you know, feminine straight women. Oftentimes when we say, "Black girls," we don't really include, you know, we don't include masculine Black girls or we are not really talking about lesbians, so I really wanted to highlight Black women who were queer as well.

While hip-hop is one vehicle to possibly cultivate Radical Black joy, it is also important to note that Radical Black joy might look different across space and place.

TOWARD A RADICAL BLACK GIRL JOY

Radical Black girl joy desires a complete upending of the carceral state. It wants a world without the conditions that have engineered the materiality of Black life as we currently know it. Radical Black girl joy calls for no foster-care system, no juvenile detention, no shelters, and no police in schools. To make Radical Black joy the default state of Black existence, capitalism must be dismantled, and Black resilience must no longer be the expectation that shapes the lives of Black (anti-)citizens. I do not envision Radical Black joy in the sanctimony of the Black professional ladder-climbers; instead, we see it in the visions of futurity held by the nonconciliatory, working-class Black girls in Columbia, South Carolina, and McKinney, Texas, who have gone to war with the state and lived to tell their stories. Black girl joy is bumping your music in the background for your TikTok hair tutorial, but Radical Black joy is collective, it is communal, it is an invitation, and it is the stuff of revolution. Radical Black girl joy is Charlene Carruthers, Pauli Murray, Audre Lorde, Angela Davis, Miss Major, Barbara Jordan, and Marsha P. Johnson. Radical Black girl joy is solidarity and healing the wounds that marked Black women and girls in the afterlife of slavery. Radical Black girl joy is not stunningly

80 DAMARIS C. DUNN

painful, it is not getting up every day and saving your own life; it is making a world where Blacklivingness is a right, it is free, and it is the Black liberatory fantasy that we wish for every Black girl. Radical Black girl joy is citizenship!

NOTES

1. Christina Sharpe, *In the Wake: On Blackness and Being* (Durham, N.C.: Duke University Press, 2016).

2. Saidiya Hartman, *Lose Your Mother: A Journey along the Atlantic Slave Route* (New York: Farrar, Strauss and Giroux, 2006), 6.

3. Carter G. Woodson, "Fifty Years of Negro Citizenship as Qualified by the United States Supreme Court," *Journal of Negro History* 6, no. 1 (January 1921): 1–53.

4. Hartman, *Lose Your Mother.*

5. Jenny Jarvie, "Girl Thrown from Desk Didn't Obey Because the Punishment Was Unfair, Attorney Says," *Los Angeles Times,* October 29, 2015, sec. World & Nation, https://www.latimes.com/nation/la-na-girl-thrown-punishment-unfair-20151029-story.html; Michael Gold, "After Report of 4 Girls Strip-Searched at School, Cuomo Calls for Inquiry," *New York Times,* January 30, 2019, https://www.nytimes.com/2019/01/30/nyregion/binghamton-school-strip-search.html.

6. Hortense J. Spillers, *Mama's Baby, Papa's Maybe: An American Grammar Book* (Durham, N.C.: Duke University Press, 1994), 67.

7. Connie Wun, "Unaccounted Foundations: Black Girls, Anti-Black Racism, and Punishment in Schools," *Critical Sociology* 42, no. 4–5 (2016): 741.

8. Monique W. Morris, *Sing a Rhythm, Dance a Blues: Education for the Liberation of Black and Brown Girls* (New York: New Press, 2019), 19.

9. Christopher L. Busey and Tianna Dowie-Chin, "The Making of Global Black Anti-citizen/citizenship: Situating BlackCrit in Global Citizenship Research and Theory," *Theory and Research in Social Education* 2, no. 49 (2021): 155.

10. Michael J. Dumas and kihana miraya ross, "'Be Real Black for Me': Imagining Black Crit in Education," *Urban Education* 5 (2016): 417.

11. Michael J. Dumas and Joseph Derrick Nelson, "(Re)Imagining Black Boyhood: Toward a Critical Framework for Educational Research," *Harvard Educational Review* 86, no. 1 (2016): 27.

12. Patricia Williams, "Spirit-Murdering the Messenger: The Discourse of Fingerpointing as the Law's Response to Racism," *University of Miami Law Review* 42 (1987): 127; Bettina L. Love, *We Want to Do More Than Survive: Abolitionist Teaching and the Pursuit of Educational Freedom* (Boston: Beacon Press, 2019).

13. Meribah Knight, Nashville Public Radio, and Ken Armstrong, "Black Children Were Jailed for a Crime That Doesn't Exist. Almost Nothing Happened to

Adults in Charge," ProPublica, October 5, 2021, https://www.propublica.org/article/black-children-were-jailed-for-a-crime-that-doesnt-xist?token=Tu5C70R2pCBv8Yj33AkMh2E-mHz3d6iu.

14. Mariame Kaba, *We Do This 'Til We Free Us: Abolitionist Organizing and Transforming Justice* (Chicago: Haymarket Books, 2021).

15. Dumas and ross, "'Be Real Black for Me,'" 417.

16. "#SayHerName," African American Policy Forum, https://www.aapf.org/sayhername.

17. "#SayHerName."

18. Spillers, *Mama's Baby, Papa's Maybe*, 67.

19. Jason Kornwitz, "Black Girls Are Being Pushed Out of Public Schools at Disproportionate Rates. This Graduate Wants to Help Fix the Problem," Boston College School of Social Work, August 3, 2020, https://www.bc.edu/content/bc-web/schools/ssw/about/bcssw-news/2020/Black_girls_are_being_pushed_out_of_public_schools_at_disproportionate_rates_She_wants_to_help_fix_the_problem.html.

20. Rebecca Epstein, Jamilia Blake, and Thalia Gonzalez, *Girlhood Interrupted: The Erasure of Black Girls' Childhood* (Washington, D.C.: Georgetown Law Center on Poverty and Inequality, 2017).

21. Epstein, Blake, and Gonzalez, *Girlhood Interrupted*, 1.

22. Epstein, Blake, and Gonzalez, 7.

23. Damien M. Sojoyner, *First Strike: Educational Enclosures in Black Los Angeles* (Minneapolis: University of Minnesota Press, 2016).

24. Mary Pattillo-McCoy, "The Limits of Out-Migration for the Black Middle Class," *Journal of Urban Affairs* 22, no. 3 (2000): 225–41.

25. Ella Baker quoted in Joy James, "Radicalizing Black Feminism," *Race and Class* 40, no. 4 (1999): 15.

26. Damaris C. Dunn, Alex Chisholm, Elizabeth Spaulding, and Bettina L. Love, "A Radical Doctrine: Abolitionist Education in Hard Times," *Educational Studies* 57, no. 3 (2020): 211–23, https://doi.org/10.1080/00131946.2021.1892684.

27. James, "Radicalizing Black Feminism," 20.

28. Dumas and ross, "'Be Real Black for Me,'" 417.

29. Frantz Fanon, *The Wretched of the Earth* (New York: Grove Press, 1963), 50, quoted in Dumas and ross, 431.

30. Katie G. Cannon, *Katie's Canon: Womanism and the Soul of the Black Community* (New York: Continuum Publishing Company, 1995), 79.

31. Cannon, *Katie's Canon*, 79.

32. Cannon, 79.

33. Audre Lorde, *Sister Outsider* (New York: Crossing Press, 2007), 56.

34. James H. Cone, *The Cross and the Lynching Tree* (New York: Oris Books, 2011), 16.

35. Cone, *Cross and the Lynching Tree*, 16.

36. Cone, 17.

37. Alice Walker, *Possessing the Secret of Joy* (New York: Harcourt, Brace, Jovanovich, 1992), 281.

38. Tricia Rosa, *Black Noise: Rap Music and Black Culture in Contemporary America* (Middletown, Conn.: Wesleyan University Press, 1994), 34.

39. Bettina L. Love, "Complex Personhood of Hip Hop & the Sensibilities of the Culture That Fosters Knowledge of Self & Self-Determination," *Equity & Excellence in Education* 49, no. 4 (2016): 414–27.

40. "Superstar," track 6 on Lauryn Hill, *The Miseducation of Lauryn Hill*, Columbia, 1998.

41. Kevin Clay, "Despite the Odds: Unpacking the Politics of Black Resilience Neoliberalism," *American Educational Research Journal* 56, no. 1 (2019): 75–110.

42. Clay, "Despite the Odds," 103.

43. Dionne Brand, "Jazz," in *Bread Out of Stone* (New York: Random House/Vintage, 1994), 161, quoted in Katherine McKittrick, *Dear Science and Other Stories* (Durham, N.C.: Duke University Press, 2021).

44. Love, *We Want to Do More Than Survive*; Bettina L. Love, *Punished for Dreaming: How School Reform Harms Black Children and How We Heal* (New York: St. Martin's Press, 2023).

PART II

SEEING THE INVISIBLE

On Youth Anti-citizenship and the Struggle for the (Under)Commons

CHAPTER 4

Coloniality and Antiblack Racism in Black Adolescent Girls' Lived Experiences

KARLYN ADAMS-WIGGINS

In middle school you gotta learn who you are, you gotta try to find good friends, and you come through a lot of kid drama. I feel like school . . . it should be important, but it shouldn't be determining our future so young.

—KHAILA

While some psychologists discuss Black children's experiences in terms of psychological processes like dehumanization, where the Black child is seen as older and lacking the characteristic innocence ascribed to white children, this perspective leaves unanswered questions regarding how beliefs related to dehumanized conceptions of Black children can reliably operate across social and historical contexts.[1] Yet, the matter of sociohistorical context is of crucial importance for those seeking to transform the conditions in which Black youth live. In recent years there has been a proliferation of research employing the concept of antiblackness, or antiblack racism, to discuss the experiences of Black youth inside and outside of school, typically embedding in the analysis the history of attempts to socially control and criminalize Black people.[2] Across this work, there are illustrations of Black youth being surveilled and criminalized as part of normalizing Black oppression. Further, this work foregrounds links between Black youths' experiences with antiblack racism, the prison system, and the reproduction of capitalist social relations. Implicit in this work is the idea that antiblack racism affects the entire life span, with no reprieve

85

during childhood. In reflecting the pervasiveness of antiblack racism, this body of work highlights the ascriptive nature of anti-citizen status for Black youth. As anti-citizens, Black youth are regularly denied access to typical childhood experiences afforded those seen as fully human. This includes being seen as lacking innocence, having one's activities seen as criminal, and being seen as a threat to community institutions, particularly schools. Research addressing antiblack racism in the lives of Black youth raises the question of what childhood means in the face of antiblack racism and how to intervene upon the reproduction of antiblack racism's underlying structures. Accordingly, the present chapter is an exploration of how antiblack racism informs development for Black girls during the middle-school years. First, I argue that antiblack racism is a sociohistorically constructed phenomenon that distorts intersubjective relations across the racial/colonial divide, creating conditions for Black invisibility. Second, I argue that antiblack racism is best understood as part of a broader racial/colonial order that coevolved with world capitalism's development, with the most recent turn being a mandate for neoliberal individualist solutions and the preservation of capitalism. Finally, I discuss interviews from ethnographic fieldwork through the lens of antiblackness as a facet of coloniality. For the analysis presented in this chapter, I draw upon end-of-year interviews at an after-school program associated with a selective public middle school in East Texas and discuss results of thematic analysis.[3]

THEORETICAL FRAMEWORK: ANTIBLACK RACISM AND COLONIALITY

To foreground my discussion of antiblackness as it relates to the experiences of the middle-school Black girls I met in East Texas, in this section, I explain antiblack racism as a facet of coloniality in a world capitalist system. While multiple theoretical orientations have been applied in addressing antiblack racism, including existential phenomenology and Afropessimism, the present study conceptualized antiblack racism using the former orientation.[4] Antiblack racism in this perspective is theorized as a pervasive form of bad faith in which intersubjective relations are distorted to construct those classified as "black" as outside of the definition of *human*. Importantly, the category of "black" was socially and historically constructed, with diverse groups of African persons being transformed into blacks. The category of "black," then, refers to the social product of persons being converted into racial objects, in contrast with the category of "Black," which is the social product of collective efforts to transform a racial object into a human subject.[5] Lewis R. Gordon contrasts his own conceptualization of antiblack racism with Afropessimist perspectives.[6] Building on Frantz Fanon's work, Gordon asserts not that blacks are ontological beings or even ontological nonbeings but rather that "black" is falsely assumed to hold ontological status in an antiblack world. People marked as black indeed have agency, hence the possibility of being Black, the possibility of persons marked as black indeed expressing perspectives aside from those prescribed in an antiblack world, and the possibility of Black resistance. He notes this as an important contrast between arguing that an antiblack world is a historically accomplished fact as opposed to an ongoing project. Further, he argues that a pessimist position implies no possibility of an antiblack world ceasing to exist and questions whether this could constitute a sufficient political act in the face of an antiblack world.

With respect to antiblack racism and an antiblack world, the purported fairness, democratic norms, and ethical superiority of Western societies is called into question by the mere presence of any blacks, which makes black (and Black) invisibility and nonexistence a key path to legitimacy for these societies.[7] Accordingly, Gordon argues that black presence is illicit, while white presence is self-justified and best conceptualized as license rather than privilege.[8] For example, unfettered ability to carry out racialized exploitation of labor, expropriations of land and property, and racialized lynchings are defining social practices associated with whiteness in a racial/colonial order. Antiblack racism produces fundamentally unequal relations that require black people to be ethically obligated to white people, with no expectation of reciprocity. Relevant to the matter of anti-citizen status, black invisibility casts black persons as interchangeable with one another, readily enabling ascription of anti-citizen status to those deemed black. The invisibility produced by antiblack racism involves having one's presence erased, personhood denied, point of view refused, plurality flattened to nonexistence, and position defined as incapable of reason. This is reflected in contradictions in capitalist social relations, as well: while black people experience antiblack racism as a structural and fundamentally social matter, the neoliberal iteration of capitalist social relations conceptualizes persons as individuals alone, complicating the matter of redress for racist outcomes. This limited conception of social change can be understood as part of a neoliberal form of subjectivity coming into dominance, obscuring the possibility of resistance in thought or action.[9] In Thomas Teo's conception, the self is an entrepreneurial entity that is responsible for self-control, engages in anticritical and antisocial forms of utilitarian thinking, frames collective expropriations as individualized dispossessions, and prioritizes economic liberty over solidarity.[10] Radically individualist framings of antiblack racism involve legitimating the turn inward to the neoliberal capitalist moral individual as the sole point of intervention and delegitimating any turn toward the social through political action.[11] In sum, the neoliberal form of subjectivity encourages the anti-citizen to attribute their own alienation to personal moral failings rather than analyze and intervene upon structural inequities.

To develop new social relations that reject antiblack racism's conception of humanity and recognize the limits of capitalist individualism, we must understand antiblack racism's relationship to the development of a world capitalist system characterized by coloniality. *Coloniality* describes a racial/colonial ordering that codeveloped with capitalism as a mode of production and involved framing the conqueror/conquered relation as a matter of inherent biological inferiority.[12] Coloniality is distinct from colonialism despite being related to it: while colonialism requires formal political relations to exist, coloniality exists after the formal end of occupation and the dissolution of colonialist political structures. Ideological justifications for these relations are linked to Spanish colonial scholars' writings, which classified humans on an initially tripartite racialized continuum of development. Those classified as black were placed furthest from humanity and in need of enslavement (i.e., Aristotle's natural slave), framing enslavement as a beneficent act by the purportedly civilized and mature human enslaver (i.e., the European conqueror), since a "natural slave" purportedly would be worse off if left without colonial intervention. Indeed, a natural slave was presumed to have no meaningful development. Further, some argue that racialization also occurred within Europe among Europeans and nonetheless reflected a colonial character, only later providing a foundation for racial/colonial mythologies employed during Western European capitalism's expansion outside of Europe.[13]

While an individualist understanding would see antiblack racism and a racial/colonial order primarily embodied in individual-level beliefs of racial superiority or in overt expressions of bigotry, coloniality is a fundamentally social process tethered to material relations of production that manifest beyond solely the level of individual persons. The definition of black people as slaves manifested as a material relation of production in which African people were literally enslaved, treated as a commodity, and dispossessed of land at the communal level through colonialism as part of capitalist expansion. This process played a vital role in accumulating capital for the development of Western Europe and the United States under their respective ruling classes.[14] In the United States, the abolition of slavery as a mode of production was followed by the conversion of formerly enslaved Black people into wage workers and practices like sharecropping and convict leasing facilitated the super exploitation of Black workers. Importantly, these relations helped construct and redefine other racial classifications. For example, the racial classification of Mexican immigrants, Mexican Americans, and Anglo-American people reflected stratification in the tenant farming system versus sharecropping systems in Central Texas but also shifted as labor relations changed.[15] The interdependence of racial classifications has continued to be illustrated over time, highlighting the importance of understanding racial/colonial orders in capitalist development holistically when attempting to explain antiblack racism.[16]

FRAMING THE INQUIRY

The present study addressed the question of how Black girls' development is informed by antiblack racism during the middle-school years.

The context of the present study was an after-school program associated within an ethnically diverse and selective public middle school in an East Texas city. The ethnographic fieldwork for this project took place from 2016 through 2017. While a teacher had already been facilitating the girls' group class, the teacher indicated that my own youth work, life experiences, and positionality as a Black and female-bodied person might help revise the class to increase its relevance and impact for the girls involved. In response to the girls' stated preferences, I implemented a discussion-oriented approach in which I asked girls to discuss their own ideas and pressed the group to identify actions that could be taken. Topics discussed throughout our time included LGBTQ rights, Black Lives Matter activism, ensuring culturally responsive practices in local schools, and promoting mental health specifically in the face of depression, family crises, and experiences with abuse. The original teacher remained present throughout and primarily interjected with additional questions to promote more discussion, and due to the teacher's larger role in the school, she also offered updates regarding how the girls' remaining days of the school week had gone to help me identify areas of support.

A total of ten girls were in the class, with the majority being Black/African American or Latina. All ten youth in the girls' group class were eligible to participate in interviews. Girls' ages ranged from eleven to fourteen years. Of all eligible youth, only those with both parental consent and child assent were interviewed. This resulted in interviews with five girls, all of whom identified as Black/African American. Girls created their own pseudonyms: Khaila (eighth grade), Unicorn (sixth grade), Rap City Flow (seventh grade), Jade (seventh grade), and Kenzo (eighth grade). Semistructured interviews were conducted near the end of the school year. Interview protocols addressed girls' experiences in school, as well as their understanding of how race, gender, and class related to their own lives in and out of school. Two research assistants accompanied me during the second half of the school year for the interviews and engaged in similar volunteer activities. Both research assistants were Black/African American women, with one being an undergraduate student originally from another city in the region and the other being a graduate student originally from a neighboring state. Interviewees were permitted to bring a friend to sit with them during their interview.

Research assistants prepared verbatim transcripts of the interviews, and I conducted all analyses of the interview transcripts. I employed a qualitative thematic analysis strategy.[17]

Researcher Positionality

My approach required a recognition of broader sociopolitical and sociohistorical context. I navigated this in part through tapping into my own lived experiences: I grew up as a working-class Black/African American child in a rural town in Western Pennsylvania that was over 80 percent white and predominantly working-class. In this project, I sought to avoid painting my own experiences over those of the girls I interviewed, despite our shared experiences of growing up Black, being female-bodied, having been high-achievers in schools that did not expect that from us as Black people, and, in some girls' cases, strongly identifying with being "country." Accordingly, in reflecting on both my past and then-present positionality, I considered my firsthand knowledge of the antiblack racist dismissiveness toward "country" Black persons as backward and even passive in the face of oppression, and I intentionally struggled to counter my own classed and regionalized assumptions as a professor and regional outsider about what consciousness development ought to look like. (See Robin D. G. Kelley's discussion of past disconnects between Northern urban perspectives on what organizing should look like and Southern Black working-class people's consciousness and social practice.[18]) Thus, the findings presented here are limited by aspects of my positionality that must be taken into consideration. I did not grow up in the South or in Texas. Crucially, I occupied a classed positionality very different from the participants as a tenure-track professor, regardless of any working-class past I had, ongoing Black racialization I experience, or political commitments to the contrary. Further differentiating my classed positionality, I did not live in the same neighborhoods where participants lived outside of school. I also did not share the girls' position as youths in a context where adults held greater institutional power, particularly in the school the girls attended.

In the present study, I acted as both researcher and a volunteer after-school program class instructor. My own ethical orientation in youth work is one reflecting a critical theoretical perspective. I sought to meet youth where they were, while striving to provide tools to extend their understanding of structural bases of social problems, by promoting girls' dialogue over the relationships between three things: local manifestations of broader economic relations within capitalism, racialization as a process occurring within capitalism, and their own lived experiences as early adolescent girls in East Texas. This orientation came with its own tensions in relation to conducting the project itself, though, as I came into this project with some knowledge of the regional histories. Specifically, I was very aware of the region's antiblack racist violence and only more recently aware of the anti-LGBTQ violence regionally.[19] During the fieldwork, the city become a target for white-nationalist leafleting for the organization Identity Evropa. The fieldwork for the study also overlapped with the 2016 U.S. presidential election.

CONSTRUCTING BLACK GIRLS IN A RACIAL/COLONIAL ORDER

In their interviews, girls discussed the role of local social practices for reproducing antiblack racism's intersubjective relations, contextualizing their discussions of their own development within a racial/colonial order. In the following sections, I present results of the thematic analysis. Thematic analysis of the end-of-year interviews produced three themes: constraining identity construction via racialized surveillance in school, gendering the racial/colonial divide across contexts, and criminalizing adolescent social activities outside of school. Across themes, girls discussed being set apart from white youth inside and outside school and from Asian American youth inside school. Only Latinx youth were discussed as sharing this experience, and girls only mentioned that in the context of racialized surveillance in school. Finally, I discuss contradictions that emerged across interviews regarding how the girls understood the role of antiblack racism in their development.

School-Based Surveillance Constraining
Black Girls' Identity Construction

A consistent theme across interviews was the role of teacher surveillance during the school day. As a backdrop for this, Rap City Flow indicated that even peer social relationships were contingent upon one's compliance: "In school, what I think makes me fit in is I do what the teacher says and just follow the rules, basically." Unicorn described this compliance as primarily a matter of teachers' regulation of youths' movement within the school during the day. Unicorn specified that she changed her movement through the school building in response to the punishment that corresponded to surveillance due to the importance of teachers' perceptions of her:

> Honestly, I think to fit in this school you have to be liked by a teacher because the teachers are . . . they're strong against what kids do and what kids don't do. Not telling them, "Oh, don't do this," or, "I-I'm the teacher I-I rule you for this period," or whatever. No, I mean like if a teacher doesn't like you, people get down about that and they're like this teacher doesn't like me, I don't want to walk down this hallway because if she sees me she gonna give me the stank eye or something like that. And I know people who think like that and are my friends and they're all like, "I don't want to walk down that hallway, she doesn't like me," and when we pass her or that teacher or whoever it is, they be like, "Don't talk to her, she don't like me, I don't want to mess with that or whatever." And I think it's based on mostly what teachers do because some of the teacher I don't think like me and I don't like passing their rooms. But, like, some teachers make it very noticeably [*sic*] when they don't like you or they do like you or when they're like, "I rather not have her in my class right now," . . . and it's really mainly the teachers. Like if you were here, you would understand.

Unicorn's comments indicate a widespread fear of a basic activity of the school day, walking down the hall. In a selective middle school that regularly celebrated its students' academic accomplishments publicly, the level of disdain and oversight experienced by Black students on a normal school day operated like a colonial school nested inside a larger school, with staff showing resentment of Black girls' mere presence. In line with the concept of Black presence as illicit in an antiblack context, Black girls became a problem when school staff were reminded they existed. In addition to the importance of teachers' perceptions to one's experiences during the school day and ability to move freely within the school, Jade noted the surveillance of ideas.

Jade described the racial/colonial order being reproduced through an enforced silence around the topic of racism.

> JADE: Sometimes at our school people just keep on going back and forth talking about that and then. But then we been start talking about it, they want to get mad at us. Sometime it's students and sometimes it's adults.
>
> KARLYN: Okay. You're saying sometimes if you were talking about it and a teacher or some other student walks by, they might get mad at you?
>
> JADE: Always happens at the school.

According to Jade, discussion of racism was off-limits, despite it being a defining characteristic of the girls' lived experiences. This suggested an institutionalized attempt at foreclosing the possibility of Black youth transforming the conditions of their own development, although girls' comments indicate foreclosure had not been fully accomplished. Yet, Khaila discussed how difficult it was to move past teachers' judgments, suggesting further surveillance as a consequence. Khaila emphasized the pressure this created for her on a daily basis and its corresponding academic toll:

> It's very short leash, very short. 'Cause I feel like once you mess up, they always looking for you to mess up again. So, it's like, I talk in class and teacher gives me a warning. Talk again and get another warning, talk again gettin' written up. Alright, even though that was just talking, they're going to take it as insubordination, which is my fault or whatever, and then they're gonna be looking for you to do it again every time you come to their class . . . You know they're going to get on you for little things because you already gotten in trouble before, so it's kinda like you gotta tip-toe around everything . . . Like, if you come here, people already have a judgment on you, then you're not going to feel very welcomed. You're probably going to be more closed off and it's going to be more opportunities for you to mess up because everyone already has that bad idea . . . Teachers already have that past pinned on you, so it's like you don't really focus in their class, 'cause you know you're trying to make sure your behavior is completely

perfect, spotless. Or you're focused in their class, but you're doing the wrong things because of the stereotype that they already gave you from your past, or whatever. It's kinda like you can't really just fully be yourself or the better version of you because of what they put on you from the past.

Khaila explained that the cost of the racial/colonial order included loss of opportunities to engage in activities generally understood to facilitate positive youth development, as well as physical health. Here, further elaborating the persistence of how she was positioned in school by teachers, Khaila discussed being unable to participate in athletics at the end of the school year because of what had happened early in the school year:

> KHAILA: Because this year I didn't get into any track, I didn't get to do anything because of behavior and all that, so *[laughs]* you know the thing is, this year I've been doing a lot better than I was last year. 'Cause last year I'm gone . . . no, let's not get into it. *[all laugh]* I was not the best student last year, so I walked in this year thinking, you know, I know I'm gonna have a bad rep, but I'm gonna try to change that. I did not know that in athletics you can have *one* write up and not even make it. And I was like oh, okay.
>
> KARLYN: That's pretty strict.
>
> KHAILA: Yeah, we had gotten one write up, you're not gettin' in. And I'm going for track season, so that's like midyear; is that midyear or close to the end?
>
> KENZO: It's the end.
>
> KHAILA: Yeah, it's close to the end of the year, so you gotta be tip-toeing for the whole year.

Finally, Khaila described this racial/colonial order as going beyond Black students to ensnaring Latinx students, as well:

> KHAILA: I feel like whenever you walk into the school, your name could be Abigail and you're African American and they're already gonna have a judgment on who you are. It's kinda like I'm a good student, like just because I'm African American does not make me any less of a good

student than Caucasian or Hispanic or whoever. I feel like that's another way teachers look at it, and also if, like, you're a good student and you're, like, making good grades, then that's some teachers' view, too.

KARLYN: Okay, interesting. And so you said being African American, they might judge you negatively in terms of whether you're a good student or not?

KHAILA: Right.

KARLYN: Do you feel like other groups get the same *[pauses]*?

KHAILA: Uh, Hispanics.

In sum, girls' opportunities to construct identities as competent in academic content areas and as belonging in school spaces were cut short by antiblack racism. Also, opportunities for further development were taken away as a form of punishment. This dynamic reflected antiblack racism's framing of Black presence as illicit and mirrored the conception of blacks as natural slaves without capacity for any meaningful human development. Girls did not fully internalize how they were positioned within a racial/colonial order, but they indeed struggled with the day-to-day impact of persistent demands for invisibility.

Gendering the Racial/Colonial Divide in Out-of-School Contexts

Girls' discussions also revealed the ways that a racial/colonial order was intertwined with their gender. In another instance of teachers' restriction of girls' movement within the school, Unicorn's teacher suggested she had an inappropriately antagonistic demeanor when she asked to use the restroom:

I honestly think my teacher is racist because the class that I'm in she has . . . four Black kids and one kid that's mixed with Black and Mexican. And I'll raise my hand or something and I'll be like, "[Teacher]," and she be like, "What do you want?" 'Cause she knows my voice 'cause I'm always talking. She'll be like, *[irritated tone]* "What do you want?" I'm like, "Can I go to the restroom?" And she is like, "Yes, you didn't have to take attitude with me." What did I do? And then a white kid will raise their hand. They'll be like, "[Teacher]." She says, "Yes?" 'Cause she knows their voice, she know that they're white or something like that. Yes, "May I go to the restroom?" or "Can I go pee?" Something that's nothing like what I said. That was way more disrespectful. She be like, "Yes sir, you can go, whatever, it doesn't matter to me." And once we were watching a movie, and I raised my hand after someone had got back from the restrooms and she was signaling, "Hold on," and, "Okay," like she shook her head "yes" like after the movie is over or after this video is over you can go. Um, so a little bit gets in—a little bit after the movie, another white girl raises her hand and she's like, "Can I go to the restroom?" She goes, "Yeah," and I'm thinking it's after the movie, you said that I could go. This white woman or, I mean not woman, this white girl raises her hand, and you say that she can go.

Referencing experiences outside of school, Khaila explained the role of gender in ascribing anti-citizenship through regulating Black girls' sexuality. In addition to experiencing harassment from older boys and adult men in public, she also experienced regulation of her clothing and appearance while participating in a community institution—her church. Her experience here aligned with notions of Black respectability in regulating Black women's and girls' sexuality:

Whenever you wear a shorter skirt or a skirt that is above your knees in church, it doesn't have to be no super short skirt, but if you're wearing a skirt above your knees at church, some people will take that as being slutty or whatever. . . . Oh yeah. Especially in church. I don't even know why, like it be older women . . . We went to church, and it was like some older women, like whispering and like doing the hand over their mouth, the side eye and the, I'm like it's a keyhole [collar dress], it's a keyhole chill, chill . . . You can't really pay attention to the pastor 'cause people are talking. I'm like, come on, this church.

Of note, Khaila mentioned her experiences with regulation of her clothing and appearance when asked about sexism, but when asked about racism focused on criminalization, she spoke first about a boy—her brother. It is unclear whether she understood experiences with respectability and harassment as connected to racial/colonial constructions of

Black women and girls or as somehow separate. While the girls readily discussed their gendered experiences within a racial/colonial order, it was less clear how much they interpreted these experiences as the product of racial/colonial processes. The erasure of Black women's and girls' experiences with capitalist state violence has become commonplace in public discourse. This kind of disconnect highlights the importance of understanding antiblack racism as a gendered process and raises the question of why girls are seeing criminalization within antiblack racism as primarily something affecting boys and men when they have directly experienced it as well. In the wake of Sandra Bland's, Breonna Taylor's, and Ma'Khia Bryant's deaths while in contact with police and prisons in recent years, and the criminalization of Black women like Marissa Alexander in Florida for her response in a situation of domestic abuse, the idea that Black women and girls do not experience criminalization is untenable. Beyond these cases, there are also school-specific cases, such as a sixteen-year-old girl in South Carolina named Shakara who was body slammed by a school police officer while her school desk was still wrapped around her body, as punishment for noncompliance.[20] If antiblack racism and invisibility are understood as feminized processes, as Gordon suggests, the matter of Black girls' relationship to notions of Black criminality warrants further exploration.[21]

CRIMINALIZING ADOLESCENT SOCIAL ACTIVITIES OUTSIDE OF SCHOOL

In addition to the girls' discussion of teacher surveillance's role in school and the gendering of antiblack racism in their daily lives, the girls also highlighted how antiblack social relations characterized their developmental contexts outside of school via criminalization of typical adolescent social activities. When questioned about whether she had personally experienced racial oppression, Khaila discussed the role of criminalization, alluding to criminalization's connection with poverty:

> One time I was in the mall and me and my friends were trying on dresses and jewelry and all this in the dressing room. And we had went in there

Coloniality and Antiblack Racism

and this white woman was standing with a clerk, you know how they give you the number and they tell you how many items you have. So, my cousin Shay, she goes in there, she has, like, a dress and a shirt. And, uh, I think she had a jacket over her arm, which was hers, and the lady gave her the number two, and this white lady that don't even work there just talking to the lady that gives her the number. Whenever Shay comes out, she's like, oh she had three why she come out with two, and Shay was like no this is my jacket, and these are my shirts and my dress . . . I said, "You ain't got nothing to prove to her, let's go, let's go." I called mom when we left and I was so heated 'cause I'm like, it's-it's her jacket why, why does it matter? Why, why? Even if she was taking it, you never know the situation with people . . . Even if people do steal or do something, you know, that they're not suppose to do, you never know the situation they're in.

Importantly, Khaila did not discuss her own experience of criminalization until after having already discussed an experience by her brother. Here, she explained a time her brother was falsely accused of bringing an illegal substance to an extracurricular event:

KHAILA: My brother once was with his friends and my brother hangs around a lot of, like, a lot of, he had a bunch of different friends. He got Asian friends, Puerto Rican friends. He got a lot of friends, but the people that he hang around most is this guy named Max. And Max recently got caught up with, uh, some marijuana. And my brother was around him at the time, and they were placing it as if he was the one that gave it to Max when my brotha ain't never did no drugs, he ain't never had to do a drug test, 'cause did nobody suspect him for doing drugs. He ain't never got caught with drugs, he ain't never been around drugs. In my house, we don't even smoke, we don't like drinking, we don't like doing none of that. But, you know, for some reason Max could have not have had this weed. It had to be Jason. It had to be Jason. And, you know, Jason was like, "Man, Max, imma—I have to stop hangin' around you," and all this. I guess he was kinda mad about it. And the friend that Jason thought he had was like, "Yeah, Jason did have it, Jason did have this weed, he gave it to me . . ."

KARLYN: And so wait, this other kid though who did have it, why did everyone think he didn't do it anyway?

KHAILA: Because he wasn't the type of kid to, like, always be into trouble or anything, you know. He was a good kid, like, in school, but outside of school is when he wasn't. The teachers don't know that, parents don't know that, not really.

KARLYN: And that kid is Black too?

KHAILA: No, he's white.

Khaila's comments illustrated the way antiblack racism operated to enable a white student to offload his own punishment onto a Black student. Khaila asserted her family's respectable behavior as a preface to this story, yet this did not protect her family from harm. Yet, Khaila also recognized instances in which these social relations were being reproduced in her own family members' interactions with other Black youths in her city. Here, she highlighted the distortion of the child–adult trajectory for Black youth, in which Black children cease to be ascribed with qualities like innocence and instead must preempt violent overreaction to perceptions of criminality within a racial/colonial order:[22]

So after we left Walmart, we went to the Walmart gas station, and there was this group of Black boys and she locked the door. And I said, "Why are you lockin' the doors?" She's like, "You see them, you see them boys ova there, them hoodlums." I said, "Hoodlums?" I said, "They're Black like us, they're still kids." Nah, they're kids, they can be reckless, and she tried to make it seem like just 'cause they were kids that they were reckless . . . And I was like, "Alright, but if there was a group of white kids wearing sandals and khaki pants and polo shirt, would you be locking your door then?" And she was like, "No, but they're kids," right . . . I was like, why did she lock this door? So I unlocked the door. Not just the guys were kinda cute [both laugh] but because I felt like it was kinda wrong of her to just lock the door. 'Cause whenever I walk past a car and I see that they locked the door and I'm walking pass, I'm like, oh man, they think I'm dangerous, you know, 'cause you can hear that little click . . . I kinda keep tryin' to keep my head straight 'cause I don't want to turn and make it seem like I'm more aggressive, so I'm like, alright, just keep walking, smile a little bit.

Continuing her story, Khaila further discussed the demand to preempt white overreaction even in the face of false accusations of criminality. Khaila changed her demeanor and extended extra courtesy for white strangers in a grocery store to communicate herself as nonthreatening and hopefully improve how she was perceived. Notably, she also explicitly identified a contradiction in antiblack racism as enacted by her Black mother's treatment of Black boys and her mother's own outrage at seeing her own child criminalized:

> Sometime . . . if I'm on a aisle and I see a older white woman or a older white man down the aisle, I try to be extra friendly, man, like extra friendly. Like, I walk down the aisle, my buggy might accidently touch them, I'm like, "Oh, I'm sorry, ma'am, I'm sorry, I'm so sorry, I'm sorry," and push the buggy, "sorry." And then I'll go get my stuff and maybe this lady is trying to grab her soda from the top [shelf], she can't reach it and she white, I'm like, if I do this she gonna have different perspective of me and who I am. So I grab the soda for her. "Here you go, ma'am." "Ahh, thank you, that was so nice." Even though she might not even be thinking that I'm a dangerous black predator, that's just the way that I feel that I come across to people . . . I was always raised that you have to respect white people just because they're white people. You know, I ain't never tried to like cross them, but I've been in a few situations where I was crossed, and I was like what, what, what, I ain't did anything. And I was walking in Walmart one day . . . and I didn't have a buggy or a basket or anything . . . put [a jar of pickles] under my arm right here . . . And this lady goes to the front and says that someone is stealing a jar of pickles. And I'm like, stealing? *[Kenzo laughs]* Come on, come on now, and my mom was really mad about it, but I'm like, back to the point where she locked her doors, I'm like, oh, but you lock your doors whenever a group of Black kids walk around, but it's not okay whenever someone places judgment on *your* kid.

These examples demonstrate that Black girls' outside-of-school time, too, was interrupted by antiblack racism in the form of criminalization and fundamentally nonreciprocal ethical obligations. Criminalization transcended gender lines, leaving girls burdened with concerns about not only themselves but also their male family members. These instances of criminalizing Black youths' leisure time and social norms requiring performance of black deference to justify Black presence highlight two aspects of antiblack racism's role in Black youths' developmental contexts. First, Black youths' criminalization occurs preemptively to protect capitalist private property relations, which themselves are racialized. Second, racial/colonial relations mark blacks as interchangeable racialized objects who are subject to both stereotyping and the whims of white license; in the case of the Black youth discussed here, this includes taking punishment for white classmates who break the law and performing servility while in private businesses.

Legitimating Ascribed Anti-citizenship: Black Girls' Struggling and Encroaching Neoliberal Subjectivity

Finally, while girls discussed frustrations with their experiences, they also at times voiced conflicting perspectives in how they responded to antiblack racism, reflecting the pervasiveness of the neoliberal form of subjectivity. For example, Kenzo expressed a clear goal of enrolling in college as well as graduate school. She named a specific elite private college, stating she sought to become a psychologist, and noted the importance of having "a high enough degree" to "choose any other job" in case she wanted to change careers later in life. She also described her idea of a prototypical "good student" in the school, placing herself outside of that group despite saying she had previously been in that category:

KARLYN: So, in your school what do you think it means to be counted as a good student?

KENZO: Oh, NJHS, all As, never gets in trouble, does all work, volunteers for things, teacher's pet.

KARLYN: And what's NJHS?

KENZO: National Junior Honors Society.

KARLYN: Okay.

KENZO: I mean, I used to be in that, man, and but then life hit me.

KARLYN: Did anything change whenever you weren't in it anymore?

KENZO: I was like damn, oh well, hm, that's it. And my momma, "Do better." I'm doing alright.

Kenzo implied that this all was a matter of choice: "They got the control, if you want to be a good student, do what you gotta do. . . . I do what I gotta do, and I don't want to." Yet, Kenzo framed her current school as a place that was wholly bad, despite it being a selective school in the district that her family had to opt her into:

KARLYN: Do you feel a strong connection to your school?

KENZO: No.

KARLYN: *[laughs]* So why not?

KENZO: 'Cuz I . . . how should I say it . . .

KARLYN: Well, I mean, you could be honest.

KENZO: I hate this school with so much in me, like, ugh, the teachers here, booboo, trash, garbage. I'm barely passing, my friends are the thing that keep me smiling in this H-E-double-hockey-sticks hole.

KARLYN: Okay. *[laughs]* Um, is there anything else you want to say about that, or is that good?

KENZO: I'm ready to get to high school.

Rap City Flow similarly asserted that being a "good student" was a matter of choice:

RAP CITY FLOW: I need to study more and pay attention more in class . . . They follow the rules, listen in class, make good grades, and is respectful too.

KARLYN: How much control do you feel like students has over whether they're a "good student"?

RAP CITY FLOW: They have a lot of control.

KARLYN: Okay. And why do you say that?

RAP CITY FLOW: 'Cause you have choices, and you can choose to be, like, disruptive or respectful. So you should be able to choose, like, whether you want to be that or not.

104 KARLYN ADAMS-WIGGINS

Nonetheless, Rap City Flow discussed her own situation as affected by her lack of connection to the school and feeling left behind by her teachers:

> KARLYN: Yeah, so earlier you mentioned you really didn't feel connected. Um, for a person to feel connected and like they belong, what do you think has to happen for them to feel like that here?
>
> RAP CITY FLOW: Teachers, like, going to their speed in the classroom. Um, and I guess making sure that you understand the—what's going on.
>
> KARLYN: Oh, okay. So, do you feel like your connection to school affects how you feel about schoolwork and achievement and grades and all that stuff?
>
> RAP CITY FLOW: Yeah.
>
> KARLYN: Okay. So, can you tell me a little bit more about that?
>
> RAP CITY FLOW: Like, when I like don't wanna, like, be at school, and I, like, kinda not pay attention in class as much as if I wanted to be in school, so that's it.

Across interviews, girls expressed a keen awareness of antiblack racism's existence, framed it as unjust, and yet at times voiced the belief that the situation was first a matter of self-control, warranting individual self-management as a solution. The neoliberal form of subjectivity's encroachment on girls' daily lives, then, operated as a basis for the reproduction of ascribed anti-citizenship. Here, Rap City Flow's own school facilitated her internalization of neoliberal individualist explanations of academic performance and positioned her as antisocial as a function of her lack of access to meaningful participation, despite her own explicit statement that teacher practice played a role in constructing opportunities for participation.

Taken together, the perspectives voiced by the girls in this chapter highlight the role of antiblack racism as part of a racial/colonial order in Black girls' developmental contexts. First, in discussing the role of surveillance and criminalization, Black girls illustrated the distortion of normative developmental trajectories across the racial/colonial divide in antiblack racism. Second, the girls' stories highlight the connections between the

Coloniality and Antiblack Racism

reproduction of capitalist private property relations and antiblack racism as experienced by adolescent Black girls. Third, while the girls were able to discuss these dynamics, contradictions in their responses were evident, possibly reflecting their wrangling with individualist ideologies about Black life under neoliberal capitalism and their confrontation with the material reality of needing to maintain access to future employment in a society that punishes Black youth like themselves for violating the racial/colonial order.[23]

The racial/colonial order that is embodied in antiblack racism today is deeply rooted in the development of today's capitalist relations of production. While Black resistance has been pervasive across different forms of exploitation and domination, there has also been a move to ascribe a status of anti-citizen to those who opposed these social relations (e.g., Black socialists and communists, revolutionary Black nationalists, and Black supporters of anticolonial struggles outside the United States). Much like antiblack racism, coloniality, and capitalist development's relationships to each other, anticolonial and anticapitalist politics often were expressed in tandem, and likewise punished in tandem, with Black radicals being targeted with particularly severe repression to the long-term detriment of grassroots political organization.[24] Yet, antiblack racism is not uncontestable, and neither is the rejection of a racial/colonial order (and anti-citizenship, by proxy) impossible. New social relations can be constructed, but the reproduction of capitalism must be addressed in any solutions offered considering antiblack racism and coloniality's origins in the capitalist mode of production.

Notes

1. Phillip Atiba Goff, Matthew Christian Jackson, Brooke Allison, Lewis Di Leone, Carmen Marie Culotta, and Natalie Ann DiTomasso, "The Essence of Innocence: Consequences of Dehumanizing Black Children," *Journal of Personality and Social Psychology* 106, no. 4 (2014): 526–45, https://doi.org/10.1037/a0035663.

2. Michael J. Dumas, "'Losing an Arm': Schooling as a Site of Black Suffering," *Race Ethnicity and Education* 17, no. 1 (January 2014): 1–29, https://doi.org/10.10 80/13613324.2013.850412; Damien M. Sojoyner, "Another Life Is Possible: Black Fugitivity and Enclosed Places," *Cultural Anthropology* 32, no. 4 (November 18,

2017): 514–36, https://doi.org/10.14506/ca32.4.04; Connie Wun, "Against Captivity: Black Girls and School Discipline Policies in the Afterlife of Slavery," *Educational Policy* 30, no. 1 (2016): 171–96, https://doi.org/10.1177/0895904815615439.

3. Virginia Braun and Victoria Clarke, "Using Thematic Analysis in Psychology," *Qualitative Research in Psychology* 3, no. 2 (2006): 77–101, https://doi.org/10.1191/1478088706qp063oa.

4. Lewis R. Gordon, *Bad Faith and Antiblack Racism* (Amherst, N.Y.: Prometheus Books, 1995); Lewis R. Gordon, "African-American Philosophy, Race, and the Geography of Reason," in *Not Only the Master's Tools: African American Studies in Theory and Practice,* ed. Lewis R. Gordon and Jane Anna Gordon, 3–50 (New York: Routledge, 2015); Lewis R. Gordon, "Writing through the Zone of Nonbeing," in *What Fanon Said: A Philosophical Introduction to His Life and Thought* (New York: Fordham University Press, 2015), 19–46; Jared Sexton, *Amalgamation Schemes: Antiblackness and the Critique of Multiracialism* (Minneapolis: University of Minnesota Press, 2008); Frank B. Wilderson III, *Red, White & Black: Cinema and the Structure of US Antagonisms* (Durham, N.C.: Duke University Press, 2010).

5. Lewis R. Gordon, *Freedom, Justice, and Decolonization* (New York: Routledge, 2021).

6. Gordon, *Freedom, Justice, and Decolonization.*

7. Lewis R. Gordon, "Black Aesthetics, Black Value," *Public Culture* 30, no. 1 (2018): 19–34, https://doi.org/10.1215/08992363-4189143.

8. Gordon, "Black Aesthetics, Black Value"; Gordon, *Freedom, Justice, and Colonization.*

9. Thomas Teo, "Homo Neoliberalus: From Personality to Forms of Subjectivity," *Theory & Psychology* 28, no. 5 (2018): 581–99, https://doi.org/10.1177/0959354318794899.

10. Teo, "Homo Neoliberalus."

11. Gordon, *Freedom, Justice, and Decolonization.*

12. Aníbal Quijano, "Coloniality of Power and Eurocentrism in Latin America," *International Sociology* 15, no. 2 (2000): 215–32.

13. Cedric J. Robinson, *Black Marxism: The Making of the Black Radical Tradition* (Chapel Hill: University of North Carolina Press, 2000).

14. William Edward Burghardt Du Bois, *Black Reconstruction: An Essay toward a History of the Part Which Black Folk Played in the Attempt to Reconstruct Democracy in America, 1860–1880* (New York: Harcourt Brace, 1935); W. E. B. Du Bois, *Fire This Time: The Watts Uprising and the 1960s* (Charlottesville: University of Virginia Press, 1995); Quijano, "Coloniality of Power and Eurocentrism in Latin America"; Eric Williams, *Capitalism and Slavery* (Chapel Hill: University of North Carolina Press, 2014).

15. Neil Foley, *The White Scourge: Mexicans, Blacks, and Poor Whites in Texas Cotton Culture* (Berkeley: University of California Press, 1997).

16. Tomas Almaguer, *Racial Fault Lines* (Berkeley: University of California Press, 2008); Natalia Molina, *How Race Is Made in America* (Berkeley: University of California Press, 2014).

17. Braun and Clarke, "Using Thematic Analysis in Psychology."

18. Robin D. G. Kelley, *Hammer and Hoe: Alabama Communists during the Great Depression* (Chapel Hill: University of North Carolina Press, 2015).

19. Claire Cardona and the Associated Press, "Racist Killer Executed Decades after Dragging James Byrd Jr. to His Death Near Jasper," *Dallas Morning News,* last modified April 24, 2019, https://www.dallasnews.com/news/crime/2019/04/25/racist-killer-executed-decades-after-dragging-james-byrd-jr-to-his-death-near-jasper/; Bruce Glasrud, "Anti-Black Violence in 20th Century East Texas," *East Texas Historical Journal* 52, no. 1 (2014): 14; Lauren McGaughy, "Texas Leads the Nation in Transgender Murders. After the Latest Attack, the Dallas Trans Community Asks Why," *Dallas Morning News,* last modified September 30, 2019, https://www.dallasnews.com/news/2019/09/30/texas-leads-nation-transgender-murders-according-national-lgbtq-organization/.

20. Jenny Jarvie, "Girl Thrown from Desk Didn't Obey Because the Punishment Was Unfair, Attorney Says," *Los Angeles Times,* last modified October 29, 2015, https://www.latimes.com/nation/la-na-girl-thrown-punishment-unfair-20151029-story.html.

21. Gordon, *Bad Faith and Antiblack Racism*; Gordon, *Freedom, Justice, and Decolonization.*

22. Karlyn R. Adams-Wiggins and Daphne V. Taylor-García, "The Manichean Division in Children's Experience: Developmental Psychology in an Anti-Black World," *Theory & Psychology* 30, no. 4 (2020): 485–506, https://doi.org/10.1177/0959354320940049.

23. Kevin L. Clay, "'Despite the Odds': Unpacking the Politics of Black Resilience Neoliberalism," *American Educational Research Journal* (August 2018), https://doi.org/10.3102/0002831218790214.

24. Gerald Horne, *Black and Red: W. E. B. Du Bois and the Afro-American Response to the Cold War, 1944–1963* (Albany: State University of New York Press, 1986).

CHAPTER 5

Queering the Citizen?

Exposing the Myths of Racial Capital Fantasies

DIANA GAMEZ AND DAMIEN M. SOJOYNER

The aim of our contribution is twofold. First, utilizing Los Angeles, California, as a social and historic backdrop, we discuss the manner in which a tawdry collective of real-estate developers, elected officials, legislators, and popular press organs sought to undermine Black sociality in order to maintain a most heinous racial regime.[1] The basis of this regime was the multifaceted suppression of Black life in order to maintain and indulge racial capitalist projects that included racially coded suburban land development and the expansion of the military defense system. This discussion is made complicated by the fact that Black people did not passively accept violence as the norm. Rather, they uprooted the terms of order, fomented a rebellion, and posited new social visions. As a means to reify the preexisting social order, state-governance procedures through legislative processes, propaganda, and ideological manipulation invoked the citizen as an agent of discipline in an effort to mask the inherent violence that was needed to maintain racial hierarchies within the city.

Moving the citizen out of its taken-for-granted liberal context, we transition to the second aim of this chapter. Detailing the experience of Salvadoran migrants to Los Angeles during the 1980s, we situate the citizen—a tool of dispossession established to corral Black liberation—as a primary strategy utilized to ensconce Salvadorans in a subjugated status within established racial hierarchies. This discussion is complicated by the governing logics of anti-Blackness inherent within the Salvadoran

109

nation-state ideological project that proved to be a key impediment to collective action against violence emanating from the United States. As a way out of this conundrum, we argue for a position that we describe as "queering the citizen?" Embracing anti-citizenship as a platform that seeks to undermine the violence imbricated in state governance and disavow difference-making projects that fuel nationalism, we utilize "queering the citizen?" as a frame to contest the binaries that are central to the "civic"—and thus to the suppression of Black life. These binaries are the foundation of Western epistemology and are based upon an intentionally limited framework that informs the gross power imbalances of socially constructed hierarchies. Based upon a two-dimensional plane, the binary formations of "good/evil," "black/white," "man/woman," and a host of other configurations have become naturalized patterns of thought and are consequently made irrational through the logics of anti-citizenship.[2] Rather than follow binary models, we explore the possibilities that have been established by communities that relish the complexity of life and embrace multiple ways of being as not only liberatory but necessary.

RACE, VIOLENCE, AND THE CITIZEN: THE CASE OF LOS ANGELES

The 1960s were fraught with intense racial animus in Los Angeles, California. The unspoken known was that Los Angeles was openly hostile to the thousands of Black people who migrated to the city during the 1940s and 1950s. The multiple forms of violence were fueled by politicians, land developers, and an insecure white middle class, who sought to suppress Black mobility, cultural expression, and communal traditions for a variety of sordid reasons. The rationale varied from financial interests to psychological hysteria. There were a host of economic, political, and social punitive policy initiatives and a milieu of general suppression that defined the experience of Black life during the middle of the twentieth century in the City of Angels.

The ironic reality was much more complex than propaganda spouted via outlets such as the *Los Angeles Times* that portrayed Black life in a constant state of disarray. Black people were actively recruited to Los

Angeles as a means to bolster an expanding war-based economy. Such movement carried with it the possibility of destabilizing racial sensibilities through a cohesive class and labor solidarity. However, the material rewards associated with whiteness usually kept those who abided by draconian formations of race-making in line with the needs of real-estate speculation and economic bottom lines. Toeing the line of a social formation (such as race) that kept them within marginal positions of power yet with distinctive advantages over Black people, the burgeoning white middle and upper-middle classes constantly chased their own tails in the name of social progression. Black people, however, by and large did not ascribe to the value of their self-worth as being attached to fleeting material conditions that satiated the shortsighted vision of whiteness. In contradistinction, Blackness was informed by traditions that sat in the multiplicity of being. The bitter containment of Black people kept in shanty housing dwellings on the fringes of Downtown Los Angeles bleeding into Watts coincided with an explosion of an artistic scene that spoke to a vision that could only be understood in sonic imaginaries. Collections of metal, steel, and iron alongside a cacophony of music and spoken word were forged to create masterpieces that paid ode to African diasporic traditions that utilized art as the tools to galvanize thought and action. In the midst of violence so profound, freedom was never forgotten. It could not be contained, it was not washed away, and, most fundamentally, it did not die.

Being illegible to western epistemological traditions, Blackness was called "uncivilized," "savage," "deviant," "criminal," and then, when tried and true tactics failed, it was called "dead." Blackness never died; it simply could not be read. Mapping Black ontologies would necessitate the destruction of the western project. A project based upon the construction of myths that necessitated difference-making tactics was inherently flawed and thus ripe for exposure. Black ontologies are not the antidote to western modalities; rather, they are practices that critically dissect the inner workings of western thought and simultaneously construct social visions, languages, and habitats that reveal the genius of the unseen, rarely spoken, yet always present. Black life, a brilliant tapestry of multiple worldviews, could not readily be contained by the racial regime of mid-twentieth-century Los Angeles. The literal and proverbial explosion of Watts in 1965 represented the city's inability to corral Blackness.

Citizen and New Racial Projects

Out of this failed paradigm, an old trope was brushed off and retooled. As argued within an ascribed anti-citizenship framework that exposes the reactionary nature of civic projects (as positioned against Black liberation), the invocation of the citizen—as the governable subject formation—was forced out of the bowels of the tattered state apparatus. Via all channels of governmentality, the citizen was reinforced as the foil to the logic of Black revolt and, by logical conclusion, Black ontology. A key rupture, the citizen attempted to mend the violent exploitative tendencies of racemaking. In this manner, the (re)invention of the citizen was crafted as a way to promote a new multiracial state formation that situated Blackness as the constant point of departure against all other racial formations. A maddening multiracial panacea, the citizen created boundaries and provided a new set of highly illusory, but much desired, material rewards to discipline the logics of Black ontology. A grand experiment of the most vile sort, the citizen ironically was designed to smash Blackness and, thus, pathways to a radical democracy.

The citizen was brought from the depths into a new regime. A new regime that was imbued with the past lives of violence, torment, destruction, and death. Violence was the precondition for acceptance, violence was the precondition for yearning, violence was the precondition for that which appeared normal. The citizen—born from miscreant seeds— took shape in the form of a rough amalgamation of undescribed harm. A harm so vile, it must be hidden. Culling through DNA strands tethered together by lies and deceit, the formation was ruthless in its approximation to its unmitigated past. Purported claims of justice and morality dressed the spectacle in tattered linens. Bespoken artifacts reveled in being able not only to construct the mythological pedestal but also to ascend to its summit, perched high on mountainscapes that could never be seen, only imagined. The facade could never be exposed. Exposure was antithetical to its nature. Linear paths formed straight trajectories

Queering the Citizen? 113

that pierced through jagged, uneven, and polygenic time formation. The citizen thus walked along the trajectory carving away at histories that did not align with the straight path. The citizen fed the beast and thus demanded erasure of the possibility of ways of life that deemed the civil project invalid. The citizen had to keep the nightmare alive.

In contemporary times, the constant reformulation of the citizen is an ongoing shell game that attempts to divert attention away from the notion that the game is rigged. An ideological farce, the citizen as the governor of civil discourse disappears subjectivity within ruthless claims of objective reality. Certain children are no longer understood as children, certain communities are suitable for destruction, certain ways of being are deemed immoral, and certain people are allowed to violently express discontent. The notion of participation in the civil process obfuscates mechanisms designed to maintain a violent political hegemony.

There is no true participation within the civic, there is only adherence. The logic of ascribed anti-citizenship points to the misleading illusory nature of inclusion within the civic process as a means to engage and negotiate with racial capitalist projects. The historical record demonstrates that while particular Black class subjectivities and their ideological adherents have made headway into matters of state governance under the banner of racial advancement via civic reform, they have done so only to discipline the liberatory ethos of Black masses who cannot be contained within the realm of the civic. The only space for meaningful dissent is in the vast silences that occupy tiny cages and large classrooms. The citizen has to occupy the role as blissfully ignorant, partake of the magical elixir, or suffer a fate far worse—willingly participate in a decrepit world-making process that will ensure suffering.

It is thus here that we arrive at the counterpoint. Given that anti-citizenship makes known the severe limitations of the citizen, what are the particulates that form a coherent, long-standing possibility to maneuver outside of the strict confines presented as the civil? In this manner, the counterformulation must be life-affirming social visions of radical possibility. They will be slandered as both heretical and, in many cases, illegible to state-sanctioned lived experiences. The heresy they proselytize demands freedom of binary modalities and embraces the multiplicity of being. It is a metaphysical invocation to live within simultaneous realities while listening, breathing, and extolling the virtues of empathy, love, and compassion. Chaffing against the notion of rational thinking, the formulation of this metaphysical journey is illegible to western constructions of knowledge production. Akin to the gathered masses, high in jagged mountains of a Haitian moonlit night, the counterformulation speaks in rhythms, repeated utterances that function as conduits to undo the violence that has been done. It is the sudden disappearance of thousands of workers from an ironically beautiful southern plantation landscape to the muddied waters in search of freedom. It cannot be understood, for it cast aside modernity's most cherished prizes. It registers across space, time, and lived experiences and breathes needed life into liberatory processes.

The Fallacy of Citizenship: The Case of Salvadorans

The illogical desire for citizenship as the given pathway to freedom is made plain with the experience of Salvadorans who have had to navigate the treacherous racial, national, and gendered politics of the United States imperial project. Further, the unrelenting anti-black logic of El Salvador's national narrative has been a major impediment to diasporic liberation efforts. As Los Angeles continued to unleash its disdain for Black life during the middle of the twentieth century, the boundaries of citizenship as a project embedded in racial capitalism and the disciplining logics of Black ontology expanded. The (re)production of racial practices intended to naturalize hierarchies of power and difference were at the core of the incorporation/assimilation process that simultaneously subjugated Black southern migrants and Salvadorans—who were used as a foil against the proper decorum of the assimilable immigrant citizen-subject.

Contextualizing Salvadorans in the United States

Since the 1970s, the United States has intervened in Salvadoran governance and social order. An intervention that has included training grounds for soldiers and death squads at the School of the Americas and extractive-based foreign policies and military aid schemes. The U.S. support of the Salvadoran national project has resulted in multiple massacres of Indigenous people, as well as deteriorating economic conditions for working people and environmental threats that caused thousands of Salvadorans to flee to the United States and Mexico. Free-trade policies, such as the North American Free Trade Agreement (NAFTA) and the Dominican Republic–Central America FTA (CAFTA-DR) that directly benefited the United States, destabilized El Salvador and the majority of Central America. Coupling free trade, particularly the free circulation of goods, such as clothing, and the elimination of agricultural subsidies with security, NAFTA policies contributed to creating the conditions for one of the largest trading zones and economic and environmental conditions that exacerbated and expanded border security measures.[3] CAFTA ushered in deteriorating economic and environmental conditions, drying several regions in the Americas and disrupting crop cycles.

The nation-building discourse in the nineteenth and twentieth centuries informed the formation of El Salvadoran state centered *mestizaje,* an abjection of Indigenous and Black roots and languages. Its anti-blackness is part of a bigger epistemology of race and the ways that race travels when people migrate. Anti-Blackness in El Salvador's formation aligned itself with the ideological and material conditions needed to further entrench Blackness as an ideological enclosure beyond U.S. borders.[4] The United States centers race as a juridical-legal status that produces a nationality and individual rights and obligations, a status that is informed by its relationship with Blackness.[5] However, in contradistinction to U.S. racial formation, El Salvador's lack of documentation of how race operates exacerbated sanitized racialized discourses of pan-ethnicity and the erasure of diasporic Blackness and Indigeneity—a violent erasure that has contributed to Central America's unwillingness to center its Black and Indigenous histories and their deep-rooted organizing and rebellions, some of which have been in conversation with Black organizing in the United States.

The violent rupture of California and the undergoing change in Los Angeles severely affected the political, racial, cultural, and social landscape that Salvadoran migrants came into. While white and Black people were working in the same industries, anti-black violence denied Black people basic needs and resources. This was further amplified by the war staged against Black people by police and the increased robust carceral expansion of the prison fix that addressed the surplus in capital, land, labor, and state power as the crucial characteristics of California's crisis in the 1970s.[6] Salvadorans migrating to the United States entered a reality that the United States was not committed to freedom outside of their borders or within their borders, as shown in their commitment to producing their precarious legal statuses and continuing to criminalize them via legal and quasi-legal methods. The logic embedded in anti-black violence in combination with myths of El Salvador being raceless, along with false claims that Black and Indigenous people did not exist there and that the slave trade never made it to what is now El Salvador, (re)produced racialized exclusions of people of mostly Indigenous and African descent. Racialized U.S. interventions within a country that did not document race contributed to the Salvadoran state's efforts, such as changes in the constitution to center race in an effort to be more inclusive.[7] However, the contradictory racialized hierarchies between El Salvador and the United States, with a shared exacerbation of anti-blackness, have resulted in exacerbating existing forms of racial and gendered criminalization.

The very presence of Salvadorans contested U.S. logics of racial formation and citizenship. U.S. notions of Blackness as monolithic would continue to be challenged with migration from Latin America and the Caribbean, where rebellions and sovereignty and land struggles are inextricably connected to Blackness and Indigenous struggles. The racialization and incorporation of Salvadorans into the U.S. nation-state were made via the tropes of communists and guerrillas, a racial collectivity of threats and dangers to civil society, informed by the criminalization of Black youth, such as the labeling of gangs.[8] The citizenship project for Central American youth has been marked as pathologically dangerous, which dismisses the conditions of young people's efforts to survive the various state-sanctioned violence. Through the inscription of Blackness as supposedly uncivilized, savage, deviant, and criminal, the United States produced Salvadorans as gang members and as dangerous. The dichotomy of assimilation and othering expanded notions of disposability, relegating

Salvadorans, including children, to be contained, controlled, and removed. This racialized production of fear in order to legitimize the contradictions of the Other, and ignore the root causes of violence, such as U.S.-sponsored interventions and forced displacement, has produced an intensified moral panic of Salvadorans for the white imaginary, specifically of a young male figure.[9]

Reagan's immigration reform policies were reactionary to both Salvadoran immigrants and Black organizing, particularly in the face of international and transborder organizing. Under the guise of supporting immigrants with the first legalization program in U.S. immigration history, the 1986 Immigration Reform and Control Act (IRCA) directly sought to address migrants as a problem through the expansion of harsher policies at the border and for employers hiring undocumented folks. However, the legality of IRCA 1986 has been primarily enacted against individual undocumented migrants and rarely against employers. The anti-immigrant landscape of the United States and California continued to intensify with the back and forth of Proposition 187, which denied services to undocumented folks but was later ruled unconstitutional. Although the proposition did not go into effect, its aftermath continued with anti-immigrant sentiment and anti-Black violence that led to the passage of IRCA 1986 and the 1996 Personal Responsibility and Work Opportunity Reconciliation Act. These policies sought to continue providing naturalization as the only route. However, U.S. recognition was dictated through a racialization of the mythical conglomerations of people as an invention needed to uphold citizenship.

Through the configuration of the term *Latino* as a hegemonic panethnic term, and with its reinforcement of whiteness and denial of Black and Indigenous roots, Salvadorans were faced with a denial of their existence in order for the possibility to obtain any type of legal permission to exist within U.S. borders. Legal routes for citizenship only continued to expand their impossible standards and simultaneously intensified the power of federal authorities to police racialized bodies, even when they were citizens, because citizenship does not protect them from policing and surveillance. These policy expansions were never intended to incorporate Salvadorans; instead, they are representative of the United States'

118   DIANA GAMEZ AND DAMIEN M. SOJOYNER

commitment to reject peoples' livelihood, a rejection that has deep roots in the militarization, policing, and surveillance of the United States and El Salvador. While it is clear that these expansions amplified immigration restrictions and enhanced the power of immigration officers, these policies also set up the foundation of one of the largest reorganizations in the government under the guise of national security and public safety. Through the Homeland Security Act and under the guise of responding to deadly attacks perpetrated on 9/11, the Immigration and Naturalization Service changed to Immigration and Customs Enforcement.

The year 2002 marked a drastic turning point for the treatment of Salvadorans, particularly for children and youth. Such an expansion was reactionary to the historical organizing of Salvadorans within the United States and was a specific reaction to Los Angeles, which has been part of larger movements organizing multiple communities that have sought legal protection for undocumented youth seeking higher education. Existing organizing celebrated Assembly Bill 540 that was signed into law in October 2001, a year before the expansion of Homeland Security, which allowed eligible undocumented, permanent resident and U.S. citizen students to be eligible for in-state tuition at public colleges and universities. While the Homeland Security expansion was justified through a commonsense expansion of national security in response to 9/11, it was an expansion that further foregrounded the manufacturing of Salvadoran gang members of MS-13 as a transnational security threat that had been in the making since the 1990s without addressing the root causes of violence.[10]

The production of Salvadoran youth as a threat is part of a deeper history within the United States and El Salvador. Despite many of the cases involving children and young people migrating from El Salvador during late 1970s and 1980s, their acknowledgment as children fleeing state-sanctioned violence was neglected. In the early 2010s, the United States officially acknowledged the term *unaccompanied minor* to refer to children migrating from El Salvador and the larger Central American Isthmus.[11] While that term brought attention to young people fleeing Central America, and to some extent it brought attention to the severity of children being forced to migrate, at its core the term was used to criminalize and dehumanize children. Unaccompanied minors were produced as criminals rather than as children seeking refuge. The narrative of criminality that was upheld with the labels of Salvadorans as gang members, better known as *mareros*, was extended and informed the treatment and inclusion of youth Salvadorans migrating in the 2010s. The invocation of *gang* is part of a larger history of a racially charged term that has manufactured Black people as collectively representing the opposite of U.S. civil society. "The Gang Enhancement Law in California, which defines a gang as 'three or more persons,' has been used to sweep city streets from East Palo Alto to Downtown Los Angeles in preparation for the glorious coming of a technocrat managerial class and designer lofts."[12] Interestingly, the Spanish translation of *gang, mara,* has been used by political candidates both in the United States and Central America and is used by the media and even the Pentagon. The word *mara* dates back to the early 1950s as referring to groups of friends.[13] The manufacturing of Salvadorans and other immigrant groups as inherently criminal has been informed and supported by the languages used by the media, politicians, and policymakers to define Blackness as criminal. The invocation of *gang* and *unaccompanied minors* has denied everyday lived experiences of those deemed to be criminal and seen as causing a national security crisis.

Salvadorans' migration has been forced by gendered violence, forcing many women, especially with children, to leave El Salvador.[14] "Women had to risk their lives to escape, knowing that they would not achieve justice in their country. If they were lucky enough to make it to the US, they might try to file a claim for political asylum. This process, however, also often involved a re-traumatization."[15] Salvadorans' migration has been gendered, classed, sexualized, and racialized, and many of them have made Los Angeles their home and have high participation rates in the labor force.[16] Salvadorans' family and communal formations thus have always defied the heteropatriarchal U.S. formations of family and communities. Those at the forefront of challenging the citizen have been Salvadoran women, especially single mothers. On the one hand, the lack of acknowledgment of children migrating during the late 1970s and 1980s was directly aligned with El Salvador's deep history of criminalizing young victims of violence. Young people in El Salvador are part of a larger history of youth who have been failed by the Salvadoran state and criminalized for finding alternative ways to survive, particularly those who have joined gangs—criminalization that has failed to acknowledge its state-sanctioned violence against the people of El Salvador, a very racialized, sexed, classed, and gendered violence. On the other hand, the use of the label of "unaccompanied minor" in the early 2000s was used to further expand the production of the Salvadoran gang members while enforcing and limiting the boundaries of asylum seekers, particularly at a moment in which U.S. higher education institutions were expanding their admissions and funding for undocumented students.

Political pressure by Central Americans in the United States, including young Salvadorans, has resulted in Temporary Protected Status and the creation of programs that provide a legal temporary protection to undocumented folks, such as Deferred Action for Childhood Arrivals. While these programs have been celebrated for the legal protection and the material conditions it creates, they have produced a "liminal legality."[17] For legal protections associated with U.S. education, it has produced a very educated and neutralized population and (re)produced precarities, an intensification of state surveillance, a perpetual state of insecurity (the opposite of what a temporary status claims to do), and the constant re-application process with ongoing changes in fees and legal contestations regarding its renewal. With the exception of a small group of Salvadorans obtaining citizenship under IRCA 1986, the majority of cases have led to a very expensive temporary status that is always at risk of being eliminated.

QUEERING THE CITIZEN?

Multiple communities that have been forced to live within the United States have an extensive history of rejecting the citizenship project. The civil rights movement expanded the possibilities of citizenship for Black people under the guise of inclusivity. Nonetheless, citizenship has instead simultaneously expanded the already impossible expectations and obligations of citizens and its exclusion and criminalization of those outside of unnatural citizenship boundaries—expectations and obligations that are racialized, gendered, sexed, and classed. Regardless of how Salvadorans have acquired citizenship, they enter structures that are embedded in impossible normative standards and structures. These expansions have a wide range of consequences, materially and ideologically. On the one hand, the incorporation has provided a shift in access to a legal structure, but on the other hand, as stated by pontifications of ascribed anticitizenship, such incorporation exacerbates citizenship as a weapon of genocide that kills anything outside of whiteness. As citizens are recognized as members of the U.S. nation-state, its mutual recognition has been inherently linked to misrecognizing Salvadorans' Blackness and Indigeneity, including misrecognizing their self-determination when it falls outside of sanitized frameworks. "Within this framework, citizenship is not only a strategy of containment implemented by the state to regulate access to power and privilege, it is also a set of political strategies used to make popular demands for participation and inclusion."[18]

Building on Fatima El-Tayeb's theorization of queering ethnicity that describes "a practice of identity (de)construction that results in a new type of diasporic consciousness neither grounded in ethnic identifications nor referencing a however mythical homeland," we can understand how Salvadorans have transformed and queered citizenship.[19] "Central American migrant activists make claims to citizenship, but reject the notion of citizenship as simply a status that is transferred to and passively accepted by individuals."[20] Through various strategies and responses, particularly the various forms of resistance that span national borders and draw upon a host of diasporic practices and resources, Salvadorans queer the citizen. Building on El-Tayeb's usage of *queer* as a verb and as a process that uses the body and community to create responses to problematic and oppressive dominant beliefs and imaginaries about race and the myth of colorblindness in Europe, Salvadorans, including those who defy heteronormative gender and sexual norms, have queered the citizenship with their communal and organizing practices.[21] Salvadorans' family and communal formations have been disrupted and they have been forced to create and participate in formations of family and communities that support their livelihood outside of conceptions of biological family formations. Faced with the reality of surviving the daily violence in Los Angeles, as seen through the Rampart scandal and immigration officers working with local police and the impossible dynamics of citizenship, Salvadorans have done just about everything to survive and are the eternally undocumented, as Salvadoran poet, essayist, journalist, communist activist, and intellectual Roque Dalton, reminds us in "Poema de Amor."[22]

Communities engage in multiple meanings of citizenship, which include tensions and contradictions. Arely M. Zimmerman refers to this as a citizenship from below, "citizenship as an enactment of membership in cultural and political community."[23] Building on this, as knowledge producers Salvadorans have also responded by queering the citizen and using a wide range of approaches to build community and establish safety networks that protect individual and communal livelihoods outside of so-called legible U.S. structures. Using multiple strategies, including gaining legal status, has allowed communities to support their own wellbeing and enact alternative ways of living that provide access to basic needs, although not always successful and not always without contradictions. The political upheaval and revolutionary landscape of El Salvador continued with Salvadorans migrating into Los Angeles.

With the majority residing in neighborhoods with low housing costs where they interact with diverse populations, including Black, Asian, and Mexican people and other folks from Central America, coalitions and solidarities have been built over the years.[24] Regardless of their legal status, Salvadorans, with the support of the existing organizing landscape of Los Angeles rooted in Black struggles especially in the midst of the 1992 uprisings, created several avenues to support the livelihood people in Los Angeles in both the informal and formal economies. The existing landscape that Salvadorans experienced in the 1980s was very different from El Salvador's cultural surroundings—specifically, their traditional concepts of community, both with regard to the physical landscape and to *community* as a verb. Many of them were exposed to people who were intentionally and strategically excluded from the Salvadoran national imaginary. In Salvadorans' efforts to seek community, they constructed communities in new multiracial and multiethnic metropolitan environments around shared experiences locally, nationally, and transnationally.

Queering the Citizen? 123

These efforts included the establishment of Central American, and specifically Salvadoran, cultural spaces with street vendors, markets, restaurants, and other stores with specific services for Central Americans, such as ways to send remittances. Salvadorans reshaped Los Angeles's political, economic, racial, and cultural landscape.

Salvadorans formed communities in various spaces with diverse groups and multiple institutions supporting the broader public. Despite the tensions in political agendas, some of them being more radical while others sought to work with and within the state, their various efforts resulted in creating their own service institutions with more of a grassroots foundation, such as El Rescate, Central American Refugee Committee, and many others promoting mutual aid.[25] Salvadoran organizing was met with reactionary anti-immigrant policies that changed the demands for resources, which gave way to private and nonprofit organizations and took attention away from grassroot organizing efforts. Under the guise of democratization, the citizenship project was a reaction embedded in interrupting the possibilities of building community across racial and ethnic groups and across local and transnational boundaries—an interruption that was further supported by the buildup of the nonprofit complex and private foundations promoting assimilation.[26] The efforts of nonprofits and foundations in focusing on citizenship was completely removed from engaging citizenship as a project bounded by race- and difference-making, despite their commitment to uphold U.S. multicultural tropes. While the imperialism and valorization of new American (settler) identity was celebrated for freedom and democracy, democracy did not actually appear until 1968 with the Civil Rights Act as a liberal representation of democratic notions. It established a structure of domination to colonial incorporation where it further expanded its structural violence beyond physical violence by recognizing Black people but not transcending the oppressive and violent relationship—a very similar, yet different, approach with Salvadorans.

Salvadoran efforts have also included silence(s)—silence(s) around the violence and repression under the Salvadoran government, which forced thousands to flee.[27] Similar to the ways that the Salvadoran government opted for silence and denial of the violence they have historically (and currently) enacted against Indigenous and Black folk, the United States has also enacted silence. They have systematically denied their involvement in the destabilization of El Salvador and failed to acknowledge Salvadorans within the United States, including the denial of protection of Salvadorans and other Central Americans as refugees and asylum seekers.[28] These multifaceted silences, by both nation-states and Salvadorans themselves, have resulted in a lack of services and denial of access to Salvadoran histories.[29] The realities of these silences have also resulted in a misrecognition and cultural genocide of Salvadorans through the production and preservation of mestizaje that have migrated to the United States with *latinidad* that carries centuries of anti-Blackness and violence, a physical and epistemological erasure of Salvadoran subjecthood. In the face of these silences, Central Americans in the United States have organized against limited narratives that only further misinformed who Salvadorans are in multiple spaces, including in the mainstream media and through public education, including U.S. educational institutions.

Salvadorans' various successful efforts in organizing within Los Angeles and transnationally were met with the United States' reactionary policies that intensified the existing violent reality. Salvadoran efforts were actually meeting the needs of people, which were already limited because of the high demand for basic needs that the United States failed to provide.[30] Mutual aid organized by Salvadorans and the various communities they were working with would be further challenged by U.S. efforts to militarize Los Angeles and other cities for immigration, a violent response that was informed and building on the existing declaration of wars on drugs and gangs that sought to sustain the myth of Black people as inherently criminal and as a justification of high incarceration rates. Access to entering the workforce was not as difficult considering the market for low-wage jobs, but many workers faced inhumane and violent working conditions and had very limited access to mid-level jobs. Their participation in the workforce became more obvious in the national imaginary as their participation strengthened labor movements resulting in a knowledge of rights and the addressing of exploitive labor conditions. They also challenged and reclaimed public spaces by expanding the existing street vending landscape of Los Angeles, which resulted in the El Salvador Community Corridor in the Pico Union area that established short-, medium-, and long-term diversity of Salvadoran and Latin American products and service companies.[31] Such state-sanctioned public acknowledgment was accomplished via individual and collective efforts that included a mix of involvement from grassroots organizing, churches, and charity groups, with many tensions in their agendas, and the majority of people involved were undocumented.

Alternative formations of communities for Salvadorans, especially young people, are rooted in enhancing and supporting human lives and practicing very different forms of the reality of displacement as a result of a series of U.S. interventions. Diasporic populations across the world have (re)created a diasporic consciousness as a "third space" that is purely distinctive from North American, South American, and Central American as an embodied location and identity.[32] Social media sites, like WhatsApp, Facebook, and Twitter, have been key in building community for Salvadorans and other Central Americans who have been displaced across the world. These communal formations that are outside of one-dimensional conceptions of home are informed by diasporic silences, memories, and histories. Their movements and efforts are a conceptualization of diaspora with folks who may or may not have a place to call home or blood-related family members. They have directly challenged formations offered by nation-states. Following the genealogical impulses of contemporary anti-citizenship theorization, queering the citizen is not a mythical linear approach to establishing an alternative route to be recognized by the state. Rather, it is constantly changing as ideological and material conditions change, particularly the constant legal changes of citizenship and of Temporary Protected Status. It is also embedded in a complex web of power in which states' reactions to queering the citizen often exacerbate the policing and criminalized conditions. Salvadorans queering the citizen have created and continue to find ways to provide vital structures and systems that support people with resources they need in the face of interlocked systems of oppression and exploitation. Salvadorans queering the citizen craft communities premised on multiple and contradictory positions and identities through fusing transborder organizing strategies, resisting logics of inclusion and multicultural

126 DIANA GAMEZ AND DAMIEN M. SOJOYNER

representation, drawing on art and poetry, and building a diasporic consciousness that is not national or oriented to a homeland.

Transborder organizing efforts directly challenge and stand in opposition to those systems and structures provided by the citizenship project that have become dominant narratives to ameliorate structural problems that are imbricated within the citizenship process itself.

DIASPORA TO THE FUTURE

The research of anthropologist Juli Grigsby indicates that the overall quality of life for Black women in Los Angeles County as determined by health outcomes is akin to living in countries whose gross domestic product is multiple sizes less than that of the United States.[33] Grigsby's work, however, is not based upon the commonsense position that such a dynamic can be remedied by policy changes and increased education opportunities made available to Black women. Rather, Grigsby points to the lived realities that Black women face whether in Los Angeles or Rio de Janeiro or Lagos. Specifically, the experience of being a Black woman is quite similar across geographic spaces. While the particularities of place are very important for the development and implementation of strategies to undo the specificities of racial capitalism, the logics of race carry across boundaries and inform the direction of Western civilization's most exploitative tendencies. Thus, knee-jerk reactions to incorporate racialized subjectivity into the civic as a means to address matters of borderless violence are often absurd.

The material and psychic violence aimed at Black women is only heightened when situated within a paradigm that removes it from its totalizing force. The function of the citizen within this arrangement is to dislocate exposure as to the root causes of the multiple forms of violence and, conversely, relocate power back to the mythical tropes of normativity inherent within the national state-governance structure. With the demand of adherence to national myths, the citizen attempts to demobilize liberatory ontological practices in order to provide cover for the grotesque schemes of a truly vile Western epistemological project. Stated plainly, citizenship as a framework becomes moot when understanding that there is a particular fact of Blackness within social structures that are governed by the logics of racial capitalism.

Reflecting back upon Grigsby's work, the formation of the citizen within the paradigm of Black women's health blurs the extreme violence levied against Black women and demarcates it with the normative moral governance structures of specific locations. In the case of the United States, much of the locus of blame is attached to the individual failures of Black women, in Rio claims to Black women's well-being are muted within a refrain of racial democracy, and in Lagos, traditional knowledge formations that center Black women have been made subservient to the whims of philanthropic-informed health-based practices. As made known through the logics of ascribed anti-citizenship, the adherence to the citizenship framework precludes an actual engagement with the multifaceted realities that have shaped the positionality of Black women with respect to the violence that is inflicted upon them. In its place, narratives have developed to protect the sanctity of national projects.

It is from the positionality of Black women that the queering of citizenship is not only a logical but a necessary position. As made abundantly clear in the writing and thinking of scholars such as Connie Wun, Sabina Vaught, Savannah Shange, and Maisha Winn, the extreme layers of violence enacted upon Black women and girls are boundless and have had tremendous consequences upon Black women and girls who are forced to engage with state-sanctioned violence-making processes that have been made compulsory, such as schools.[34] The positionality of Black women and girls demonstrates the incongruous nature of the citizenship paradigm with Black life and, further, makes queering of citizenship the rational first step toward a radical democracy.

Grigsby's methodological insights to connect Black women's relationships across geographic localities directly relates to the violent enclosures of life possibilities presented to Central American migrants arriving into the United States during the 1980s. The configuration of citizenship represented a set of foreclosed options that negated the material reality of their lived experience. The claiming of citizenship to home countries such as El Salvador rang hollow due to the interference of large power brokers—namely, the United States. Under the banner of democracy, the

United States' intervention within El Salvadoran governance was a thin veil to protect particular financial interests. Directly connected to the extraction of natural resources from soil, the logics of capitalist extractive technologies could not abide by the nationalization projects implemented by the El Salvadoran government. As a result, the United States fomented military conflict that resulted in the destabilization of Salvadoran social relationships that still rings true nearly forty years later.

The violent disruption of El Salvadoran governance was further exacerbated by a fundamental problem with nation-state consolidation throughout the region during the nineteenth century. Unwilling to grapple the "fact of Blackness" and multiple forms of violence related to the forced relocation of Africans from West Africa into the region for purposes of labor extraction, the silencing of Blackness has continued to ring loud. Given that no burgeoning nation in the "New Americas," aside from Haiti, seriously engaged with the issue of abolition during independence struggles, the question of Blackness was largely avoided as a means to not disturb the flow of extractive labor economies. As a result, the multiple forms of violence that had demarcated the time period prior to independence rang loudly in the century-plus following independence movements. Thus, the inherent flaws related to the citizenship paradigm resonated even louder as the ironic calls for liberation from Spain were not lost upon the largely disenfranchised Black population.

In the immediate aftermath of independence and as nation-state ideological formations took on mestizaje narratives, the particularities of Blackness became erased from the liberated landscapes. Always present, yet not identifiable or legible to the state, the citizenship projects demanded genuflection to a mythical past that did not recognize Blackness. Shaped by ideological configurations that negated Blackness, Salvadorans were displaced to a new nation-state project that had firmly embraced the subservience of Black subjects. Rather than matters of erasure, the codification of Blackness into U.S. citizenship practices situated the new experience for Salvadorans arriving into Southern California. Bordering on existential crises, the interpolation of Salvadoran migrants ranged from the dismissive catchall "Mexican" to being squarely located in the pit of Blackness as violent gang members.

Forced to engage with a set of bad options, the citizenship paradigm reflected the inherent flaws located with the nation-state process. Governed by Western epistemological binary formations, Salvadoran migrants were situated as both "illegal" and "gang terrorists," and they were welcomed with the full range of policy and social agendas that had been the normative reality for Black people in the United States. In line with the citizenship narrative, the only option was (and continues to be) to maneuver away from Blackness as a means to prove one's viable legibility to the state as a rational-acting subject. However, given that the fact of Blackness was never about a rational set of politics, such maneuvering has always been a Sisyphean task, as the established racial mantras would continually be exercised through the 1990s and early 2000s as a means to mitigate labor, housing, and health crises.

Faced with the impossible, the project of queering citizen-based schemes undoes the veiled threats that undermine Black freedom movements. Further, they relocate the formation of the citizen as a derivative of racial capitalism's insistence on differentiating along lines of mythical normative standards. Thus, the queering process forces a relocation of power away from the reproduction of the state and instead toward the generative locus of differentiating techniques and strategies. Out of such a practice, a new radical imagination emerges that fundamentally alters relations of being and community and demands new formations of political and social collectives.

NOTES

1. David Halberstam, *The Powers That Be* (New York: Knopf, 1979); Mike Davis, *City of Quartz: Excavating the Future in Los Angeles* (New York: Verso Books, 2006); Ruth Wilson Gilmore, *Golden Gulag: Prisons, Surplus, Crisis, and Opposition in Globalizing California* (Berkeley: University of California Press, 2007); Cedric Robinson, *Forgeries of Memory and Meaning: Blacks and the Regimes of Race in American Theater and Film before World War II* (Chapel Hill: University of North Carolina Press, 2007).

2. Writing about the intimate connections between western philosophical traditions to western Christianity, Cedric J. Robinson notes that the binary has been crucial in the development of western thought:

The ancient civilizations of the Old World, in Asia as well as Africa, became legends, preserved most constantly in the obscure and recondite histories of biblical narrative. As knowledge became more and more a monastic preserve, secular reconstructions assumed a certain rarity due to the church's commitment to the interpretation of history in accord with its perceptions of divine Ethnocentrism, legitimated by the authorities of church and ignorance, the two fountains of medieval knowledge, became the basis for world knowledge. Ultimately, with the evolution of Christian ideology into a worldview, it was enough to know that mankind was divisible into two collectivities: the army of Light and the army of Darkness . . . Europe was God's world, the focus of divine attention; the rest of mankind belonged for the moment to Satan. For perhaps a thousand years or more, western European world historical consciousness was transformed into theosophy, demonology, and mythology. And, indeed, in a most profound sense European notions of history, both theological and pseudo-theological, negated the possibility of the true existence of earlier civilizations. The perfectability of mankind, the eschatological vision, precluded the possibility of pre-Christian civilization having achieved any remarkable development in moral law, social organization, or natural history (science). (Cedric J. Robinson, *Black Marxism: The Making of the Black Radical Tradition* [Chapel Hill: University of North Carolina Press, 2000], 86).

3. Leisy Abrego analyzes President Obama's administration and the construction of Central American migrants as a "crisis." She argues that his administration expanded their unwillingness to protect and fulfill human rights protections across the region's nation-states, including Mexican and Central American states:

In conjunction with free trade, the US government must also implement security measures to protect profits and facilitate border crossings for goods while blocking the path for potential migrants. Shortly after CAFTA was ratified by the countries of the so-called Northern Triangle of Central America, in 2007 the Bush Administration implemented the Mérida Initiative, a bilateral partnership with Mexico focused among other things on "(1) disrupting organized criminal groups, (2) institutionalizing the rule of law, (3) [and] creating a 21st-century border." To protect US interests through the North American Free Trade Agreement (NAFTA), the program provided funding mostly for Mexico but shaped the experiences of Central Americans, as well. Besides also providing limited funding to Central America, the Mérida Initiative's goal to create a "21st-century border" helped to militarize Mexico's southern border with Guatemala, leading to increased risks for Central American migrants on that journey. (Leisy Abrego, "Central American Refugees Reveal the Crisis of the State," in *The Oxford Handbook of Migration Crises* [New York: Oxford University Press, 2018], 220).

4. Peter Wade, "Mestizaje, Multiculturalism, Liberalism, and Violence," *Latin American and Caribbean Ethnic Studies* 11, no. 3 (2006), https://doi.org/10.1080/17442222.2016.1214368.

5. Engin Isin and Bryan Turner, *Handbook of Citizenship Studies* (London: SAGE, 2002).

6. Gilmore, *Golden Gulag*.

7. Leisy Abrego and Alejandro Villalpando, "Racialization of Central Americans in the United States," in *Precarity and Belonging: Labor, Migration, and Noncitizenship*, ed. Sylvanna Falcón, Steve McKay, Juan Poblete, Catherine S. Ramírez, and Felicity Schaeffer, 51–66 (New Brunswick, N.J.: Rutgers University Press, 2021).

8. Abrego and Villalpondo, "Racialization of Central Americans in the United States."

9. Steven Osuna, "Transnational Moral Panic: Neoliberalism and the Spectre of MS-13," *Race & Class* 61, no. 4 (2020): 3–28.

10. Osuna, "Transnational Moral Panic."

11. Osuna.

12. Shana Redmond and Damien Sojoyner, "Keywords in Black Protest: A(n Anti-)Vocabulary," *Truthout* (blog), May 29, 2015, https://truthout.org/articles/keywords-in-black-protest-a-n-anti-vocabulary/.

13. Roberto Lovato, *Unforgetting: A Memoir of Family, Migration, Gangs, and Revolution in the Americas* (New York: Harper, 2020).

14. Adrianne Aron, Shawn Corne, Anthea Fursland, and Barbara Zelwer, "The Gender-Specific Terror of El Salvador and Guatemala," *Women's Studies International Forum* 14, no. 1–2 (January 1991): 37–47, https://doi.org/10.1016/0277-5395(91)90082-S; Shannon Drysdale Walsh and Cecilia Menjívar, "Impunity and Multisided Violence in the Lives of Latin American Women: El Salvador in Comparative Perspective," *Current Sociology* 64, no. 4 (2018): 586–602, https://doi.org/10.1177/0011392116640474; Leisy Abrego, Mat Coleman, Daniel E. Martinez, Cecilia Menjivar, and Jeremy Slack, "Making Immigrants into Criminals: Legal Processes of Criminalization in the Post-IIRIRA Era," *Journal on Migration and Human Security* 5, no. 3 (2017): 694–715.

15. Abrego et al., "Making Immigrants into Criminals," 78.

16. Nora Hamilton and Norma Stoltz Chinchilla, *Seeking Community in a Global City: Guatemalans and Salvadorans in Los Angeles* (Philadelphia: Temple University Press, 2001).

17. Cecilia Menjívar, "Liminal Legality: Salvadoran and Guatemalan Immigrants' Lives in the United States," *American Journal of Sociology* 111, no. 4 (January 2006): 999–1,037, https://doi.org/10.1086/499509.

18. Arely M. Zimmerman, "Contesting Citizenship from Below: Central Americans and the Struggle for Inclusion," *Latino Studies* 13, no. 1 (2015): 40, https://doi.org/10.1057/lst.2014.71.

19. Fatima El-Tayeb, *European Others: Queering Ethnicity in Postnational Europe* (Minneapolis: University of Minnesota Press, 2011), xxxvi.

20. Zimmerman, "Contesting Citizenship from Below," 40.

21. El-Tayeb, *European Others*, 40.

22. Roque Dalton, "Poema de amor," in *Las historias prohibidas del pulgarcito* (Mexico: Siglo XXI de España Editores, 1974), 199–200.

23. Zimmerman, "Contesting Citizenship from Below," 28.

24. Susan C. B. Coutin, "In the Breach: Citizenship and Its Approximations," *Indiana Journal of Global Legal Studies* 20, no. 1 (2013): 109; Elana Zilberg, *Space of Detention: The Making of a Transnational Gang Crisis between Los Angeles and San Salvador* (Durham, N.C.: Duke University Press, 2020).

25. Hamilton and Chinchilla, *Seeking Community in a Global City*.

26. Hamilton and Chinchilla.

27. Abrego et al., "Making Immigrants into Criminals."

28. Suyapa G. Portillo Villeda, "Children of the Diaspora: For Peace and Democracy," *Latino Studies* 14, no. 3 (2016): 413–13; Abrego et al., "Making Immigrants into Criminals."

29. Cecilia Menjívar, *Fragmented Ties: Salvadoran Immigrant Networks in America* (Berkeley: University of California Press, 2000); Villeda, "Children of the Diaspora."

30. Hamilton and Chinchilla, *Seeking Community in a Global City*.

31. Hamilton and Chinchilla.

32. Karina Oliva Alvarado, Alicia Ivonne Estrada, and Ester E. Hernández, *U.S. Central Americans: Reconstructing Memories, Struggles, and Communities of Resistance* (Tucson: University of Arizona Press, 2017), 36.

33. Juli Grigsby, "Grim Sleeper: Gender, Violence, and Reproductive Justice in Los Angeles" (PhD diss., University of Texas, 2014).

34. Savannah Shange, *Progressive Dystopia: Abolition, Antiblackness, and Schooling in San Francisco* (Durham, N.C.: Duke University Press, 2019); Sabina E. Vaught, *Compulsory: Education and the Dispossession of Youth in a Prison School* (Minneapolis: University of Minnesota Press, 2017); Maisha T. Winn, *Girl Time: Literacy, Justice, and the School-to-Prison Pipeline* (New York: Teachers College Press, 2019); Connie Wun, "Against Captivity: Black Girls and School Discipline Policies in the Afterlife of Slavery," *Educational Policy* 30, no. 1 (January 1, 2016): 171–96, https://doi.org/10.1177/0895904815615439.

CHAPTER 6

Black ~~Youth Organizing~~ for the Destruction of Schooling, the Citizen, and the World

MICHAEL DAVIS

In recent years, educational scholars, practitioners, activists, and community organizers have included explicit ontological theorizations of (anti-)Blackness into practical and analytical frameworks. This chapter will examine Blackened ontological theorization through projects such as Afropessimism, which exposes a particularly antagonistic relationship between the Human and the Anti-Human or the Master and Slave. More important, this chapter highlights how ontological theorizations of anti-Blackness shift our work as scholars, educators, activists, and community organizers. This chapter ultimately considers what it might mean to embody ways of existence against and through the citizen and the Human. To be clear, there are projects and concepts like "anti-Black racism" and "misogynoir" that claim to center Black specificity in understanding oppression and liberation from that oppression. However, kihana miraya ross points out, while "racism" is not conceptually "meaningless," it "oversimplifies" and "defangs" the severity and reality of anti-Blackness.[2] Ross asserts, "The word 'racism' is everywhere. It's used to explain all the things that cause African Americans' suffering and death. . . . But 'racism' fails to fully capture what black people in this country are facing. The right term is 'anti-blackness.'"[3] How might our (educational) analyses and

---

* Trigger Warning: I make the suffering and death of Black ~~youth~~ a spectacle in order to demonstrate empirical evidence to support my arguments.[1]

practices change if we center ending anti-Blackness, which is to say the end of the World, as we think about survival and liberation?

There are extant projects that purport to center Blackness analytically and politically. For example, critical theory writ large is composed of projects and theories that aim to expose how oppression operates within the confines of this World. Critical theory also provides space for addressing this pervasive violence on all levels. However, Human projects of critical theory such as critical race theory, feminisms, intersectionality, psychoanalysis, postcolonialisms, Marxisms, and other so-called critical projects do not reckon with the ontological position of Blackness that is inextricably linked to Slavery and Slaveness. This lack of Blackened theorization obscures anti-Black violence and freedom from that violence. Anti-Blackness cannot be ended through policy, law, or any other Human-centric measure or method of supposed progress. Since Humanity is guaranteed within the assumptive logics of all critical theory projects, the experiences of the Slave are guaranteed to be excluded and erased. This reorients how we think about violence. For the Slave (Blackened sentience), violence operates at the level of existence. Black liberation is therefore not possible without ending the Human and the World. What does this all mean for the vastness of Black ~~education and schooling~~?

The existence of American schooling is not possible without the mundanity and spectacularism of anti-Blackness. Like all American institutions, schools require anti-Blackness to function. Considering this, the argument here is that schools are irredeemable and inherent sites of anti-Black violence and suffering.[4] Of course, there are examples of powerful work being done within the context of schools aimed at helping young Black ~~folx~~ survive American schooling contexts. However, these examples of school-based resistance and survival are not enough to allow Black ~~youth~~ to be perpetual lab rats for (neo)liberal and anti-Black education policy, practice, training, and reform, which oftentimes lead to more violence. To be explicit, the goal of this chapter is not to focus on the immeasurable ways in which Black ~~youth~~ suffer in schools and other institutionalized educational contexts. Rather, the goal is to center some of the tactics and strategies employed by Black ~~youth~~ aimed at resisting, refusing, and surviving the school plantation. These tactics should be used to theorize and actualize political projects and schools of thought that

Black ~~Youth Organizing~~

better equip Black ~~youth~~ to not only survive current schooling contexts but also imagine Black radical ~~educational futures~~ on their terms.

Before moving on, it is important to make a note about the strike-through or bar written through Humanist identity markers and categories (*youth, boy, girl,* etc.) as it relates to Blackness. The strikethrough here is used to represent what Calvin Warren calls the "double bind" of Black (non)existence (being caught between Humanity and fungibility).[5] Since the Slave (Black) does not have access to Human identity markers and categories and therefore is outside of projects and analytics that purport to name and address anti-Black suffering, Warren suggests that we strikethrough and write "with and against" this language until we develop (if ever possible) new language that allows us to better understand and address anti-Black violence in all its manifestations. The strikethrough is a method that allows for anti-Black violence to be considered alongside Human categories from which Blackness is inherently excluded. Similarly, because of Blackness's permanent (non)ontological exclusion from Humanity, words, ideas, concepts, and physical things that require access to Humanity such as *schools, body,* and *agency* will also be struck through. The goal here is to demarcate the chasm between Blackness, Humanity, and all of Humanity's productions. This is a discursive critique of attempts to achieve redemption/liberation within the confines of an inherently anti-Black World.

Moreover, drawing on data from a qualitative study on Black ~~youth organizers~~ in schooling and community contexts in a midwestern college town, the subsequent sections will highlight the ways in which Black ~~youth~~ embody and display abolitionist and World-ending politics against the citizen, the school, and the Human. The study took place in a midwestern college town that is presumed to be liberal and progressive. The population of Black ~~folx~~ is about 6 percent, yet this town and county have some of the most severe forms of statistical anti-Blackness (violence measured by numbers) in every category imaginable. The liberal and progressive mantra that is associated with the town overflows into the local school district. This school district has invited some of the top educational scholars, even those focused on abolition, but has made national and global headlines for its atrocities against Black ~~children~~. Since being here, the police have killed five Black ~~men~~ and ~~boys~~. We are left with deader Black physical flesh while the city and its school districts celebrate their so-called racial equity and justice programs. At schools with "excellence plans" for Black ~~students~~ and "restorative justice" circles as opposed to punitive school punishment, it is still normal and necessary to rip hair from the heads of Black ~~girls~~, throw elementary-aged Black ~~boys~~ up against lockers and call them devils, celebrate "high-achieving" Black ~~youth~~ who have mastered anti-Black curricula, have respectability projects like "Boys to Men" clubs, and generally punish and dishonor Black ~~students~~. To be Black is to be both visible and invisible in the inherently violent structure of schooling. The Black ~~youth~~ at the center of this story are Ayanna and Cardi. At the time of the study, Ayanna was a junior in high school and Cardi was a senior. Ayanna and Cardi also both identify as queer, which is central to their organizing and radical politics in addition to identity. Ayanna and Cardi both demonstrate what a radical Black abolitionist project might look like for Black ~~students~~ in their everyday schooling experience. These everyday acts of educational deviance and destruction, as demonstrated by Cardi and Ayanna, can assist young Black ~~folx~~ in surviving school spaces and actualizing their hope for learning and liberation.

Additionally, there will also be a brief theoretical section that will focus on projects of Black (non)ontology such as Afropessimism and Black nihilism, the concepts of so-called deviance and fugitivity, and reflections on what an anti-citizenship and antischooling project means for the anti-Human.[6] The final section offers a call to action to scholars, activists, organizers, educators, and all lovers of Black ~~children~~ to seriously and genuinely consider what an abolitionist politic might look like against the citizen, the school, and the Human for the sake of Black ~~children~~.

THEORIZING IN BLACK: DEVIANCE, DESTRUCTION, AND HOPE FOR THE ANTI-CITIZEN AND THE ANTI-HUMAN IN SCHOOLS

Remember, Blackness, which is to say anti-Blackness, is an imposed ontological position made possible through Slavery and New World-making. Thus, to be "Black" means that every subsequent Human-contingent identity marker (race, class, gender, sexuality, ability, etc.) that follows is disrupted and made impossible by the very structure of the modern,

Western World itself. How we, Black ~~folx~~, see ourselves is irrelevant here. The World and its Humans commit prenatal robberies of Black ~~child-hoods~~, which means we enter the World as civil society's permanent problem. This plays out in education policy, discourse, and praxis. Thus, Black ~~youth~~ rightfully and righteously resist this violence. Through intellectual and political projects such as Afropessimism, the theoretical aim here is to further explain how the (non)ontological position of Black ~~young people~~ makes schools an always-already permanently violent space, place, and plantation. This will be followed by a theoretical reflection on Black so-called deviance and fugitivity to further examine the various political acts Black ~~folx~~ employ to resist anti-Black school violence that do not align with accepted forms of resistance such as voting, a peaceful protest, letter writing, etc. The section will end with insight with regard to how we might understand antischooling as a branch of anti-citizenship and what a project of anti-Humanity might consist of as we strive to "destroy the World" and get free outside of and beyond a Worldly/Humanly context that denies Black ~~agentic capacity~~ in schools and everywhere else.

Furthermore, to better understand the positions taken in this chapter, it is important to note how (*anti-*)*Blackness* is being defined here in relation to Humanity and the World. If you ask most folx to define *Blackness,* responses might include some explanation of race, ethnicity, nationality culture(s), and a "social construction."[7] Racial Blackness is always already under attack in the political and civil society that permanently excludes Black ~~folx~~. However, the gratuitous violence (violence at the level of existence) that renders Black ~~folx~~ anti-Human is ontologically different from the contingent violence (violence as punishment for disrupting the oppressive social order) that leads to de-Humanization. Blackness is not a racial/cultural category alone, it is a paradigm all on its own.

Building on the work of Orlando Patterson, Afropessimism asserts that Slaveness, which is to say Blackness, is undergirded by "social death" which forces the Slave outside of all Human or ontological positions.[8] Social death is marked by gratuitous violence (violence without transgression—no rhyme nor reason—just because one is Black—no crossed border or terrorist attack needed), natal alienation (no recognition of familial ties or ancestry), and general dishonor (an automatic and inherent disregard and disgust for Blackness in all of its manifestations).

In the same vein, Garba and Sorentino further explicate why the violence of the Slave (a fungible object) should not be conflated with the violence of non-Black people of color (exploited colonized subject).[9] In their critical examination of Eve Tuck and K. Wayne Yang's *Decolonization Is Not a Metaphor*, they refute the claim that "slavery is internal to settler colonialism" and instead suggest that the existence of the settler and the colonized is contingent upon the ontological incoherence of the Slave that occurs pre-1492.[10] In this view, "slaves are stuck in a treadmill of political indecipherability—both victims and antagonists, essential to the clearing of land and inessential to its return."[11] The possibility of land recovery and sovereignty speaks to the nonfungible status of the colonized subaltern. In other words, there is no "project of recovery" within the structure of this World that would set the Slave free. Freedom itself is possible in the World because the Black is the Slave. There is nothing to be returned to the Slave (culture, land, resources, etc.) ~~whose~~ existence equates to nothingness. In this frame, Tuck and Yang's lack of theorization of Slaveness (Blackness) is anti-Black just as the metaphoric decolonization (nonland decolonial projects) is anti-Indigenous as the "slave enables the very possibility for the settler to accumulate land and wealth."[12]

From this vantage point, Humanity is not a liberating epistemology, ideology, or practice. Humanity is the beating heart of anti-Black violence. For the Slave, a (no)thing who is permanently locked outside of Humanity and therefore citizenship, this understanding is critical to the theorization and praxis of anti-citizenship. Being against the (good) citizen is not enough. If we worked to undo and destroy Humanity and the World (a project of anti-Humanness), its citizenry will also be unmade (anti-citizenship). With that being said, Afropessimism offers an "unflinching paradigmatic analysis" on (anti-)Blackness that shifts Slavery from an event (bound by time and space) to an ontology (Slaveness, a metaphysical time breaker).[13]

Not only is there "disdain" and "disregard" for Black ~~folx~~, but the project of modernity and Humanity relies on the social death of Blackness. In other words, Slavery is not merely a historical moment with a definitive beginning and end, it is a "nonevent" that always already informs the condition of Black ~~folx~~. Connected to that, the grammar of Black suffering (or how and why Black ~~folx~~ suffer) can be defined and distinguished through the concepts of fungibility or exchangeability (being bought, sold, traded, disposable, murdered, brutalized, celebrated, etc.) and accumulation (the ontological, ideological, material, etc., benefits for white/non-Black folx that are possible because of anti-Blackness). Fungibility and accumulation describe the grammar of Black suffering while mere alienation and exploitation describe the grammar of Human suffering for non-Black people: exploited workers, colonial subalterns, women, queer folx, and other Human registers made inherently unavailable to the Slave. Human suffering and oppression are politically conflictual (which indicates the possibility of an end like the Jewish Holocaust) as opposed to politically antagonistic/ontological (which indicates unending metaphysical and ontological suffering). Therefore, ending Human-first systems like white supremacy does not inherently lead to the end of anti-Blackness. Like race, class, gender, and sexuality, white supremacy assumes guaranteed Humanity for all, even if that Humanity is de-Humanized. Therefore, "ending" racism, classism, sexism, etc., still leaves the ontological grammar of (anti-)Blackness intact.

Additionally, there is a certain respectability politic, even among supposedly critical folx, that surrounds the ways in which Black ~~folx~~ resist and refuse anti-Black violence. Even though Black sentience (flesh/~~body~~) is always already under attack in schools and elsewhere, we are condemned for engaging in resistance practices that are deemed "too radical," like slapping a violent teacher, burning down a police station, skipping class, abolishing schools, etc. In education scholarship and discourse, it is commonplace to make the suffering of Black ~~youth~~ a spectacle of repetitive violence. There is also a perpetual desire to recount stories and scenes of Black suffering, death, and violence with little to no offerings on how to address and, most important, end the systemic and ontological harm that is unique to Black ~~folx~~ and Black ~~children~~ specifically. However, Black ~~youth~~ are punished and critiqued for resisting anti-Black (school) violence outside the purview of what is considered "respectable" or even "critical" forms of resistance. Through a Black ~~queer~~ lens, Cathy J. Cohen's piece "Deviance as Resistance" calls on researchers and scholars to take seriously the ways in which every day Black ~~folx~~ operationalize their "limited agency" that is marked as "deviant" by the state and the World.[14] Cohen argues that this "intentional deviance" should be rearticulated as forms of Black radical resistance and, I would add, survival. For Cohen, "deviants" are Black ~~folx~~ whose "rule or norm-breaking behavior" is framed as an inherent problem to society and the World. Deviance as defined by the anti-Black World makes an inherent connection between Blackness and being the problem. These Black "acts of nonconformity" can lead to sustained refusal, resistance, and survival and may also be more feasible as a strategy than engaging respectability politics or "playing the game." To be clear, even though "these choices are not necessarily made with explicitly political motives in mind,"[15] Black folx are precisely aware of the violence and consequences that they/we will and do face when resisting the normative terrain of an anti-Black society and World. It is important to quickly note that Black folx who are marked as deviant are typically fighting for basic Black desires, such as pleasure and survival, as well as living and moving freely.

This chapter attempts to at least partly address the contradiction Cohen points to between the "crisis facing Black communities" and the "routinization of much of what passes for the academic study of Black people," especially within the nice field of education. Thinking deviance in Black engenders "new radical politics of deviance [and the possibilities to] create new or counter normative frameworks by which to judge [Black] behavior."[16] The possibilities of thinking deviance as Black ~~resistance~~ and ~~survival~~ leads to "the creation of spaces or counter publics, where not only oppositional ideas and discourse happen, but lived opposition, or at least autonomy, is chosen daily. Through the repetition of deviant practices by multiple individuals, new identities, communities, and politics might emerge where seemingly deviant, unconnected behavior can be transformed into conscious acts of resistance that serve as the basis for a mobilized politics of deviance."[17] As I will demonstrate in subsequent sections, it is critical that we support Black ~~youth~~, in education and elsewhere, when they employ politics and practices that deviate from accepted forms of supposedly critical resistance. A by-any-means-necessary approach is a normative requirement in this work.

Black ~~Youth Organizing~~ 141

Similarly, Damien Sojoyner asks education scholars and practitioners some critical questions around Black ~~fugitivity~~ that are typically dismissed as "impractical" or even "dangerous" for Black ~~youth~~ to engage in. For Sojoyner, Black ~~fugitivity~~ "is based on the disavowal of and disengagement from state-governed projects that attempt to adjudicate normative constructions of difference through liberal tropes of freedom and democratic belonging."[18] Black ~~fugitivity~~, while built on the shoulders of those who resisted before us, is not a static historical practice. It is a radical Black ~~present~~ and ~~future~~ practice that informs the ways in which many Black folx decide to resist and refuse anti-Black violence. This is incredibly important in an anti-Black "enclosed place" such as a school. Sojoyner raises a particular question that informs the analysis in this work: "What damage is done by reinforcing a narrative that Black students should not drop out of school . . . [and] by no means [is this statement] hyperbolic?"[19] As I will address below, Black ~~youth~~ rely on radical deviance and fugitive refusal as daily practices against anti-Black schooling violence. There are essential lessons to be learned from their work. More important, there is a need for institutional and organizational support for Black ~~youth~~ who decide to employ a radical deviance or fugitive refusal into their (educational) resistance. Black ~~youth~~ also offer essential lessons around what it means to resist not only the state and the citizen but the Human and the World as well. The anti-citizen project must include a project against the anti-Black Human and World that requires the citizen in the first place.

Of equal importance, everywhere in the World, Black ~~citizenship~~ is marked by its position outside the category itself. In other words, regardless of context, to ~~be~~ a Black ~~citizen~~ means to not ~~be~~ a citizen at all. This is true even for Black ~~Africans~~ whose Africanness cannot shield them from the reality of being marked Black. How should we make sense of this? What is it exactly that inherently forces those who we call "Black" outside of citizenship in the first place? The designation of a non-Black supposedly unpatriotic and lawless anti-citizen is driven by discourses based on some type of transgression according to the colonizer/oppressor— a border was crossed, a building was bombed, jobs are taken, crime is rising, etc. For Black ~~folx~~, there is no transgression necessary. The Slave is a "bad" or "anti-" *citizen* before and beyond the physical womb.

142   MICHAEL DAVIS

The obliteration of Black flesh gives legibility to and coheres the World's conception of good citizenship. How should we then conceptualize and theorize "citizenship" in relation to Blackness (Slaveness) when Blackness is simultaneously terrorized by and permanently outside of civil society, law, politics, education, Humanity, etc.? Projects like Afropessimism allow us to (re)think the ways in which the (non)ontological position of Blackness permanently denies Blackness citizenship and argues that Black (non)existence is always already anti-citizen as we exist within the interstices of social life, Humanity, and the World. Anti-citizenship as theorized in this book must consider what a project of Black anti-citizenship might look like compared to a project of anti-citizenship for non-Black people of color. Therefore, this chapter also explicates the ways in which the moniker "of color" fails to adequately explain and address the different ways in which Black and non-Black (nonwhite) youth are oppressed and subsequently engage in revolutionarily practices that are anti-citizen and what I call anti-Human (sentience against the Human) since we are positioned outside of the World.

"I Knew It Was the Right Thing to Do": Black ~~Youth~~, Black ~~Fugitivity~~, and Rebel ~~Resistance~~ in School Contexts

There is a growing body of theoretical and empirical work in educational research and literature that is in rigorous and deep conversation with projects that explicitly theorize anti-Blackness (not to be confused with anti-Black racism). The logics and epistemological assumptions that undergird anti-Black racism (typically understood as racism specific to Black ~~folx~~) reinforce the Human, which is to say anti-Blackness, because it lacks an ontological theorization and analytic of Blackness in the first place.[20] It is critical that we examine racialized Blackness, of course, but it is typically divorced from the fact that anti-Blackness subsequently creates the desire for race and racism. However, education research is inundated with scholarship that imagines and envisions a World, or at least society, in which schooling and education will one day be supposedly equitable or justice-centered, especially for Black ~~youth~~. Even further,

Black ~~Youth Organizing~~ 143

there are educational scholars and practitioners who are more interested in what anti-Black violence looks, feels, and tastes like, as opposed to using all means necessary to address and end anti-Black violence. With that being said, it is necessary to understand the ways in which Black ~~youth organizers~~ in American schools resist and refuse not only anti-Black school violence but the structure of schooling itself. While their resistance is always already read as deviant, we must take a lesson from Cohen and articulate these acts as necessary forms of Black resistance. This section therefore aims to focus on how Black ~~young people~~ respond to and recount these stories of violence through nonrespectable, non-conforming, anti-citizen, and anti-Human approaches, which is central to a project against the anti-citizenship project.

Additionally, this section will draw on a qualitative research project that examined the educational programs and educational grassroots organizing and activist efforts in what I refer to as a radical, queer, and womyn-led Black liberation survival organization pseudonymously called Assata's Children (AC). The data from this project is used to (re)imagine anti-schooling and anti-citizenship as projects underneath a broader anti-Human imperative. This includes doing away with the Human in our attempt to survive and destroy the World. As demonstrated below, there is no happy ending with a definitive solution in this approach. There is no hope for Humanity, Black ~~agentic capacity~~ is always a myth, empiricism could never fully capture anti-Black violence, and spirit work, "Wake Work," and other Black ~~survival~~ tactics and ideologies are prioritized.[21] An anti-Human approach is still inherently limited and anti-Black because the nature of political projects already forecloses possibilities in this World for the Slave (the Slave is political currency, not a political subject). While anti-Humanness is not a perfect frame or praxis, it helps us move closer to truths and further away from frameworks, disciplines, and political contexts that force and coerce us into lying—most times unknowingly. One of the major goals here is to reduce the extent to which we reinforce anti-Blackness when trying to survive the World and Humanity. For the sake of time and space, the following subjection focuses on just two Black ~~queer youth organizers~~ at AC. The interviews included a total of twenty-seven participants, but Cardi and Ayanna summed up the general thoughts

144 MICHAEL DAVIS

and actions well. Since all political projects of survival will reinforce anti-Blackness, the goal here is to engage in as little anti-Blackness as possible. This means that how we survive and resist matters.

"Is This a School or a Plantation?"

Schools are inherent sites of anti-Blackness and unquestionably irredeemable and that is all they could ever be in the structure of this World.[22] Schools must be abolished. This is neither metaphor nor hyperbole. This is a political sentiment among Black ~~youth organizers~~ and ~~activists~~ that is often ignored, even in what is considered the most critical educational scholarship. This section outlines how Black ~~youth organizers~~ describe ~~their educational experiences~~. We have heard countless stories of spectacular and quotidian (the spectacular is the quotidian for the Slave) anti-Black school violence come from the flesh of Black ~~young people~~. There is no need to recount this terror considering that sharing videos, stories, and experiences about the Slave's violence can never generate sympathy or reprieve and thus only further normalizes the World violence that lies at the center of the Slave's nonexistent existence. The goal here is to show that everything must be anti-Black for schooling to function, even those with commitments to Black excellence and abolitionist teaching. In this work, abolition functions as the end—for example, an end to schooling that cannot be gained through Black educational excellence or even abolitionist teaching. While both approaches may be positioned differently in the political and social sense, they both hold up the anti-Black institution of the school.

The following subsections will emphasize the politics and practice of two Black ~~queer youth organizers~~ at AC—Cardi and Ayanna (pseudonyms). Cardi is a gender nonconforming young person who uses all pronouns but mostly *they/them*. They have been with AC for the last six years and have recently graduated from high school. Cardi now does full-time work with AC while attending college. Ayanna is a ~~queer~~ Black ~~womyn~~ who has been at AC since its inception, since she was a younger young person. At the time of the study, Ayanna had just finished high school. She now does programming and services for Black ~~girls~~ and queer folx at AC. They both do very powerful work and make critical

Black ~~Youth Organizing~~ 145

educational interventions that we must pay attention to. To be clear, this does not end anti-Blackness in schools—that is impossible—but it gives us a more radical and ethical way to survive.

It is important to start off by saying that both and Cardi and Ayanna forefront Blackness over queerness in their interviews. Cardi mentioned that "it's okay to be queer, just not queer and Black." Ayanna mentioned that "being queer makes a lot of things hard, but being Black on top of everything just makes the whole situation worse." This is not to say that queerness does not inform their experiences—it just does so in a different way that is inseparable and illegible without considering social death. It also suggests that Blackness (inherently queered at the ontological level) ruptures and disrupts what might be commonly known as a "queer experience." Unlike the non-Black queer person, Cardi and Ayanna cannot seek reprieve within the confines of civil society or its schools. With that being said, the following excerpts from their interviews emphasize their schooling in experiences in relation to being Black. This is not a race-first argument and it is not intersectional. It allows us to begin the process of thinking Black ~~difference~~ without Human logics and rubrics.[23]

Moving on, Cardi and Ayanna speak to the everyday anti-Blackness of schooling. They both had been suspended and kicked out of class routinely. After mentioning repeated suspensions I asked, "Can you tell me about a specific time where you got suspended or kicked out?" Cardi responded, "Where should I start! In high school now and middle school the teachers would say that I was, like, gifted, but I was suspended a lot for 'talking back.'" Mundane anti-Black school violence happens this way often. Teachers and school actors will supposedly celebrate Black ~~students~~ just to make their attacks seem less anti-Black. This also takes all responsibility away from the school and its structure. The idea suggests that Black ~~youth~~ who are smart lack the cultural and social ability to apply that intelligence. This type of celebratory destruction undergirds most school-based reward systems. Any celebration of academic success that is not understood as a project of anti-Blackness and violence to Black ~~students~~ is just successful death. If schools are ideological arms of the anti-Black state, schooling will almost always create students who reinforce the structure of society and the Human. This is not to say that Black

~~youth~~ should not have graduation parties, finesse high standardized test scores, get high GPAs, or achieve valedictorian. However, the Slave has to be under attack in the Human's schools and all celebrations are entangled with deep levels of anti-Black violence. Schooling is not a benign process. What are we celebrating when we did not go and learn how to get free?

Cardi and Ayanna were both kicked out of class and school for standing up to white bullies who terrorized their Black ~~classmates~~. Cardi was kicked out of class for defending Megan, a Black ~~girl~~ who was called a "hoe" by a white woman teacher. After being called a "hoe," Megan slapped the white woman teacher. Cardi then held the teacher back from Megan and condemned the teacher for calling Megan a "hoe." In Cardi's view: "Everybody was, like, criminalizing Megan. They was calling her violent and aggressive but . . . the teacher had called her a 'hoe,' literally." Megan was expelled. Cardi was moved to a different class and forced to pick up trash after school for a week. Similarly, Ayanna was suspended for fighting a white boy who was bullying a disabled non-Black student of color named Mark at lunch. Mark used a cane and needed more time to navigate the chaos of a high-school cafeteria. In Ayanna's account, she gave the white boy time to stop and walk away, but he began to bully her as well:

AYANNA: The white boy started cursing at me and pushed me. I fell to the ground, got up, and punched him. He punched me back and I blacked out. They told me I punched him again. Two police officers lifted me up by each arm, and I tried to get my arms loose and one said, "You don't want to do that." The officers were screaming in my face, so I screamed back.

MIKE: What happened after the situation?

AYANNA: I was like, "You don't have to talk to me like that," and they said, "You shouldn't have been fighting." Then my biological dad came to the school and they started following him because they said he "looked angry." There was a social worker, my dad, and the principal in the room. The principal said he couldn't see the boy push me, but they saw me punch him, but we were in the same location. I said, "Let me see," and they said, "No, we have to send this to investigators, and they

Black ~~Youth Organizing~~ 147

determine what to do." They suspended me for more time because they said I was pushing and had teacher contact. I was suspended for five days. They said I could talk to the boy about it too if I didn't want to get suspended. I came to talk, and they all ganged up on me. They blamed me, saying I didn't have to throw the punch. If you punch back, both people get suspended. I ended up walking out the room and didn't come back. The teacher told the social worker that if I could do it, I would do it again. The white boy was nineteen and I was fifteen. I just walked out and decided to get suspended.

MIKE: What happened with the lil white boy?

AYANNA: He went back to lunch and got his lunch. That was it.

MIKE: Anything else happen?

AYANNA: Oh yeah. My friend got a $300 ticket for screaming trying to help me.

Black ~~students~~ are always already guilty in the schema of mundane and everyday anti-Black school violence. Action in response to this violence is always framed as unacceptable and unnecessary, especially when the response does not fit the liberal Humanist frame. When murderers and abusers apologize, Black ~~people~~ are demanded to accept the apology and immediately move on. There might also be a liberal call for futile training and cultural understanding as well. The point here is that Black responses to anti-Black (school) violence are always deemed excessive, while the actual violence that caused the response is tolerated and accepted. Ayanna chose suspension over a bully and Cardi chose suspension over allowing a Black ~~girl~~ to be disrespected and degraded in her presence. To defend yourself while Black is always a crime.

School curricula and pedagogy is always anti-Black whether it includes a Black-~~centered~~ curriculum or not. Cardi and Ayanna attended different high schools in the same district. In the mission statements and discourse of both schools are claims to "social justice," "antiracism," and "Black excellence." At Cardi's school, according to a monthly newsletter, there was also curricular programming aimed at making "Black history a year-round goal." These supposed commitments will not and cannot address the anti-Black suffering that is required for schooling to function. In fact, many of these supposedly Black-centered programs and initiatives end up reinforcing the very systems that we need to dismantle and destroy. Even the most so-called critical or radical educational initiatives and activism create different portals of violence through which Black ~~youth~~ suffer.

Cardi goes on to talk about two other times in which they were removed from class for confronting a teacher about the inaccuracy of course material and refusing to engage a Donald Trump speech for a class assignment. This was common across all classes. Cardi was forced to consume anti-Black ideologies regardless of the context or curricular focus. In a contemporary issues class, a Republican white woman teacher created an assignment based on President Donald Trump's inauguration speech. As a ~~community organizer~~ and ~~activist~~, Cardi felt an extreme sense of frustration and pain having to "consider all sides." Cardi refused the teacher and the very premise of the assignment. They were then removed from class by a Black security guard for being "disrespectful." The security guard asked Cardi why they were being kicked out of the classroom. Cardi responded: "I spoke up. I'm like, because I didn't want to listen to Donald Trump. That's the reason why. And she stood there and gasped and said, 'That's not why,' but why are you kicking me out then, because that's the only thing that I've done. The teacher was like, 'She was just being very disrespectful using vulgar language.'" Black ~~students~~ are oftentimes forced to engage in debates, class material, and school discourse that completely disregard ~~their~~ existence in all forms. Black ~~folx~~ have to debate, through assignment or intellectual exercise, whether ~~we~~ deserve to exist. The World's answer is always already "no."

Cardi also mentioned being kicked out of a ~~history~~ class that claimed to center Black history. In Cardi's account: "The teacher was sayin' something historically inaccurate. Basically, like [Abraham] Lincoln 'freed' the Slaves or whatever. Something that I knew was not true. We kept goin' back and forth and then I just said, 'Fuck it I'm done,' and stop talking. I was kicked out and was mad, but deep down, but I was happy for sayin' what was right." Refusing this type of ideological anti-Black violence almost always guarantees punishment for Black ~~young people~~. Similarly, Ayanna recalled an incident in which she confronted a teacher about why believing that "all lives matter" is problematic. Ayanna had been kicked out of this particular class several times. According to Ayanna:

> I got a referral. She didn't kick me out this time, so she let me stay in the class, and then I found out the next day that she had wrote a referral on me, talking about I was being disobedient and not doing my class work. This was my first period class. The class I go to every morning. I had to sit in the dean's office from the beginning of the school day till lunch. So that's four hours. And so, I also had to serve a lunch detention. Which is where you have to sit in the dean's office for thirty of the fifty minutes for lunch. When I asked about the referral, she was like, "I don't feel like that's respectful, and I feel like I would know those things or else I wouldn't be in my position."

Ayanna was punished and disciplined for pushing back against a politic that denies ~~her existence~~. Black ~~youth~~ are framed as not "respectful" when attempting to defend their ~~bodies~~ and ~~minds~~. Those "things" that the teacher claims she "knows" force Ayanna outside of epistemological and ontological possibility. The teacher's comments can be also read as: "I know you don't matter, and I know the 'things' that make you not matter." Blackness is too heavy and hated in the classroom, which is why schooling must go. Schools and their actors are not only standing in the way of their supposed rights as citizens (inherent impossibilities). Schools antagonize Black ~~life~~ under the guise of "progress" and "inclusion." Cardi's and Ayanna's (non)existence makes them permanently ineligible for citizenship and therefore ineligible for any political relief in schools or elsewhere. Cardi's dismissal of Trump and refusal of an anti-Black curriculum and ideology, along with Ayanna's critique of anti-Black teachers and bullies, are projects inherently against the type of citizen that schools desire to create. This refusal does not stop at the political level. Ayanna and Cardi embody a spirit of refusal and survival that aims to expose and expel the ontological impossibility for the Slave on the school plantation.

Similar to the theoretical and epistemological realms of the academy, Black specificity is always sacrificed and deemed regressive, which consequently leads to POC legibility and resolve and total Black erasure. As mentioned, this chapter belabors this point, so the following paragraphs will just briefly discuss the ways in which Cardi and Ayanna talk about the (ontological) difference between Black and non-Black People of Humanity (POH) or "POC." There is a plethora of educational scholarship on the hyperexcessive discipline and punishment practices and ideologies that scaffold Black ~~schooling~~. Ayanna points out some of the experiential differences that she noticed during a typical school day between Black ~~folx~~ and non-Black POC:

> You could be Black and have a pass, but you would get harassed . . . You could be white and you could not have a pass at all and be cool. Hell, you could even be a person of color and not have a pass, and you would not get harassed most of the time. That's just how the police and teachers be . . . they target the Black kids way more.

In most educational literature, the harassment and targeting of Black ~~students~~ in schools is understood through Humanistic empiricism or tautological concepts like "anti-Black racism." This scholarship is mostly descriptive (where, when, how, how many participants, how much something occurred, how much time passed, what are the colors on the wall while the Black ~~kids~~ are harassed, etc.). The rubrics cannot begin to think about anti-Black violence if Black ~~Humanity~~ is assumed or stated as a desirable goal. In other words, it forecloses the ability to understand why the condition of Blackness leads to "way more" violence. So, how might we understand the differences that Cardi and Ayanna mention between Black ~~folx~~ and non-Black folx of color as a difference in ontology as opposed to experience alone? We must understand this harassment and violence beyond (anti-Black) race/racism, xenophobia, white supremacy, and other Human-centric ways of thinking about and addressing Black oppression. This might lead us to the Black specificity necessary to at least make some spaces, even though temporarily, more bearable—this includes the school plantation.

Both Cardi and Ayanna do community-organizing work with non-Black POH or POC. Their relationships are strong, and they see each other as family. Here is Cardi speaking to why, in their view, making

Black ~~Youth Organizing~~

distinctions between Blackness and people-of-colorness, in this case Black and Southeast Asian (SEA), is important as an organizer on the ground fighting for Black liberation:

> I feel like there's different things that has to be dismantled before thinking about Black and SEA liberation into one. There's just a lot of different things going on in our communities. You know, a lot of it is similar. We've all been oppressed by the white man. A lot of us are here because we've had to escape, and we've had to come somewhere where we already knew was bad, but it was better than where we was [referring to SEA folx]. But a lot of us didn't even have a choice to come here, a lot of us was forced here. I'm specifically talking about Black people and our enslavement. I don't like to compare us in the same group because we've had so many different things happen to each different culture. Before we combine and go forward, we have to know there's a lot of difference between the two. Thinking about police, Black folx, we targeted off bat, but SEA folx, they have a little more leeway. They don't have to duck and dodge like we do.

Cardi is not denying that non-Black POC endure structural violence. In fact, they have committed themself to what might be called a coalitional politic. What Cardi implies, though, is that coalitions oftentimes cohere at the expense of the Slave. Cardi does not "like to compare [Black ~~folx~~ and SEA folx] in the same group" because there is an understanding that anti-Black violence becomes further entrenched in "POC" types of concepts and politics. The Human-adjacency and capacity afforded to non-Black POC means that coalitions are likely to fail or reinforce anti-Blackness (i.e., there are calls to abolish ICE, but a refusal to abolish police and prisons generally). To use Cardi's words, there is "a lot of difference" between Black and POC (in this case SEA) ~~folx~~ that starts with "enslavement" and Slaveness. To be three-fifths of a person and citizen means to be nothing at all, or even the outside of nothingness. This is the incalculable calculus of anti-Black violence. We must work alongside ~~young~~ Black ~~folx~~ like Cardi and Ayanna to find the language to explain this difference and why "leeway" is granted to some and permanently denied to others. In understanding and addressing anti-Black violence, Cardi and

Ayanna help us shift from a white/POC binary to a Black/non-Black or Human/Slave framework. As Cardi avers: "[Non-Black POC] don't got white privilege, but they ain't Black either."

Again, it is important to quickly note that both Ayanna and Cardi attend schools with explicit claims to "diversity," "social justice," and even "Black excellence." Some might mistake this type of work as a commitment or a step forward for Black ~~students~~. Black-~~centeredness~~ is always violent in the mundaneness of anti-Black school violence. Anti-Blackness is so mundane and diurnal that it works as the foundation to how we think about progress and even social justice, especially in schools. These programs and initiatives do not dismantle or decrease anti-Black violence. The ideological and political aspects of these initiatives work to actually reinforce anti-Blackness. They are most times predicated on respectability politics, linear understandings of "racial" progress, Black bourgeois excellence (Black students simply getting 4.0s and high test scores), carceral restorative justice plans, cultural Blackness (i.e., hanging up a picture of Martin Luther King Jr. and Rosa Parks for a week or a whole year), etc. These structural adjustments, or the World's illusionary justice, promise work to do more harm. The violence that is forced on Black ~~students~~ like Cardi and Ayanna is necessary and needed to justify schooling as it stands. To be clear, there were contextual differences between Cardi's and Ayanna's schools (e.g., policies, practices, curricula, lunch, teachers, administrators, and general school experiences). However, Ayanna's and Cardi's conditions expose the irrelevancy of such a concept in making sense of and ending anti-Black violence.

The fact of the matter is that Blackness is generally dishonored in the everyday project of anti-Black schooling. Black hair, skin, cultural aesthetic, attire, and language are always already marked as disgusting and are even banned in a large majority of schooling and educational spaces. Always, our hair is too big, our skin too dark, our pants too low, our culture too lazy, and our existence too much. Blackness in schools and elsewhere is too much for the World to handle, but it is also not enough in terms of satiating the World's and the Human's fatal desire to consume Black flesh to give their bodies life. Schooling is always central here. Cardi and Ayanna unquestionably push back against the obedient, patriotic, socially mobile, and law-abiding citizen that schools aim to create. Black ~~politics~~ that aim to destroy the World are inherently against the citizen, since Blackness is always outside of citizenship, regardless of any legal status. However, Cardi's and Ayanna's conditions do not change if the citizen is dismantled. For Ayanna and Cardi, being a "good citizen" is never possible, regardless of what Black ~~folx do~~. The Slave is not concerned with second-class citizenship. The Slave's concern is whether folx can be counted as "citizen" (good or bad) because of anti-Blackness. Anti-citizenship projects must therefore reject the Worldly tendency to make sense of anti-Black violence through Human rubrics like white supremacy and race/racism alone. For Cardi's and Ayanna's sake, we must take seriously what it means to think about Black experience and violence beyond the Human.

There are countless studies on dead and dying Black ~~youth~~ that unveil much of what we already know, yet we still call on empiricism, context, and other Human calculations as if there is something substantially different to be found. Like many Black ~~young people~~ in these studies that we do, Cardi and Ayanna both started out mentioning much of what is known—anti-Black violence is essential and necessary to schooling. Cardi helps us understand what a Black radical politic of refusal and survival might entail as they summed up a response to an interview question:

MIKE: Anything else to add about your own educational experiences before we move on?
CARDI: *Fuck school!*
MIKE: Fuck it!

Embodying a "fuck school," "fuck citizen," and "fuck Human" politic might allow our (Black ~~folx~~) chests to pump just a little while longer.

THE ANTI-HUMAN APPROACH FOR THE ANTI-CITIZENRY AND THE ANTISCHOOLER

Black ~~youth~~ make sense of the World with the tools made available to them and with the tools they create. Cardi and Ayanna offer us pivotal

154   MICHAEL DAVIS

insight into how we might survive the World en route to its destruction. Cardi and Ayanna teach us about what it means to be against the state, the citizen, the Human, and the World. This section begins to theorize a project of anti-Humanness (a survival project not to be confused with liberation) based on Cardi's and Ayanna's community organizing and activist work. This is not to say that they explicitly make claims against the Human, but their condition (as Slave) and Black radical politics come together to make this type of theorizing possible. Also, thinking about their work through an anti-Human lens might help us more accurately understand and name the actions that we take against the World. Anti-citizenship must allow space for Black specificity if the Slave is to be accounted for within its theoretical and epistemological terrains—especially if the goal is to end or survive anti-Black violence that is citizenship-specific. This starts with a Human/non-Human (Master/Slave) dichotomy as opposed to a white/Black or Black/non-Black binary.

Why anti-Humanness for the anti-citizen and the antischooler? While we are in search of language that might move us closer to a Black (non) ontological truth, it is also understood that Human rubrics might serve as stand-ins or placeholders in the meantime. When utilizing Human methods, methodologies, or frameworks, we cannot simply apply these rubrics in typical or usual ways. We must bend and break the rules and logics of liberal Humanist projects in order to begin to think about the Humanizing violence that is anti-Blackness. We must also engage the "exceptionally violent tradition, humanism, to provide intellectual and philosophical space for [the Slave, queer or otherwise]."[24] Anti-Humanness might help better finesse the Humanistic and contextual bounds of the academy. This is not a perfect concept or method. It is simply an otherwise direction in understanding specificity within the grammar of Black suffering for the Slave in all its manifestations. This is not a liberation project but a project that is survival-based and with World destruction as a guiding practice.

A project of anti-Humanness for the anti-Human and its non-Black co-conspirators includes: centering modernity, Humanity, and the World as the starting place for anti-Black violence; positioning anti-Blackness as a paradigm all on its own, as opposed to a mere racial/cultural category or

Black ~~Youth Organizing~~ 155

identity; refusing claims of Black ~~agency~~ (the ability to end anti-Black violence in this World) and instead focusing on Black sentient ~~survival~~ (the Slave's attempt at surviving until Humanity ends); thinking about anti-Blackness at (non)ontological and metaphysical levels; rejecting liberation and survival projects that attempt to salvage the World and integrate the Slave into Humanity, such as intersectionality; breaking and bending the extant rules of empiricism, method, and methodology to move closer to addressing and ending anti-Black violence; creating new methods, methodologies, and other practices that are meant to address (not redress) anti-Black violence but think against and past the "Human" in doing so; advocating and fighting for liberation and survival without the "Human"; and insisting on Black specificity to rethink how violence functions at the Human level. An anti-Humanness project does not end here. This is just a start to thinking about an ever-expansive anti-Humanness project. Just to quickly note, this list does not imply that each strategy is disconnected or separate from the others. The strategies are all closely related and interdependent.

Finally, the following demonstrates what operationalizing an anti-Human politic and project might look like at the school level. The same strategies and approaches could and should be centered in a Black anti-citizenship framework, as demonstrated by Cardi and Ayanna. In the framework presented here, chattel Slavery is a material manifestation of the Human, which is born before the Columbian advent. For Cardi, while whiteness, or, as they put it, the "white man," certainly terrorizes racial Blackness and non-Black POC, "our enslavement" or Slaveness positions Black ~~folx~~ outside of the Human spectrum to give it coherence (anti-Humanization) as opposed to merely facing violence within the confines of the World (de-Humanization). Cardi recognizes that non-Black POC are not "white" but they "ain't Black either." Why ain't they Black and why do non-Black POC not have to "duck and dodge" like Black ~~folx~~? This is not an argument about "more" or "less"—the Slave is outside of the logic of reason and measure. What separates Blackness from people-of-colorness is the ability to achieve Humanity, even if de-Humanized. Again, Cardi still engages coalitional work but also recognizes that non-Black POC can navigate civil society and the public sphere only at the expense of the Slave. This is why Black ducking and dodging looks ontologically different from ducking and dodging for non-Black POC. This distinction matters as we engage survival projects like anti-citizenship and anti-Humanness. There is nothing for the Slave (the embodiment of nothingness) to reclaim or go back to in the ontological and metaphysical confines of this World. How we frame what we do and how we do it matters. The liberal Humanist academy is full of political refutations that deny Black specificity and take an all-lives-matter approach to thinking about anti-Black violence. Cardi and Ayanna teach us the importance of recognizing how some liberation and survival projects are connected but also require separation when necessary. Centering Humanity and the World as root causes for the Slave condition also allows for the positioning of anti-Blackness as a paradigm all on its own, which might allow us to see and address anti-Black violence differently.

Cardi and Ayanna embody this politic in their daily refusals of anti-Blackness in the classroom. They both reject liberation and survival projects that attempt to salvage the World and integrate the Slave into Humanity (the Slave cannot integrate into a class or Humanity). Ayanna repeatedly mentioned "skipping" not to avoid learning or education (assuming that learning is taking place) but to avoid the mundane anti-Black violence that occurred. Her political education as a community organizer led to an important internal question: "What's the point of me being here [in school]?" Ayanna understands schooling as a tool in the game but also disconnects schooling as we know it from Black ~~liberation~~ and ~~survival~~ as "schools can't get us free."

For Cardi, who got security called on them for wearing headphones because they "didn't want to hear" anti-Black historical perspectives, and for Ayanna, who "got suspended one time for laughing too loud . . . and one time for tapping [her] pencil too much," schools must go, and not in a metaphorical sense. Abolishing schools will not get Black ~~folx~~ free, but it is necessary in Black sentient survival projects. Cardi and Ayanna were constantly kicked out of class and school for asserting ~~their~~ knowledge. We know that Black ~~students~~ are not allowed to be learners. While schools rely on a banking model of education, we know that Black ~~youth~~ resist this model, and the schooling model in general, every day. While some might recognize anti-Black school violence, there is still a demand for Black ~~youth~~ to attend schools that still goes unchallenged. We must consider the anti-Black violence that is inherently embedded in that desire.[25] Thus, anti-citizenship must seek to destroy the school and the Human.

Thinking about Megan, who "smacked the hell outta that teacher," what would it mean if we embraced a revolutionary politic of self-defense in the form of smacking a white woman teacher? How might this smacking politic be essential to projects against the citizen and the Human? This is not to say we should teach Black ~~kids~~ to slap school-based abusers like a white woman teacher in this case (at least not yet), but we should be prepared at the institutional level to defend them when they do. Many educational scholars, so-called critical or not, might deem this suggestion as impractical or dangerous. But when has Blackened schooling ever been practical or safe in this World? Never. There are some who might agree with the slapping but not advocate it. It is also understood that anti-Black violence is a school requirement. We cannot sit back and expect Black ~~youth~~ to take ~~blow~~ after ~~blow~~ while we dance in the fanciful imagination of "better schools." Ayanna talked a decent amount about the school halls and spaces like the back of the class as a place and space of insurgency, insurrection, and anti-Black violence. We must understand that skipping class, talking back, putting heads down, putting headphones on, arriving late, supposedly cheating on assignments, missing assignments, missing school, and so on are fugitive survival practices.[26] Ayanna asserts, "I don't like school and don't think it's really needed for what we trying do." What is it that we are trying to do? For the Slave, surviving while keeping World destruction in mind is key. If we want Cardi and Ayanna to survive (we can never thrive in this World context), we must end the school as we know it. Schools must be set ablaze just like those police stations and precincts during summer of 2020.

It should be clear that Cardi and Ayanna did not just give up because schools must go. Their Black survival educational imaginations include what education buildings might look like (or if we need such a physical space in the first place), curricula, pedagogy, teachers, teacher training, etc., but also goes beyond these structures. Their education dreams were partly formed by their political education at AC. Cardi mentioned, "I finally found someplace that I knew was gon' take initiative into, like, hearing my voice and hearing what I had to say and what I was trying to teach. And some place where I won't be judged. This is just a place where I could come be around people who are like family to me and stuff like that." Ayanna mentioned that: "During my first action, I was already at the front. I knew people who were leading. So I knew all the girls up there, so I felt comfortable. I felt comfortable in my skills." Ayanna went on to talk about how AC allowed her to facilitate critical conversations with other Black ~~youth~~:

> [AC is] a place where people can be open and express themselves and their concerns. Take the girls group, for example. We have a wide range of girls. For different ages and knowledge bases. I feel like if we get all of those girls to a level where they can explain to us what certain things are—like what is oppression, what does it really mean? what do these definitions of things really mean?—we can start to see some little change in our community at the very least.

While their desire to lead and teach was suppressed in school, Ayanna enjoys being a learner-teacher: "[I'd like to] educate people my age. I like educating people. At lunch, I would sit in a corner by myself and read. I was such a bookworm. And then I tried to start, like, telling people about real facts, real shit. The stuff that we learn at AC, I tried teaching it to them and they was down! And so, with that, you—you start to wake up and you start to learn a lot of things, you start to dig deeper, you do a lot of research with the people." Both Cardi and Ayanna engage educational imaginations that are rooted and centered on Black ~~folx~~ and our ~~communities~~.

Cardi and Ayanna were also aware that there are school changes that are necessary now. They mentioned demands for "better school lunches," "getting cops out of all schools," and being able to "control what we learn more." They did not confuse this type of work with progress. Ayanna envisioned a learning space where "all the kids in the hood would go to that place, right. So, and the parents, the grandmas, the aunties would contribute to the learning in some way." More frankly, Cardi expressed the desire to create a Black educational space where "actually, everybody give a fuck about everybody for the most part." The point here is that their desire for learning and education goes beyond what is possible in a school. Their learning objectives embody a politic of destroying the citizen, destroying the school, and destroying the World. Cardi proclaimed: "I know it's unrealistic. I know schools can't even give us the basic things we ask for. I know as much as we want our people to have their own spaces in the school, it's unrealistic. To be real, the school shouldn't be doing none of this for us in the first place. Just give us what y'all owe and let us do it." While we are trying to destroy schools in every sense of the word, Black ~~youth organizers~~ and their adult co-conspirators continue to provide pivotal lessons on the distinction between Black ~~survival~~ and liberation. We must consider what a praxis of anti-Humanness and anti-citizenship look like in education contexts. We must allow Black specificity and start with school abolition at the very least.

ANTISCHOOLING, ANTI-CITIZENSHIP, AND ANTI-HUMANNESS AS "HOPE"

Hope and progress narratives have been highly detrimental to Black families and communities—especially in education. Landmark legal decisions like *Brown v. Board of Education* are celebrated as milestone moments in education, which in turns reduces and covers the extent to which American schools inherently lack the capacity to hold and love Black ~~youth~~. However, there is a different kind of hope that exists in these projects that refuse every edge of the state and World. These Worlds are actualized through Black tactics and strategy that will always be deemed deviant and destructive. There is a hope in Black deviance and destruction as it aims to undo and reimagine not only education but existence too. Again, it must be restated that scholars, researchers, activists, and organizers must provide intellectual, theoretical, institutional, and practical support when taking up radical and deviant acts of fugitivity. Anti-Humanness focuses on Black sentient ~~survival~~. These are daily practices and politics that can only temporarily (if that) assuage anti-Black violence but will inevitably create new portals of violence through which the Slave suffers.

160   MICHAEL DAVIS

There is a desire to do more than survive, but "more" is simply Black excess or futile claims to World on behalf of the Slave. The "more" relies on the Human and civil society to allow the Slave to live, but these are the very entities that make the Slave die on repeat. Let us end the school, the citizen, and the World for the love and sake of Black ~~children~~ who this World always will deny.

NOTES

1. This chapter employs the strategy of strikethrough formatting throughout—that is, the author crosses out words so that they appear "under erasure," at once expressed and (not quite) eliminated.

World: *World* refers to the epistemological, ontological, social, political, and cultural that govern the structures, institutions, economies, and lives of those who are in, on the periphery of, or permanently on the outside of Humanity. This world must end for the Slave to be "free."

Human/Humanness/Humanization/Humanity/Master: *Humanity* (capitalized) is understood as an anti-Black and violent process of modernity that synonymizes *Blackness* and *Slaveness* (dehumanization versus anti-humanization).

Slave: *Slave* (capitalized) makes a point that Blackness cannot be separated from Slaveness in terms of ontological/metaphysical condition. *The Slave* is synonymous with *the Black* and *the Nigger.*

People of Humanity: *People of Humanity* (POH) is used in this chapter as opposed to *People of Color* (POC) or *BIPOC* because the latter terms assume a universal regime of violence and oppression through which "racialized" violence can be understood. This further erases and obscures anti-Blackness. Since Blackness is Humanity's opposite (Master/Slave relationship), all-encompassing terms are themselves anti-Black. POH theoretically aligns with Black specificity by making an ontological distinction between anti/Blackness and race/ism and white supremacy. It speaks to ontological position as opposed to identity.

2. Kihana miraya ross, "Call It What It Is: Anti-Blackness," *New York Times,* June 4, 2020, https://www.nytimes.com/2020/06/04/opinion/george-floyd-anti -blackness.htm.

3. Ross, "Call It What It Is."

4. Michael J. Dumas, "'Losing an Arm': Schooling as a Site of Black Suffering," *Race Ethnicity and Education* 17, no. 1 (2014): 1–29.

5. Calvin Warren, "Onticide: Afropessimism, Gay Nigger #1, and Surplus Violence," *Journal of Lesbian and Gay Studies* 23, no. 2 (2017): 391–420.

Black ~~Youth Organizing~~ 161

6. On deviance, see Cathy Cohen, "Deviance as Resistance: A New Research Agenda for the Study of Black Politics," *Du Bois Review: Social Science Research on Race* 1, no. 1 (2004): 27–45; on fugitivity, see Damien M. Sojoyner, "Another Life Is Possible: Black Fugitivity and Enclosed Places," *Cultural Anthropology* 32, no. 4 (November 18, 2017): 514–36.

7. Michael Omi and Howard Winant, *Racial Formation in the United States: From the 1960s to the 1990s* (New York: Routledge, 2014). Eduardo Bonilla-Silva, *Racism without Racists: Color-Blind Racism and the Persistence of Racial Equality in America,* 5th ed. (London: Rowan and Littlefield, 2017).

8. Orlando Patterson, *Slavery and Social Death: A Comparative Study* (Cambridge, Mass.: Harvard University Press, 1982).

9. Tapji Garba and Sara-Maria Sorentino, "Slavery Is a Metaphor: A Critical Commentary on Eve Tuck and K. Wayne Yang's 'Decolonization Is Not a Metaphor,'" *Antipode* 52 (2020): 764–82.

10. Eve Tuck and K. Wayne Yang, "Decolonization Is Not a Metaphor," *Decolonization: Indigeneity, Education & Society* 1, no. 1 (2012): 1–40. Garba and Sorentino, "Slavery Is a Metaphor," 774.

11. Garba and Sorentino, 772.

12. Garba and Sorentino, 772.

13. Frank B. Wilderson, *Red, White & Black: Cinema and the Structure of U.S. Antagonisms* (Durham, N.C.: Duke University Press, 2010), 31.

14. Cathy Cohen, "Deviance as Resistance: A New Research Agenda for the Study of Black Politics," *Du Bois Review: Social Science Research on Race* 1, no. 1 (2004): 27–45.

15. Cohen, "Deviance as Resistance," 30.

16. Cohen, 28.

17. Cohen, 32.

18. Sojoyner, "Another Life Is Possible," 517.

19. Soyjoyner, 518.

20. Michael J. Dumas and kihana miraya ross, "'Be Real Black for Me': Imagining BlackCrit in Education," *Urban Education* 51, no. 4 (2016): 415–44.

21. Christina Sharpe, *In the Wake: On Blackness and Being* (Durham, N.C.: Duke University Press, 2016); Calvin L. Warren, *Ontological Terror: Blackness, Nihilism, and Emancipation* (Durham, N.C.: Duke University Press, 2018).

22. Dumas, "'Losing an Arm'"; ross, "Call It What It Is."

23. Warren, "Onticide."

24. Warren, 413.

25. Sojoyner, "Another Life Is Possible."

26. Sojoyner.

CHAPTER 7

We Have Nothing Left to Prove, Yet a Whole New World to Accomplish

CHRISTOPHER R. ROGERS

I have a lot to accomplish. I don't have anything to prove. Subtle difference there.

> —STEPHEN CURRY, quoted in Scott Polacek, "Warriors' Steph Curry: I Still Have 'a Lot to Accomplish' but Nothing 'to Prove'"

We are virtually forced into the invidious position of proving our humanity by citing historical antecedents; and yet the evidence is too often submitted to the white racists for sanction. If there is to be any proving of our humanity it must be by revolutionary means.

> —WALTER RODNEY, *The Groundings with My Brothers*

Let us begin: We have nothing left to prove, yet a whole new world to accomplish. We must no longer cyclically repeat ourselves or the truths of our ancestors, denying the sacred inheritance that has already set forth what we are called to do and become in this moment. We must stop explaining, stop negotiating, stop counternarrativizing, and shift our energies toward being immersed within and possessed by our own Africana ways of knowing and being to transform our worlds.[1] Critique is no substitute for organizing and is easily accumulated into academia's capitalist calculus that prizes circulation and eschews authentic engagement.[2] Turning toward new horizons, Toni Cade Bambara teaches us that revolution is never something that begins "out there" but in here with "what the community is doing" or what Hortense Spillers terms "the intramural."[3]

163

What's happening between us, y'all? Are we even aware of an "us"? Do we want to be well? Are we interested in the messy, chaotic work of constructing alignment? How does an attunement to our collective self-governance prefigure the necessary future strategies and movements to come, if we are to have a future at all?

Bambara and Spillers remind us of the present opportunity: it's always already our time to become unavailable for servitude (as reinforced by Avery F. Gordon), to immerse ourselves into the intersectional care work of the intramural, to claim our indifference to the adulation of entrenched, yet never indestructible, empire.[4] To move beyond its gaze, Eduardo Galeano best articulates the cynicism to the fetishization and commodification we've grown to abhor: "Let us be wary of applause. Sometimes congratulations comes from those who think us harmless."[5] Certainly, this is not the time for harmless half-steppin', not the time for seeking legitimacy and awaiting validation, not the time for confusing sympathetic surveillance for substantive solidarity.

Like Gwendolyn Brooks taught us, this has to be the time of Big Poems.[6] We must avail ourselves into installing this era as one of radical resurgence in reciprocity with the many who've put their bodies and livelihoods on the line to widen the rupture of white supremacist imperialist heteropatriarchy. Thank you, bell hooks. We must claim our individual and collective responsibility as the midwives for a new world struggling to be born. It's the Robesonian time of knowing that we be the decisive force in this effort. "That's why they're afraid of us!"[7] We can be complete within each other when we refuse to see ourselves through the West's broken windows. We must no longer disavow the sovereignty of our imagination (see George Lamming, study Sylvia Wynter) by lowering ourselves to merely make do in a world order that enshrines itself in making death.[8] We must no longer compromise ourselves and our futures by dressing up in ill-fitting nation-state uniforms (get them cops out ya heads and hearts too . . .) and treasuring their colonial adornments.[9] We must know that while every police station, Target, and CVS that burns at breakfast will inspire more #representation, lifetime achievement awards, and small-business funding by dinnertime, what we do won't add up to shit if we gamble our soul abandoning the struggle to undo what lies at the root.

We Have Nothing Left to Prove 165

We can reclaim how to stand upright and practice walking freely. These wandering thoughts go out to the ones like me, scratching and surviving as cyborgs in the machine, as everyday, ordinary folk who find purpose, righteousness, and integrity within the liberatory vision of Black studies as a global project of transforming "the entire order of things."[10]

Becoming Unavailable for Servitude and Choosing Community

All we must have now are songs of freedom, which sends me reminiscin' on my own youthful anti-citizenship praxis revealing how I got over, how I came to learn we were more than what they showed us. Much more. You see, it was hip-hop that first possessed me as a cis-hetero Black male growing up in Chester, Pennsylvania, not too far outside Philadelphia. Between the 1990s and early 2000s, we lived under constant judgment by media portrayals of our town as wholly "negative," "lacking," and "dangerous," but never "oppressed," "sequestered," or "subjugated." It was the single story attributed to my city, to the Village that reared me. Years later, that same single story would serve as the social currency of some sort of psychological debt that I made payment upon by achieving a sense of upward class mobility. *Chris, see, but you made it out.*

Don't get gassed, y'all. Either side of that coin ain't got nothing to do with me. Yes, the realities of drugs, crime, and violence had their impact upon our community just as more rarely articulated state-sponsored political corruption, failed educational policy, and environmental racism. These were the structural ravages of organized abandonment cruelly projected onto Black families as evidence of disorder and deficiency.[11] To accept individual praise is to refute the collective offense. We have not been saved.

What I came to cherish the most from my upbringing in this Black-ass city, to which I later found language for through Black place-making, was to know that even among this ongoing acute duress, it could never wholly consume the freedom-dreaming energies of the Black community.[12] We still invented ways to make beauty in the Village. What remained, yet invisibilized to those unwilling to see us, was the Chester of neighborhood block parties, playground basketball tournaments, church revivals, candlelight vigils, etc. It was the various communally improvised ways we built community, grieved for community, and planned for a future together in this 4.7-mile city, in spite of the fundamentally racialized and racist structuring of urban space. It became a path-breaking realization to perceive that the Chester I loved and that loved me was a world away from its state-architected municipal, electoral, and economic chaos. And in some meaningful ways, my inheritance was to see that the next generation would be reminded that this place remains useful ground from which to glean world-altering possibility.

Rap became this platform where we, Black teenagers, could practice an anti-citizen poetics of landscape within the cipher and on the record.[13] I couldn't rap a lick. Still can't. I made beats and realized that even without a vocal track, those beats spoke too. We recognized our power to write ourselves and our complex social worlds into existence within, beyond, and against the dominant dictates of Black suffering. We invested our time, intellectual energies, and a couple dollars to invent our own narratives about ourselves and the city that explored the tensions in trying to make a life in a place deemed to be unlivable. We collaged language, rhythm, and style to honor a multidimensional look at our urban social realities that we never found in school textbooks or passed down from the well-intentioned but narrow mentorship offered by many of the local elders. Narrow because it often felt too missionary, too much like a civilizing mission that faulted us as being the impetus of our own premature death. We arrived into these conditions and too many of us were being blamed for attempting to experiment a way out. Yet, the best of our preceding generations, elevated by community wisdom rather than educational achievement, chose to accompany us in making sense of our environments. They honored what Toni Cade Bambara sanctified as part of the preparation for collective self-governance by "imparting language for rendering the confusing intelligible, for naming the things that warped us, and for clarifying the complex and often contradictory nature of resistance."[14] I suspect that they knew the building blocks for creating otherwise worlds required a foundation in what Kiese Laymon expresses as healthy choices, second chances, and good love.[15] They believed, if not in the music itself, in our capacity to commune, compose, and self-reflect

We Have Nothing Left to Prove   167

as necessary survival skills. Years later, I would envisage this commitment to endlessly creating ourselves in studios, on community stages, and digital platforms as our rediscovery of a very old Black epistemological tradition, a surviving blues impulse Ralph Ellison describes as "to keep the painful details and episodes of a brutal experience alive in one's aching consciousness, to finger its jagged grain, and to transcend it."[16]

Within our Chester Village, we Black youth made *something*, however ephemeral, networked across a mix of basements, park benches, street corners, and community centers, that allowed us a collective standpoint to interpret our experiences and desires fueled by an expressive freedom that formal education failed to incite. While the insights gained couldn't be made to protect us from the promised incursion of prevailing anti-Black logics, the ability to define ourselves for ourselves echoed the simple and powerful truth that "defeat or victory [remained] an internal affair."[17] It was made clear that making a commitment to community helps you survive. And just maybe, the work of a lifetime was to stay grounded as we were, sitting in that revelation, to be ever wonderful by never allowing the colonial world to change our minds. To know we can make worlds hints that we can unmake them too. Could it all be so simple?

Answering the Call:
Anti-citizenship as Black Radical Praxis

We must no longer underestimate our power in reshaping the world. We certainly know what currently *is*, but a stroll through our archives perpetually reminds us to live up to what *ought to be*.[18] With these intimate experiences as backdrop, I argue that a contemporary lived praxis of Black studies rests upon what Mary Hooks of Southerners on New Ground declared for our generation with the Mandate:

MARY: Call and response!
CROWD: Call and response!
MARY: The mandate for Black people in this time!
CROWD: The mandate for Black people in this time!
MARY: Is to avenge the suffering of our ancestors!
CROWD: Is to avenge the suffering of our ancestors!

168 CHRISTOPHER R. ROGERS

MARY: To earn the respect of future generations!
CROWD: To earn the respect of future generations!
MARY: And be willing to be transformed in the service of the work!
CROWD: And be willing to be transformed in the service of the work![19]

Do you hear, feel, sense yourself within that crowd? Do you recognize that this call is also being made to you/through you? Are you there? You coming thru? Answering the call is to "fall in step with the chorus" that Saidiya Hartman teaches us propels transformation by availing us to "make a way out of no way, to not be defeated by defeat."[20] I assemble these words, tributes, homages as a call for recommitment among those who dedicate themselves and their labor to advancing the struggle for Black liberation. We got to know that we answer the call with our lives. Shifting power means meditating upon the requirements of ourselves to be one-in-the-number. Shifting power means discovering our responsibility within shaping the horizon of ever-expanding struggle. How are we answerable to incubating glorious futures of global Black flourishing? I return to Walter Rodney, who delivered his own mandate in service of Black Revolution in 1968:

> Under these circumstances, it is necessary to direct our historical activity in the light of two basic principles. Firstly, the effort must be directed solely toward freeing and mobilizing Black minds.... Secondly, the acquired knowledge of African history must be seen as directly relevant but secondary to the concrete tactics and strategy which are necessary for our liberation. There must be no false distinctions between reflection and action, because the conquest of power is our immediate goal, and the African population at home and abroad is already in combat on a number of fronts.[21]

From Rodney then to today, we remain in battle and embattled, yet resolute in faith and principle. We must not put our stake into the easy victories of temporary and illusive rights and reforms; We Want Power. True power, as Kwame Ture reminds us, may only come through the general, improvised, collaborative activities of the organized masses.[22] And to achieve organized masses presupposes that our first work be about getting good at the freeing and mobilizing of Black minds, which demands we begin with ourselves. This requires that we find the break, a praxis of refusing to serve time to a system that only serves us death. *You wanna fly, you got to give up the shit that weighs you down.*[23] Certainly, our pledged tactics won't be without contradiction, won't be effective if the result of magical or essentialist thinking, and chiefly require us to develop critical infrastructure for amassing both visible and subterranean strategy. This is honest, serious, collective work that none but ourselves can complete. The editors of this collection lay out enacting anti-citizenship as "threatening the maintenance of a social order that functionally harms our communities." To be anti-citizen is just one articulation by which we may claim our participation in radical reimaginations, rearticulations, (re)memberings of the world to pursue a lasting exodus from subjugation.[24] And best to know who else just may be on this road with us. We cannot prize theoretical and methodological purity over rich engagement with the multiplicity of avenues folk take for studyin' freedom. There's still the radical responsibility to all who choose fugitivity: *We may not know the way through the forest, but we can pick each other up when we fall, and we will arrive together.*[25]

Toward Infinite Redemption Songs and Survival Programs

I leave readers with this call-into-action, which came to me through the work of the #LetUsBreathe Collective in Chicago and uniquely articulated by playwright Kristiana Rae Colón: "As artists, it is our duty to not simply reflect these times, but to imagine, paint, script, sculpt, sing, and perform how these times must change."[26] What (re)new(ed) visions are animating our activist labor?[27] We must redeem ourselves, our communities, our futures from writing and repeating social death sentences. We must speak life and carry on tradition, presuming our power and not our powerlessness. We must hold ourselves to the integrity and fortitude upheld by abolitionist radical thought in practice—a way of grasping, forging, working out alternatives to systems of domination and dehumanization, where Avery F. Gordon reiterates that this work inevitably

170 CHRISTOPHER R. ROGERS

and historically has always taken place while still enslaved, imprisoned, indebted, occupied, walled-in, commodified.[28] It's where we are, but never our sole vantage. That's why we turn to our ancestral archives. We've been here before. We've never let the perceived impossible overwhelm us. We've been called to survive, whereas Black lesbian mother warrior poet Audre Lorde frames:

> I have to tell you guys, I need to, to, perhaps talk a little more about survival. Because, when I say that, I have heard people say, "oh, but I'm not content to survive." . . . And implicit in that response, is a certain denigration of what survival is. That is to say, they reduce survival to a mere existence. And that is not survival . . . Implicit in survival is joy, mobility, and effectiveness. And effectiveness is always relative . . . none of us are going to move the Earth one millimeter from its axis. But, if we do what we need to be doing, then we will leave something that continues beyond ourselves, and that is *survival*.[29]

Our survival is both the urgency and the long game, our anchor between the here and now and the "beautyful ones" not yet born.[30] *If we do what we need to be doing. If we do what we need to be doing.* Let us turn away from the presupposition that our work as Black scholars be bogged down in merely narrating the shape of the wound, reiterating intergenerational traumas, and not embracing the duty of fashioning revolutionary selves, revolutionary lives. Our Black educational heritage encourages us that the generational question and its answers, which always already remains in our grasp and not that of our enemy, are revealed when we do away with distraction: *What are we doing to be free?* Let a thousand Black freedom experiments bloom. We have nothing left to prove, yet a whole new world to be won.

NOTES

1. Vincent Harding, "The Vocation of the Black Scholar and the Struggles of the Black Community," *Education and Black Struggle: Notes from the Colonized World*, ed. Institute for the Black World, 3–39 (Cambridge, Mass.: Harvard Educational Review, 1974).

2. Abigail Boggs, Eli Meyerhoff, Nick Mitchell, and Zach Schwartz-Weinstein, "Abolitionist University Studies: An Invitation," *Abolition: A Journal of Insurgent Politics* (2019).

3. Toni Cade Bambara, "On the Issue of Roles," *The Black Woman: An Anthology*, ed. Toni Cade Bambara, 101–10 (New York: Signet, 1970); Tim Haslett, "Hortense Spillers Interviewed by Tim Haslett for the Black Cultural Studies Web Site Collective," *Black Cultural Studies* 4 (1998).

4. Avery F. Gordon, *The Hawthorn Archive: Letters from the Utopian Margins* (New York: Fordham University Press, 2017).

5. Eduardo Galeano, "In Defence of the Word," trans. William Rowe, *Index on Censorship* 6, no. 4 (1977): 15–20.

6. Gwendolyn Brooks, *Winnie* (Chicago: Third World Press, 1991).

7. Paul Robeson, *Paul Robeson Speaks: Writings, Speeches, and Interviews, a Centennial Celebration* (New York: Citadel Press, 1978).

8. David Scott, "The Sovereignty of the Imagination: An Interview with George Lamming," *Small Axe* 6, no. 2 (2002): 72–200; Sylvia Wynter, "Rethinking 'Aesthetics': Notes towards a Deciphering Practice," *Ex-iles: Essays on Caribbean Cinema* (Trenton, N.J.: Africa World Press, 1992), 245.

9. Paula X. Rojas, "Are the Cops in Our Heads and Hearts?," in *The Revolution Will Not Be Funded: Beyond the Non-profit Industrial Complex* (Cambridge: South End Press, 2007), 198–214.

10. K. Wayne Yang, *A Third University Is Possible* (Minneapolis: University of Minnesota Press, 2017); Jarvis R. Givens, *Fugitive Pedagogy: Carter G. Woodson and the Art of Black Teaching* (Cambridge, Mass.: Harvard University Press, 2021).

11. Ruth Wilson Gilmore, *Golden Gulag: Prisons, Surplus, Crisis, and Opposition in Globalizing California* (Berkeley: University of California Press, 2007).

12. Marcus Anthony Hunter, Mary Pattillo, Zandria F. Robinson, and Keeanga-Yamahtta Taylor, "Black Placemaking: Celebration, Play, and Poetry," *Theory, Culture & Society* 33, no. 7–8 (2016): 31–56.

13. Edouard Glissant, *Caribbean Discourse: Selected Essays* (Charlottesville: University of Virginia Press, 1992); Katherine McKittrick, *Demonic Grounds: Black Women and the Cartographies of Struggle* (Minneapolis: University of Minnesota Press, 2006).

14. Toni Cade Bambara, *Deep Sightings and Rescue Missions: Fiction, Essays, and Conversations* (New York: Vintage, 1996).

15. Kiese Laymon, *Heavy: An American Memoir* (New York: Simon and Schuster, 2018).

16. Frantz Fanon, *Black Skin, White Masks* (New York: Grove Press, 1991); Clyde Woods, *Development Arrested: The Blues and Plantation Power in the Mississippi Delta* (London: Verso Books, 2017); Ralph Ellison, "Richard Wright's Blues," *Antioch Review* 5, no. 2 (1945): 198–211.

17. Cedric J. Robinson, *Black Marxism: The Making of the Black Radical Tradition* (Chapel Hill: University of North Carolina Press, 2020).

18. Lorraine Hansberry, "The Nation Needs Your Gifts," speech given to the *Readers Digest*/United Negro College Fund creative writing contest winners, New York City (1964).

19. "The Mandate: A Call and Response from Black Lives Matter Atlanta," Southerners on New Ground, July 14, 2016, https://southernersonnewground .org/themandate/.

20. Saidiya Hartman, *Wayward Lives, Beautiful Experiments: Intimate Histories of Riotous Black Girls, Troublesome Women, and Queer Radicals* (New York: W. W. Norton, 2019).

21. Walter Rodney, *The Groundings with My Brothers* (London: Verso Books, 2019).

22. Stokely Carmichael, Michael Thelwell, John Edgar Wideman, and Kwame Ture, *Ready for Revolution: The Life and Struggles of Stokely Carmichael (Kwame Ture)* (New York: Simon and Schuster, 2003).

23. Toni Morrison, *Song of Solomon* (New York: Random House, 2014).

24. Cynthia B. Dillard, *The Spirit of Our Work: Black Women Teachers (Re) Member* (Boston: Beacon Press, 2022).

25. Colson Whitehead, *The Underground Railroad: A Novel* (New York: Doubleday, 2016).

26. Kristiana Rae Colón, "Creating Frontlines," Poetry Foundation, December 5, 2017, https://www.poetryfoundation.org/harriet-books/2017/12/creating -frontlines.

27. Robin D. G. Kelley, *Freedom Dreams: The Black Radical Imagination* (Boston: Beacon Press, 2002).

28. Gordon, *Hawthorn Archive.*

29. Audre Lorde, "Women and the World in the 1980s: August 20, 1982-Audre Lorde," interview by Blanche Cook, August 20, 1982, Pacifica Radio Archives, available at Internet Archive, http://archive.org/details/pacifica_radio_archives -IZ1349.07.

30. Ayi Kwei Armah, *The Beautyful Ones Are Not Yet Born* (London: Heinemann, 1988).

PART III

"WHO DO YOU LOVE, ARE YOU FOR SURE?"

Rejecting Citizenship's Assimilations

CHAPTER 8

Reclaiming the "Mexican Problem"

Chicano Youth, Agency, and the
Rearticulation of Citizenship

RACHEL F. GÓMEZ AND JULIO CAMMAROTA

This chapter problematizes the ways that Chicanos' racial and ethnic identities are tightly coupled with their relationship to United States citizenry as historically defined through imperialist and colonial relationships.[1] We complicate the generations-old "Mexican Problem" narrative through the examination of the ways that Chicano youth have both resisted and reclaimed this narrative through dynamic political participation in their educational experiences. Deemed unfit to be citizens since the signing of the Treaty of Guadalupe Hidalgo, Chicano youth and their communities have historically been on the forefront of grassroots social movements to subvert white-supremacist policy and ideology in their public schooling experiences.

A QUESTION OF CITIZENRY

The 1848 signing of the Treaty of Guadalupe Hidalgo in relation to Mexico and Mexican-descent peoples has shaped U.S. public policy in education in negative ways.[2] Since this pivotal moment in U.S.–Mexican history, Chicanos have been forced into a social and economic insubordinate position within the strata of U.S. racial and ethnic hierarchy. Framed as having qualities antithetical to citizenship, Chicanos have endured generations of stereotyping as "unfit" or illegitimate citizens.[3] Considered to be genetically flawed interlopers and noncontributors to the democratic

176   RACHEL F. GÓMEZ AND JULIO CAMMAROTA

landscape of the United States, Mexican Americans were framed in the master narrative as occupying a space of anti-citizenship—the bedrock for the historical idea of a "Mexican Problem" that continues to frame the educational experiences of Chicanos and Latinos today.[4] Since the Mexican–American War, the U.S. status quo has consistently depicted Chicanos as people who do not belong, who do not care, who do not fit, and who refuse to assimilate—and therefore are unfit to be citizens. Although Chicano youth have been forced into the contours of this trope, they have also simultaneously embraced an anticolonial stance of refusing to "fit" and rejecting assimilation. As anti-citizens, Chicano youth continue to push back on some of the negative characteristics they have been assigned by demanding that their educational experiences serve their community's needs. Operating within the typecast of anti-citizens, Chicano and Latino youth have persistently found ways to engage politically to assert their own rights as legitimate beings for themselves, in spite of being systematically marginalized through anti-Mexican policy and rhetoric. As a counterstance to the Mexican Problem narrative, Chicanos and Latinos have made great contributions to this country as they rearticulate what it means to be a citizen—a different sort of citizen who refuses to succumb to de-Mexicanization campaigns. For Mexican Americans, their liberation struggle is most apparent in the areas of education where they exercise anti-citizenship through subversion, resistance, and reclaiming space for themselves. Chicano youth agency, then, is manifest through agitation, contestation, and radical transformation.

In the 1960s, Chicanos, formally identifying as Mexican Americans, renamed themselves as Chicano/Chicana—a statement of Brown pride and liberation, a counterstance to centuries of Spanish and Anglo colonial subordination. The term *Chicano*, although once considered pejorative due to its co-option by Anglos in the Southwest, has roots in Nahuatl, the language of the Mēxihkah (me:ˈʃiʔkaʔ) or Aztec people. The North American country known as México (the *x* pronounced as *j*—the letter *jota* in Spanish and the *h* sound in English) is an eponym of Mēxihkah. The Nahuatl word for the land of the Mēxihkah is *Mēxihco*, pronounced "me:ˈʃiʔko"—ʃ is the equivalent of the English *sh* as in *shoe*. The identity term *Chicano* is derived from *Mexica*, which is the Spanish spelling of

Mēxihkah, and is pluralized by Spaniards as *Me-xi-ca-nos* and then abbreviated to *shicanos* or *Chicanos.* Chicano identity embraces Indigeneity and the history and culture of the original peoples of what is now referred to as the U.S. Southwest. The claiming of Chicano positionality is the reclamation of sovereignty, of resisting further domination and exploitation, and of decolonization. Chicanos embody an anti-citizenship stance as a means to rearticulate and reimagine their rightful place in this land, although as beings for themselves.

In this chapter, we will consider the ways that Chicano youth have ignited their agency in making demands to ensure that they receive the education that is within their rights as U.S. citizens. This includes the right to history, including the ways in which Chicanos have contributed historically and contemporaneously to U.S. society. The public school curriculum is not inclusive of the historical or contemporary experiences of Mexican Americans—or any other ethnic or racial group outside of white Americans. Instead, students consume state-sanctioned curricula through a dominant master narrative that is steeped in whiteness ideology and, depending on where they attend school geographically, varies in lens and scope. Chicano youth have been actively engaged in demanding an ethnic studies curriculum since the civil rights and Chicano movement of the 1960s. As an alternative to the pattern of oppressive schooling currently experienced by students, Chicano families continue to pressure school governing bodies for a liberating and justice-centered curriculum. Some basic demands are a program of study that introduces historical counternarratives, is transdisciplinary and relevant to the culture and geography of Mexican Americans, and centers U.S. history and culture in relation to Mexico and Mexican, Chicano, and Indigenous people, land, labor, economics, social movements, and social and racial stratification through policy and practice.

This chapter is about the agency of Chicanos in resisting and asserting their rights in education for culturally responsive education, curriculum, and language instruction.[5] We cannot talk about the (im)possibility of an equitable education for everyone in this country without talking about the history of Chicanos in endeavors for change around education, such as *Mendez v. Westminster,* the Chicano Blowouts, the resistance to

English-only laws, and the continued fight for ethnic studies.[6] We draw on historical evidence of Mexican Americans reaching for equity in education while being simultaneously submerged in the abyss of a white-supremacist "American" educational system where many students still attend racially segregated, substandard schools nationwide.[7]

Through grassroots social movements and resistance to white-supremacist policy and ideology, Chicano youth and their families have been at the forefront in rejecting an educational system that is complicit in multiple forms of oppression against their bodies and identities. In the following section, we problematize the construction of the Mexican Problem narrative at the turn of the twentieth century and how this popularly accepted understanding of early Chicanos became a point of entry for academic research on Mexicans in the 1920s and 1930s.[8] The Mexican Problem–related stereotypes routinely employed to describe Chicanos during this time were grounded in racist nativist perspectives that served to uphold white supremacy and economic dominance over Mexico and Mexican-descent people. The same master narrative that grounded the early academic works on Mexico and Mexican U.S. territory continues to negatively affect the educational experiences of Mexican American youth today.

The Mexican Problem

In order to understand the state of Chicanos in education today, it is imperative that we consider the economic relationship imposed on Mexico by the United States in the late nineteenth century. Since the signing of the Treaty of Guadalupe Hidalgo, imperialist ideology in relation to Mexico and Mexican people as the Mexican Problem has shaped not only U.S. public opinion about early Chicanos but also public policy in education. As a means to justify the economic dominance over Mexico, its people, and its resources, white-supremacist discourse served to position and define Mexicans as pathological and in need of a cure, and thus needing to be segregated away. The imperialist discourse of this time was embedded with eugenics-based ideological notions that otherized Mexico and its citizens as foreigners who were continually framed as "Orientals" and peons. Nationalist discourse portrayed early Chicanos as nothing more than a backward people—a cheap labor force who were born to serve. Some of the early language used to exert dominance over Mexicans and the expansion of the United States into Mexican land was not dissimilar to language utilized to identify all colonial subjects globally. Early Chicanos were often described with animalistic and other insulting descriptors such as "apathetic," "simple," "lazy," "dense," "donkey," "oriental," "childlike," and "culturally deficient" and were thought to be in need of paternalistic guardianship.[9] During the 1920s, other descriptors of Mexicans—such as "feeble-minded," "idiot," "moron," "degenerate," "dirty," "unkempt," and "immoral diseased peons"—incited frenzy among white Californians who feared Mexican reproduction, as all of these terms spoke to who was fit to be a citizen. Health officials' perceptions of "Mexicans increasing at an alarming rate" placed Mexican women and people with mental illnesses at high risk for forced sterilization.[10] Defining Mexicans in these terms positioned them as an obstacle to American progress that merited removal. Yet other language was used to vilify early Chicanos living in the Borderlands—*borderes* as criminal, deviant, and violent—especially through racial narratives perpetuated by the Texas Rangers, who were state-sanctioned "skilled executioners (of Mexicans, Indians and 'runaway-slaves') on behalf of the white power structure."[11] Early Chicanos were generally racially framed as an imminent and burdensome threat to the "virtuousness" of whiteness, and their place at the lowest strata of the new U.S. economy made them dispensable.[12] Historically, language informed by eugenicist-based logic has been a valuable tool in rationalizing the economic, social, and political domination over colonized peoples globally. This white-supremacist reproduction of the Mexican Problem in the United States validated the extraction of resources and human labor from Mexico for the last two centuries as part of a colonial project articulated through the justification of Manifest Destiny. Centuries earlier, the Spanish used similar language to justify the religious conquest and brutal enslavement of Indigenous and African peoples throughout the Americas and Caribbean.

Around 1880, during the height of the economic subordination of Mexico and its resources, many American writers began to publish "exotic" tales of Mexico and Mexican people. Many of these works were published

180   RACHEL F. GÓMEZ AND JULIO CAMMAROTA

in monthly magazines, books, and journals, and Americans were eager to devour them. Gilbert G. Gonzalez offers a typical sample of such works:

> "That Mexican" whom we have so long contemplated from north of the Rio Grande, has therefore come to live with us. With his inherited ignorance, his superstition, his habits of poor housing, his weakness to some diseases, and his resistance to others, with his abiding love of beauty he has come to pour his blood into the veins of our national life. "That Mexican" no longer lives in Mexico; he lives in the United States. The "Mexican Problem" therefore . . . reaches from Gopher Prairie to Guatemala.[13]

These early writings were useful in solidifying the justification of the capital conquest of Mexico and Mexican people. Gonzalez describes this "emerging genre of works dedicated to Mexico, . . . later to be known in academia as Latin American Studies," as a body of work in which authors often quoted and cited one another, yet rarely critiqued U.S. foreign policy.[14] The otherization and racialization of Mexican people as pathological was carried over with them as the Mexican laborers worked on the U.S. side in segregated labor camps and colonias set up for mining and the other unskilled labor coveted by U.S. economic order.[15] Soon, this labor force and their offspring living on this side of the border would become widely portrayed as the Mexican Problem in popular U.S. discourse.[16] In a 1908 academic study of Mexican laborers printed in the official *Bulletin of the United States Bureau of Labor*, one academic, Victor S. Clark, writes:

> The Mexican laborer is unambitious, listless, physically weak, irregular and indolent. On the other hand, he is docile, patient, usually orderly in camp, intelligent under competent supervision, obedient, and cheap. If he were active and ambitious, he would be less tractable and would cost more. His strongest point is his willingness to work for low wage.[17]

Just as early Chicanos and Mexican immigrant laborers were deemed the Mexican Problem in the United States, so were their descendants in the

Reclaiming the "Mexican Problem"   181

context of education. The Mexican Problem discourse was later substantiated by academia in the form of journal articles, theses, and dissertations that cross-referenced this body of work as authoritative sources. Between 1912 and 1957, there were at least twenty-five master's theses and doctoral dissertations devoted to the Mexican Problem in the Southwest, which focused on the alleged intellectual and cultural inferiority of Mexican Americans and immigrants.[18] U.S. scholars centered the Mexican Problem as the preliminary point for their research in education and in other social arenas—never investigating the origins of the Mexican Problem itself. Educators, social workers, courts, and the police referenced these supposed data on how to deal with Chicanos in education and in other public policy. These data hinged on literature that debased Mexican peoples as a justification for their economic subjugation and subordination by the United States. Through this body of literature, the same discourse that justified the exploitation of Mexico's labor and its resources had streamed back into the United States and was being utilized to address the Mexican Problem through a lens of objectification and domination. And along with it came an identical list of cultural pathologies that had now filtered into the U.S. school boards and educational program policies designed for Chicano youth schooling.

Americanization through Schooling

Grounded in biological deficiency tropes, imperialist ideology was now informing educational policies designed to educate Chicanos.[19] Referencing these dominant ideologies and racial narratives, the United States set up schools segregated by race and language with special curricula for Mexican students in hopes of dealing with their Mexican Problem. These early Mexican schools were grounded in racialized notions of inferior intelligence. Mexican American boys were funneled into low-status and low-paying jobs through curricula that emphasized vocational education to learn building trades and factory work, and the girls were trained to emulate Anglo homemakers. The purpose of schooling for Mexican Americans was to fix the Mexican Problem through a project of Americanization and, therefore, de-Mexicanization and de-Indianization.

182   RACHEL F. GÓMEZ AND JULIO CAMMAROTA

Mexican schools in the U.S. Southwest were inferior compared to Anglo schools at the time. The school buildings and materials were substandard, and the Mexican American teachers were paid lower salaries than those of the Anglo schools. These early Chicanos, who were monolingual Spanish speakers, were forced to use Standard English curricula and were made to take standardized tests in English to assess their abilities, although these new citizens spoke no English.[20] Today, similar trends in educational policy around race and ethnic studies, English-only laws, English language learning, tracking into special education, and being discouraged from considering college, along with disparate disciplinary procedures, continue to harm Chicano and Latino students.

Americanization through Protestantization

As a remedy to the Mexican Problem, religious-sponsored campaigns to Americanize Chicanos reached from the Southwest to the Midwest.[21] These assimilation projects, or settlements, were steered by Protestant religious organizations whose goal was to Americanize the growing immigrant population. Under the leadership of upper- and middle-class supposedly progressive white women, these religious groups created and directed hundreds of settlements and settlement houses throughout the country, and dozens of those Americanization sites were located in the Southwest alone. Beginning in the late nineteenth century, settlement houses were strategically placed in the Southwest to Americanize Mexican American women through romanticized ideas of the great American melting pot. Operating on the volunteered time and fundraising efforts of the Anglo women, Mexican American women were to assimilate by emulating Anglo women in various homemaking tasks, such as cooking and cleaning, as well as hygiene practices and Bible study. The cultural messages were clear: the goal of Americanization was for Mexicans and Mexican Americans to assimilate to Anglo culture and values.

During the first half of the twentieth century, the Methodist church alone sponsored four boarding schools and sixteen settlements to coerce predominantly Mexican American women and children in the Americanization process. A force of the colonial project was to acculturate early Chicanos through a process of forced proselytization. The Protestant

Progressive Era Houchen Settlement in El Paso, Texas, operated between 1912 and 1962 and systematically indoctrinated approximately fifteen thousand to twenty thousand Mexican-descent individuals from 1930 to 1950, which was approximately one-fourth to one-third of El Paso's Mexican population.[22] The settlement assimilation project at Houchen was a Christian rooming house that obliged women and children to emulate and embrace Protestant Anglo culture and lifestyles. The Anglo female staff instructed the women and children through a "full schedule of Americanization programs such as citizenship, English instruction, cooking, carpentry, bible studies, Boy Scouts, music lessons, and hygiene."[23] Those Anglos spearheading Americanization campaigns in the Southwest, such as religious missionaries, social workers, and educators, targeted women and children for their programs, but they especially focused on young girls as they were thought to be the purveyors of Mexican culture. As Pearl Idelia Ellis of Covina City Schools in California explains in her 1929 publication *Americanization through Homemaking*: "Since the girls are potential mothers and homemakers, they will control, in a large measure, the destinies of their future families."[24]

Imperialist ideology reinforced the otherization of these early Chicanos as objects in need of a transformation toward whiteness and assimilation into Anglo culture. It was thought that perhaps once they had been whitened through a process of segregated cultural cleansing, Anglos could then live with them.[25] To this end, the link between imperialist ideologies (including racial narratives) and the historical conditions that inform current educational practice and policy must be examined. Through this historical lens, a clear trail of instances of education-related racial oppression emerges, and, therefore, Chicano historiography is incomplete without consideration of this fundamental imperial context.

Fit to Be Citizens?

The narrative around Mexican Americans as supposedly unfit to be citizens continues today, and much of the language used to describe Chicanos and Latinos in general centers around citizenship, belonging, criminality, and (il)legality. Former president Donald Trump perpetuated the Mexican Problem narrative through his description of Mexican

184 RACHEL F. GÓMEZ AND JULIO CAMMAROTA

immigrants as drug dealers, criminals, and rapists.[26] The false narrative that routinely surfaces and tends to stick is that "Latinos do not value education," and this is why their educational persistence is low compared to Anglo students. Reagan- and Bush-era education secretary Lauro Cavazos may just hold some of the responsibility for this enduring narrative when he made a wide and sweeping statement that Hispanic parents do not care about education. Cavazos, who identifies as Hispanic, declared, "We don't care.... We must have a commitment from Hispanic parents . . . that their children will be educated."[27] Historical evidence turns this conjecture on its head. The Chicano and Latino communities have always valued education and have consistently rejected its oppressive characteristics in demand for opportunity and educational policy and practice that meets the needs of their communities. It is the U.S. education system, driven by white-supremacist ideology, that has failed Chicano and Latino students since its inception.

RESISTANCE

Chicanos, specifically, have historically resisted subjugation, including through the critique of education policy that systematically perpetuates inequalities. They have resisted oppressive systems that position them in a status of second-class citizenry through their efforts in the areas of civil rights, which included affirmative-action policies that implemented race-based college admissions. Chicano students have demonstrated resilience and opposition to the conditions of their schooling. Some of these conditions include racial and ethnic segregation to Mexican schools, especially in the Southwest. The negative treatment of youth through schooling and white-supremacist curricula reinforces systems of Anglo cultural and racial dominance and imperialist ideology.

Mexican Schools and the Question of Race

In 1946, eight years prior to the landmark Supreme Court case *Brown v. Board of Education of Topeka,* existed the *Mendez v. Westminster School District of Orange County* case.[28] In this case, five Mexican American families—the Estradas, Guzmans, Mendezes, Palominos, and Ramirezes—

Reclaiming the "Mexican Problem"

challenged school segregation in the five school districts in Los Angeles, where their children attended segregated schools for Mexicans. Segregated Mexican schools were commonplace throughout the U.S. Southwest.[29] In 1945, when the Mendezes moved into the Westminster neighborhood, they attempted to enroll their children in their neighborhood school but were told to register them at the Mexican school. Yet, their lighter-skinned cousins were permitted to enroll. What followed was a class-action lawsuit against five Orange County school districts.[30]

Although "Mexican" is not a race (and was not at this time) but an ethnicity and a nationality, Anglo parents in these Orange County school districts refused to allow Mexican American children to attend schools with their children and insisted on separate schooling. These nuanced conceptions of race and ethnicity, within a white-supremacist framework, are what make the *Mendez v. Westminster* case remarkable. To offer some essential historical context, the Treaty of Guadalupe Hidalgo of 1848 granted Mexican Americans U.S. citizenship, and, until the 1930 U.S. Census, Mexican Americans had been classified as "white." Following an increase in Mexican immigration since the Mexican Revolution of 1910, a "Mexican" race category was added to the 1930 census.[31] Anglo families could, and would, petition that Mexican American children be segregated away to Mexican school under "separate but equal" doctrine.

During the Great Depression (1929–1939), Anglo rage around Mexican immigration and resources (meant for them) spurred government-sponsored sweeping raids to deport people of Mexican descent. These "repatriation drives" deported up to 1.8 million people of Mexican descent to Mexico, many of whom were U.S. citizens.[32] Certainly, to be racially marked as "Mexican" during this era, in particular, was especially hazardous for Mexican American families. In response to anti-Mexican hostilities and heightened racial climate, the Mexican American community successfully lobbied to eliminate the "Mexican" race category from the 1940 census, making Mexican Americans officially classified as "white" again. In general, however, Anglos would not accept Mexican Americans as anything other than "Mexican." In consideration of this historical context, the implications of the complexities around understanding race and ethnicity become clear. How these nuanced racialized understandings intersect with the underpinnings of racial segregation and the Fourteenth Amendment make the *Mendez* case markedly significant.

The *Mendez* attorney, David Marcus, did not claim race discrimination, as racial segregation was legal under *Plessy v. Ferguson*.[33] Rather, he argued that school segregation based on Mexican or Latin heritage was unconstitutional under the Fourteenth Amendment because they were not included in school-segregation policies, as Black, Native/Indigenous, and Asian American students were.[34] In 1947, the U.S. Court of Appeals for the Ninth Circuit ruled that the forced segregation of Mexican American students, specifically, was unconstitutional based on "separate but equal" doctrine because Mexicans were technically "white." Although this was a victory for these five families attending the separate remedial Mexican schools in Los Angeles, this decision only shielded children of Mexican ancestry from public school segregation in California and therefore did not end legal race segregation in California or elsewhere.

White-Supremacist Curriculum and the Demand for Chicano Studies

Schooling has historically been a site of violence for Chicano youth, as the persistence of Anglo cultural dominance over their minds and bodies is essential to U.S. Americanization projects. Grounded in white-supremacist conventions, school curricula have been potent regulators of the identities of Mexican Americans since the signing of the Treaty of Guadalupe Hidalgo. Through segregated Mexican schools and other de-Mexicanization projects supported by state and religious organizations, Chicanos have continually been the object of colonial projects throughout the United States.

During the height of the Chicano movement of the 1960s, Chicano youth rejected their continued subjugation to white-supremacist curricula and schooling. Cognizant of the damage inflicted upon them through their schooling experiences, Chicano youth demanded an ethnic studies curriculum that affirmed their own history and culture and rejected the white-supremacist curricula they were forced to consume and celebrate.[35] Chicano youth understood how schooling, as it was, remained a central force in the continuation of their colonization. As their demands remained

Reclaiming the "Mexican Problem" 187

unmet, students walked out of their high schools en masse. These mass student walkouts are known as the Chicano Blowouts.

The Chicano Blowouts of 1968 lasted for ten days in which more than ten thousand Los Angeles Chicano high-school students walked out of classes in protest to white-supremacist curricula in their schools. Similar blowouts were repeated in Texas and throughout the Southwest that same year. Students walked out again in California and Colorado in the 1990s, insisting that their schools hire Chicano and Latino teachers and counselors, along with implementing a comprehensive and inclusive ethnic studies curriculum.

Latino youth have historically resisted oppressive systems through their fight for civil rights in postsecondary education as well, which included affirmative-action policies that implemented race-based college admissions. Mexican American students have not only engaged in high-school walkouts to redress issues of white-supremacist schooling but also resisted the oppressive nature of higher education for Chicanos. As the Chicano movement grew in scope, student activists, educators, and administrators from the University of California, Santa Barbara created a powerful document that, at the time, was a radical demand on U.S. education and political consciousness. *El Plan de Santa Bárbara: A Chicano Plan for Higher Education, 1969* was a 155-page manifesto that called for the implementation of Chicano studies educational curricula throughout California and, importantly, demanded community control in education. *El Plan* would not only aid in the institution of previously nonexistent Chicano studies programs and departments but also act as inroads to cohesive Chicano student activism within the university system nationwide. *El Plan* expressed a new resolve in Chicano liberation. In recognition of generations of historical assaults on Chicano people, their culture, and their human dignity, *El Plan* called for the freedom of self-expression, self-actualization, and the self-determination of the Chicano community in strategic decision-making, particularly in educational policy.

Notably, the Chicano student organization MEChA (Movimiento Estudiantil Chicano de Aztlán) was founded through the implementation of Chicano studies at UC Santa Barbara. MEChA is a unified student movement and organization that "promotes higher education, *cultura,* and *historia*" and remains a vital student group in the success and dedication to Chicano studies.[36] Today there are approximately three hundred active MEChA chapters nationwide that are affiliated with U.S. colleges and universities. MEChistas, as they are commonly called, express their (anti-)citizenship through challenging institutions of higher education to recognize the latent hypocrisy in their claims of inclusivity and democratic ideals.

Nationwide, Chicano students continue to demonstrate resilience and opposition to the conditions of their schooling. As previously mentioned, some of these conditions include racial and ethnic segregation, the negative treatment of school-aged youth, and white-supremacist curricula that reinforce systems of dominance. Through resistance to substandard and racist educational systems, Chicano youth are challenging ideas of citizenship through engaging in behaviors that contest the contours of colonial schooling practices. Chicano and Latino educators, too, are active in anti-citizenship behavior in similar ways.

The Tucson Battle for Chicano Ethnic Studies

An example of revolutionary resistance work enacted by academic Latino and Chicano critical scholars is the Social Justice Education Project (SJEP) in Tucson, Arizona. Over a period of several years, a university professor worked with SJEP high-school student researchers to conduct empirical studies that exposed racism and oppressive school conditions experienced by Chicano youth.[37] Students then took their research findings to their school administrators to address the issues surfaced through their research. Although SJEP was exterminated under the 2010 Tucson Unified School District (TUSD) Mexican American studies ban, Chicano and Latino scholars continue to dedicate their research to resistance work with students through critical praxis, such as Youth Participatory Action Research. One study in particular examines the relationship between race, ethnicity, and the sociopolitical development of Chicano youth through a curriculum grounded in critical race theory.[38] Latino and Chicano scholars are involved in resistance to white-supremacist colonial schooling through their research and teaching of emancipatory pedagogies in Chicano and Latino communities and schools.

In their objection to the ban of the Mexican American studies (MAS) component of the TUSD ethnic studies curriculum in Tucson, high-school students engaged in various public acts of civil disobedience. The MAS program was exterminated in 2010 through HB 2281, a bill that stated that the MAS courses were "designed for Latinos as a group that promote [*sic*] racial resentment against 'Whites.'"[39] The Tucson Chicano community, which included students, families, teachers, professors, and other community members, pushed back.

In a public demonstration of civil disobedience in protest to the ban of the MAS curriculum, a group of nine Chicano high-school students took control of the April 2011 TUSD school board meeting by chaining themselves to the governing board members' chairs. Fed up with being ignored, the student activists (UNIDOS Coalition) derailed the evening's planned vote on the controversial resolution that would end MAS courses. While chained to the chairs, and to one another, the student activists led the crowd in chanting, "Our education is under attack! What do we do? FIGHT BACK!" The banning of the MAS curriculum was a devastating blow to the Chicano community in Tucson. The curriculum ban not only interrupted Chicano education at the high-school level but also disjointed the once-steady educational pipeline that had been created between the local high schools' MAS program and the Mexican American Studies Department and major at the University of Arizona.[40] Tucson youth continued to protest the ethnic studies ban, demanding that it be reinstated and reviewed for constitutionality. The state-sanctioned curriculum ban also included a list of more than eighty books, mostly written by Mexican Americans and other authors of color, as part of the curriculum ban.[41] The grassroots, youth-led social movement surrounding this court case garnered national attention and support from Chicano and Latino communities nationwide and gained support from educator allies across the nation. The success of the court case was due, in part, to the national attention and support the youth received through their unrelenting activism.

In 2015, the U.S. Court of Appeals for the Ninth Circuit affirmed that HB 2281 that banned Mexican American studies in the TUSD was indeed unconstitutional and in violation of students' First Amendment rights.[42]

In 2017, U.S. District Court Judge A. Wallace Tashima, ruled that TUSD had violated the students' constitutional rights by discontinuing the MAS program. Judge Tashima argued that the students' First Amendment rights were violated because they were "denied the right to receive information and ideas." In addition, the ban was in violation of students' Fourteenth Amendment rights because the decision by TUSD to eliminate the program discriminated against Latinos. Judge Tashima stated, "The Court concludes that the plaintiffs have proven their first amendment claim because both enactment and enforcement were motivated by racial animus."[43] He continued, saying that the law to ban MAS was "motivated by a desire to advance a political agenda by capitalizing on race-based fears." The judge also cited blog evidence authored by former Arizona School Superintendent John Huppenthal, stating that "several of his blog comments convey animus toward Mexican Americans generally." Undeniably, Chicano youth, and the Mexican American community in general, have always valued education. Mexican Americans have stood their ground battling for their constitutional rights in public education. At local and Supreme Court levels, Chicano resistance to racial oppression has shone a light on the hypocrisy of so-called American democratic values by illuminating the United States' hand in harming children of color through racial segregation, white-supremacist curricula, and other de-Mexicanization and Americanization projects.

Reclaiming the Mexican Problem

The master narrative of the Mexican Problem appeared in U.S. public and foreign policy shortly after the Mexican–American War and the cession of nearly 55 percent of Mexican territory to the United States. The Mexican Problem stance, imperialist in nature and vindicated through ideals of Manifest Destiny, served to justify economic domination over Mexico and Mexican people. Historically grounded in the early decades after the Treaty of Guadalupe Hidalgo, the Mexican Problem construct was reproduced over multiple generations through a double lens of economic dominance and racist nativist perspectives. Eugenics-based logic marked Mexican culture and ways of being as pathological, deficient, and therefore unfit for citizenry. Early twentieth-century scholars grounded their research in this logic, which was solidified in the Anglo-American consciousness through academic publications, books, and travel guides. The academic scholarship produced on early Chicanos situated the Mexican Problem as the preamble in the study of Mexican peoples and their schooling experiences in the United States. This white-supremacist master narrative contributed to the formation and trajectory of the ways Chicanos have experienced education.

Although the Mexican Problem narrative has endured generations since the Mexican–American War, Chicanos have resisted the racist nativist stereotypes and pathologies associated with their ethnic and racial identities by challenging those colonial education policies and practices that fly in the face of the democratic principles this country claims as inherent to its foundation. Historical evidence illuminates a clear trail of Chicanos not only problematizing U.S. claims of democracy but also harnessing a version of the Mexican Problem narrative through their refusal to de-Mexicanize or de-Indianize. Chicanos affront Anglo ideas of Americanness through self-preservation. That is to say, Mexican Americans' refusal to assimilate, even after over one hundred years of oppressive acculturation projects, is worth noting.

Chicanos embrace a version of the Mexican Problem narrative that speaks to the recognition that, because they refuse to assimilate, they just do not fit into American ideals around citizenship. This is correct—and it says as much about who Chicanos are as it does about who they are not. The persistence of Chicano ethnic identity has multiple social, political, and psychological implications.[44] Familial interdependence, attachment, and commitment to family have served as protective factors for Mexican American youth in particular.[45] Familial interdependence, or *familismo,* is considered a form of cultural wealth; however, familismo is not valued in Anglo ideology, as these values and beliefs are not congruent with American ideals of frugality, temperance, industry, and ingenuity.[46] Chicanos have historically refused to be absorbed into the hegemonic contours of U.S. citizenry by rejecting the pressure to acculturate. Thus, their anti-citizenship means the rejection of a white default notion of citizenship and a celebration of the beauty and joy of Chicanismo, insisting instead that their familial and community needs be met through anti-citizen behaviors.

Chicano youth have been instrumental in the advancement of U.S. education through grassroots activism, including protests and acts of civil disobedience. From this anti-citizenship stance, Chicano youth have been at the center in transforming public education to meet their academic and sociocultural needs. Furthermore, Mexican American parents have always cared a great deal about creating opportunity for their children and have expressed this commitment through challenging racist policies in schooling. It is important to note that it is through community organizing and litigation that Mexican American parents counterattack racism—which is antithetical to emulating Anglo women in the homemaking tasks of the settlements. Chicano youth have shaped the trajectory of their academic success through grassroots organizing and civic engagement—and especially through civil disobedience. Supported by Mexican American families, educators, and community members, they have been agents of transformation in the areas of bilingual and multicultural education and ethnic studies. Due in part to the unique history of the U.S. Southwest, Chicano anti-citizenship continues to be persistently contested, asserted, and reimagined as the "Mexican Problem."

Notes

1. We use *Chicano* interchangeably with *Mexican American*. *Chicano* is the masculine and gender-neutral noun form in the Spanish language. *Chicanos* is plural and inclusive of feminine gender. We chose to use the term *Chicano* in this paper for uniformity with the many historical references.

2. This signing marked the official end to the Mexican–American War (1846–1848). This treaty guaranteed displaced Mexicans (those who decided to stay in their homeland) who remained in the new U.S. territory the right to citizenship, the right to their property, language, and culture. This treaty was broken.

3. Natalie Molina, *Fit to Be Citizens? Public Health and Race in Los Angeles, 1879–1939* (Oakland: University of California Press, 2006).

4. Anti-citizenship here is a way of being that threatens the imposed imperialist social order through politics of community resistance and beings for themselves.

5. Julio Cammarota and Michelle Fine, "Youth Participatory Action Research: A Pedagogy for Transformational Resistance," in *Revolutionizing Education: Youth*

Participatory Action Research in Motion, ed. Julio Cammarota and Michelle Fine, 9–20 (New York: Routledge, 2010); Julio Cammarota, "Youth Participatory Action Research: A Pedagogy of Transformational Resistance for Critical Youth Studies," *Journal for Critical Education Policy Studies* 15, no. 2 (2017); Julio Cammarota, "The Social Justice Education Project," in *Raza Studies: The Public Option for Educational Revolution,* ed. Julio Cammarota and Augustine Romero (Tucson: University of Arizona Press, 2014), 107; Rachel F. Gómez, Ejana Bennett, and Julio Cammarota, "The Battle for Curriculum: Arrested Semantics and Reconciling Racism with Critical Race Theory and Ethnic Studies," *Race Ethnicity and Education* (2023): 1–18; Rachel F. Gómez and Julio Cammarota, "Taking the Teachers to School! Critical Consciousness Emerging: A Qualitative Exploration of Mexican American Youth's Social Justice Orientation Development," *Urban Review* (2021): 1–28; Michaela J. L. Mares-Tamayo and Daniel G. Solórzano, eds., *The Chicana/o Education Pipeline: History, Institutional Critique, and Resistance* (Oakland: University of California Press, 2018); Pedro Noguera, Julio Cammarota, and Shawn Ginwright, *Beyond Resistance! Youth Activism and Community Change: New Democratic Possibilities for Practice and Policy for America's Youth* (New York: Routledge, 2013), 201; David Stovall, "Foreword: Committing to Struggle in Troubling Times," in Cammarota and Romero, *Raza Studies.*

6. Westminster v. Mendez, 161 F. 2d. 774 (9th Cir. 1947).

7. Emma Garcia, "Schools Are Still Segregated and Black Children Are Paying a Price," Economic Policy Institute, February 1, 2020, https://www.epi.org /publication/schools-are-still-segregated-and-black-children-are-paying-a-price/; Harvard Graduate School of Education, *Civil Rights Project Stories,* accessed October 11, 2021, https://www.gse.harvard.edu/news-tags/civil-rights-project.

8. Gilbert G. Gonzalez, "The Ideology and Practice of Empire: The U.S., Mexico, and the Education of Mexican Immigrants," in *Latinos and Education: A Critical Reader,* ed. Antonia Darder, Rodolfo D. Torres, and Henry Gutíerrez, 19–40 (New York: Routledge, 2014).

9. Gonzalez, "Ideology and Practice of Empire," 25.

10. Molina, *Fit to Be Citizens?,* 142.

11. Americo Paredes, *With His Pistol in His Hand* (Austin: University of Texas Press, 1958); Doug J. Swanson, *Cult of Glory: The Bold and Brutal History of the Texas Rangers* (New York: Viking Press, 2020).

12. Joe R. Feagin, *The White Racial Frame: Centuries of Racial Framing and Counter-framing* (New York: Routledge, 2013).

13. Gonzalez, "Ideology and Practice of Empire," 26.

14. Gonzalez, 48.

15. A colonia is comparable to a "shanty town" specifically laid out for Mexican American laborers and their families near the U.S.–Mexico border and labor sources.

16. Gonzalez, "Ideology and Practice of Empire," 26.

194   RACHEL F. GÓMEZ AND JULIO CAMMAROTA

17. Victor S. Clark, "Mexican Labor in the United States," in *The Department of Commerce and Labor, Bulletin of the Bureau of Labor,* no. 78 (Washington, D.C.: Government Printing Office, 1908), 496.

18. Gonzalez, "Ideology and Practice of Empire," 156.

19. Gonzalez.

20. George I. Sanchez, *Forgotten People: A Study of New Mexicans* (Albuquerque, N.M.: Calvin Horn Publisher, 1967), 31.

21. Vicki Ruíz, *From Out of the Shadows: Mexican Women in Twentieth-Century America* (New York: Oxford University Press, 1998).

22. Ruíz, *From Out of the Shadows,* 36.

23. Ruíz, 35.

24. Ellis quoted in Ruíz, 33.

25. Sanchez, *Forgotten People,* 30.

26. Amber Phillips, "'They're Rapists. President Trump's Campaign Launch Speech Two Years Later, Annotated," *Washington Post,* June 16, 2017, https://www.washingtonpost.com/news/the-fix/wp/2017/06/16/theyre-rapists-presidents-trump-campaign-launch-speech-two-years-later-annotated/.

27. AP News, "Education Secretary Criticized for Questioning Hispanic Parents' Values," April 11, 1990, https://apnews.com/article/679960bb7b4d6ca2b589544aa31bf248.

28. Mendez v. Westminster School Dist., 64 F. Supp. 544 (S.D. Cal. 1946).

29. Gonzalez, "Ideology and Practice of Empire"; Ruíz, *From Out of the Shadows*; Sanchez, *Forgotten People.*

30. Maribel Santiago, "Diluting Mexican American History for Public Consumption: How Mendez Became the 'Mexican American Brown,'" *Teachers College Record* 122, no. 8 (2020): 1–30, https://doi.org/10.1177/016146812012200808.

31. G. Cristina Mora, "Cross-Field Effects and Ethnic Classification: The Institutionalization of Hispanic Panethnicity, 1965 to 1990," *American Sociological Review* 79, no. 2 (April 2014): 183–210, https://doi.org/10.1177/0003122413509813.

32. Becky Little, "The U.S. Deported a Million of Its Own Citizens to Mexico during the Great Depression," History, July 12, 2019, https://www.history.com/news/great-depression-repatriation-drives-mexico-deportation.

33. Zinn Education Project, "Teaching People's History," accessed 2021, https://www.zinnedproject.org/.

34. Santiago, "Diluting Mexican American History for Public Consumption."

35. Elizabeth Martínez, *De Colores Means All of Us: Latina Views for a Multicolored Century* (Boston: South End Press, 1998).

36. "MEChA (Movimiento Estudiantil de Chicanos de Aztlán)," Discover the Networks, https://www.discoverthenetworks.org/organizations/mecha-movimiento-estudiantil-de-chicanos-de-aztlan/.

37. Julio Cammarota, "A Social Justice Approach to Achievement: Guiding Latina/o Students toward Educational Attainment with a Challenging, Socially Relevant Curriculum," *Equity & Excellence in Education* 40, no. 1 (April 2007): 87–96, https://doi.org/10.1080/10665680601015153; Julio Cammarota, "From Hopelessness to Hope: Social Justice Pedagogy in Urban Education and Youth Development," *Urban Education* 46, no. 4 (July 2011): 828–44, https://doi.org/1 0.1177/0042085911399931; Julio Cammarota, "Blindsided by the Avatar: White Saviors and Allies out of Hollywood and in Education," *Review of Education, Pedagogy, and Cultural Studies* 33, no. 3 (July 2011): 242–59, https://doi.org/10.10 80/10714413.2011.585287; Cammarota, "Social Justice Education Project."

38. Gómez and Cammarota, "Taking the Teachers to School!"

39. An Act Amending Title 15, Chapter 1, Article 1, Arizona Revised Statutes, by Adding Sections 15-111 and 15-112; Amending Section 15-843, Arizona Revised Statutes; Relating to School Curriculum, H.B. 2281, 49th Cong. (2010); "Ninth Circuit Court of Appeals Issues Decision in Lawsuit Challenging Arizona's Ethnic Studies Ban," American Library Association, July 13, 2015, http://www.ala .org/news/press-releases/2015/07/ninth-circuit-court-appeals-issues-decision -lawsuit-challenging-arizona-s.

40. Gómez and Cammarota, "Taking the Teachers to School!"

41. "Banned Books," Arizona State University Library Library Guides, accessed August 17, 2020, https://libguides.asu.edu/BannedBooks/EthnicStudies.

42. Arce v. Douglas, no. 13-15657 (9th Cir. 2015).

43. Valerie Strauss, "Arizona's Ban on Mexican American Studies Was Racist, U.S. Court Rules," *Washington Post,* August 23, 2017, https://www.washington post.com/news/answer-sheet/wp/2017/08/23/arizonas-ban-on-mexican-ameri can-studies-was-racist-u-s-court-rules/.

44. Martha E. Bernal and George P. Knight, eds., *Ethnic Identity: Formation and Transmission among Hispanics and Other Minorities* (Albany: State University of New York Press, 1993).

45. Andrea J. Romero et al., *Preventing Adolescent Depression and Suicide among Latinas: Resilience Research and Theory* (Cham, Switzerland: Springer, 2014).

46. Tara J. Yosso, "Whose Culture Has Capital? A Critical Race Theory Discussion of Community Cultural Wealth," *Race Ethnicity and Education* 8, no. 1 (March 2005): 69–91, https://doi.org/10.1080/1361332052000341006; Guadalupe Valdés, *Con Respeto: Bridging the Distances between Culturally Diverse Families and Schools: An Ethnographic Portrait* (New York: Teachers College Press, 1996).

CHAPTER 9

Unsettling the "Good Citizen"

How Narratives of Palestinian Liberation Threatened a Liberal School

LUMA HASAN

I have a vivid memory of the moment my mother sat me down to discuss how I planned to apply for my first teaching position. She looked at me with a familiar honesty and concern in her eyes. It was an expression that I had seen on other Palestinian mothers, torn between wanting their children to embody Palestinian pride and resilience and knowing that any bold proclamation of Palestinian identity in the workplace would likely subject their children to scrutiny and skepticism. "You need to take the word *Palestine* off of your résumé," she sighed as she looked over my application materials. At first, I was taken aback. She was my first representation of a strong and unapologetic Palestinian. A woman who grew up under Israeli occupation and fiercely claimed her humanity in the face of repressive militarization, who had passed that same ferocity on to her children. In fact, her example is what led to the activism that was documented all over my résumé. The reservations my mother held were animated by her awareness of several cases in the United States where Palestinian educators were defamed and their employment jeopardized for vocalizing their stance on Palestinian sovereignty. She explained her view that being loudly Palestinian upfront would close doors to me on the job market; after I got tenure, she thought, I could stand more boldly in my convictions about Palestine as an educator and have a larger impact. The possibility that I could even attempt this in my first teaching position was severely undermined by the official and unofficial constraints my school placed on my ability to share hard truths with my students.

In this chapter, I reflect on my experience as a new teacher and Palestinian woman teaching social studies in a supposedly diverse, liberal suburban high school in the U.S. Northeast. Having just spent five years in preservice teacher training, I was grappling with what it meant to be a social-studies teacher in the American education system. The resounding yet unspoken duty we were being called to as social-studies educators was to produce "good citizens" in our classrooms. However, in my experience, sharing hard truths about the Palestinian struggle for liberation tested the archetypical boundaries of so-called good citizenship in my school, revealing the underlying conflict between "good citizenship" and anti-citizenship. I recount various ways in which my voice and the voices of my students were policed to demonstrate how high-school social studies operated as a vehicle to protect the state's image. I also discuss experiences with my colleagues and supervisors that positioned both me and my students as anti-citizens. In conclusion, I make the argument that the goal of schools to produce "good citizens" is rooted in the desire to foster compliance and legitimizes a false measure of student progress. Instead of conceding to this limitation, anti-citizenship provides an alternative pathway and opportunity to collectively decolonize the power structures in schools.

I Am Not Your Token Diversity Hire

"I'm so proud of hiring you because I maintained my Arab quota." Those were the words my supervisor, a white woman, supposedly jokingly said to me at the end of my first year of teaching in the summer of 2017, after I had endured a year full of people comparing me to the Arab woman who had resigned from the position that I was in. It was at that moment when I realized my presence was to occupy a tokenized space for the gap in this supervisor's diversity collection. While the district is in a community that is racially, ethnically, socioeconomically, and religiously diverse, the 40 percent Black students, 32 percent Hispanic students, and 15 percent Asian students are not adequately represented by the staff, which was 67 percent white. In my school, I was a diversity checkmark, and I got an extra point for being Muslim. Despite filling this quota, there was a clear limit imposed on how much of my authentic identity I could actually share in my capacity as both a colleague and an educator that was highly predicated on the extent to which my identity could be selectively deployed to benefit those who needed to prop my face up when the time called for it. Relatively soon into my position, I was seeking out safe spaces in the company of other Arab women in the district to cope with this casual orientalism. Having played a role in facilitating our connections to one another, the same supervisor publicly demanded credit for bringing together what she called the "Arabian princess club." My presence and employment validated her self-perception as a nonracist supporter of multiculturalism, but when various opportunities arose for her to participate in community conversations during times of heightened violence against Palestinians, she took to social media to declare a "neutral" stance.

Among my liberal colleagues in the school, there was a pervasive culture of needing to be perceived as nonracist and as tolerant of diversity and inclusion efforts in order for them to move up the ladder. This meant that when they stood to gain brownie points from it, my supposed diversity would be propped up as evidence of progress, but only if I refrained from sharing my personal opinions, experiences, and critiques. Ultimately, I served the same purpose as a stereotypical primarily white institution catalog highlighting its so-called diversity through the smiling faces of non-Anglo twenty-year-olds. For the majority of my tenure at the school, there was a white male principal who thought he had perfected this bleak form of inclusion. I saw it clearly when I sat with him one-on-one for a postobservation meeting. I was all ready to discuss the lesson I had carefully planned and taught; however, he decided that it was more important to shift the conversation to illegally raising probing questions about my religion, asking if I considered myself a practicing Muslim. Not sensing (or possibly ignoring) my discomfort, he then moved on to a self-laudatory conversation about the decorations in his office; he wanted to show me how much of the world was represented in the trinkets, wall displays, and ornate cultural talismans that he had amassed in that space. Noticing an image of the Dome of the Rock in Jerusalem,

I made a swift attempt to broach the subject of my identity to gauge his stance on Palestine. He caught my gaze and proceeded to tell me that his daughter had brought it back for him on one of her many trips to Israel. Failing to recognize how his assertions of an Israeli state erased Palestine and my identity as an extension, he droned on, cutting off my attempts to respond by telling him that it was illegal for me to visit the mosque myself because of Israeli apartheid laws.

Two years later, in May 2021, this principal would finally decide it was worthwhile to acknowledge my Palestinian identity; however, ironically, only for the purpose of his Asian American Pacific Islander Month celebration. The so-called celebration was a daily morning video of a different Asian person in the school reciting the Pledge of Allegiance. He made a point to sign the all-staff email with the words "This is not tokenization." After cornering me in the library to ask me to participate, with the condescending reminder that "Palestine is technically in Asia," I declined to participate. Not sensing my discomfort, again, he pressed me as to why. I tried to explain that I personally have not recited the Pledge of Allegiance in years because, to me, it represents a dangerous unchecked nationalism and is often used to unfairly discipline students of color for not participating. "That's unfortunate," was his response. I also tried to explain that geography and identity are not interchangeable, that Asia is a large continent outlined arbitrarily by colonization, and that I am sure other students and faculty who actually identify as Asian have things they want to share. "But I looked at the map and Palestine is in Asia," he insisted. Telling people how to identify and planning to squeeze 30 percent of the planet into one month is the type of diversity and inclusion that got him far. When I tried to explain later that day that I found it to be very disingenuous to ask Asian students and faculty to record themselves saying the pledge after a surge in violence against their community due in part to President Trump blaming China for Covid-19, his response was that an Asian teacher had told him it was a good idea. I responded that teachers and students might not have felt comfortable declining to participate as he holds power over them and that several people had confided their discomfort to me. He no longer felt the need to respond. My identity and cultural and historical knowledge were useless to him if

I was deploying it to question his diversity, equity, and inclusion bona fides. I could only be useful if I submitted to patriotism and acquiesced to a month of watered-down recognition.

There was a clear avoidance of my self-identification as a Palestinian on the part of administrators and colleagues. In my school, I had been referred to as "Arab," "Middle Eastern," "Asian," "Muslim," "nonwhite," "ethnic," or (the worst of them) "exotic." To me, these were reminders that nuance is not built into the diversity framework. As time went on, my role became clear: I was expected to address any questions or concerns that came up in our school related to what they considered "the Middle East," which to them included regions, nations, and cultures that spanned from North Africa to South Asia. This view of the Middle East was wedded to the false assumption that Islam is the exclusive religion of this region. Every Palestinian is very familiar with the skepticism we encounter after we publicly claim our identity. This skepticism quickly escalates into a rejection of our existence with anything from "Palestinians don't exist because there's no P in the Arabic alphabet" to "Wikipedia says Palestine isn't a country, so you should just tell people you are Jordanian." These responses reflect the reality that I and other Palestinians occupy a space in the United States as perpetually invisible foreigners, still not permitted to speak honestly about our existence. Edward Said writes, "From the beginning of Western speculation about the Orient, the one thing the Orient could not do was to represent itself."[1] My school's attempt to erase "Palestinian" as an identity and to replace it with a geographic or ethnic generalization was part of a much larger project of historical revisionism by Zionists to justify the occupation of Palestine. They impose a homogeneity on so-called Arabs that corroborates the historically flawed narrative that Palestinians have never existed. This perceived sameness is what allows the American liberal psyche to unite all forms of difference under the banner of "diversity and inclusion" rather than having to contend with the actual complexity of our differences as they operate in and through structural inequalities in institutions like my school.

As time went on, I was subjected to more blatant attempts to police my voice. I was the only teacher teaching a course on race, gender, and equity, and the administration felt an unearned sense of accomplishment that they had found someone "diverse" to lead the class. However, my vision for the curriculum and for the course's larger place in our school community were not met with the same excitement. In fact, there was an outright hostility toward my vision. For example, the first of many conflicts between me and my supervisor about my teaching arose when I proposed a simple lesson that involved comparing what students had learned about Christopher Columbus in their years of schooling to what they had (not) learned about the Indigenous Taíno people he colonized. It was also the first of many discussions where I was scolded for not teaching "both sides." In this particular case, he suggested that I present the importation of horses to the Americas as a legitimate positive to outweigh the negative of colonial genocide. After refusing to make those adjustments the following year, I was instructed to stop teaching about Christopher Columbus altogether. All the while, my supervisor spent meeting after meeting publicly praising my course and deceptively using my curriculum as evidence of his competence and leadership.

At the same time, I was learning that my school intended to weaponize my voice by manipulating me into vocally embracing Western feminist stereotypes about Arab Muslim women and girls. Perceived by my colleagues and supervisor as an example of a "liberated" Arab Muslim woman, I was expected to validate the Islamophobia that ran through the school. There exists a reductive assumption that by not wearing hijab, somehow, I am an exception and agree with paternalistic Western generalizations of Islam. The more Muslim women appear to have assimilated to a Western understanding of liberation, typically measured by the extent of the revelation of their bodies, the more they are assumed to have adopted a hatred of their own culture and selves. This was revealed during one particular incident when a social-studies teacher in my school sought out my validation as she was attempting to punish a Muslim girl for violating the dress code. "You're Muslim, right?" she asked me before she proceeded to question whether it was normal for Muslim girls to wear a hat instead of a hijab. Frustrated by the intention behind this ethnocentrically violent inquiry, I responded that it was absolutely normal and expressed further concern about the hostility of her interaction with this student. Before I could finish speaking, I was interrupted by a white male colleague who spoke over me to declare that Muslim girls decide by middle-school age whether to wear hijab and concluded that the student was lying because it was "too late." The expectation in asking me the question was that I would vindicate her intention to villainize a Muslim girl navigating whether or not she wants to make that choice. Once my answer was clearly going down the path of explaining why that is a complex decision, why it does not fit into a particular time constraint, and why this student is deserving of the space and agency to decide without judgment, my voice was cut off. It did not matter that I shared how some Muslim women begin wearing hijab in their sixties or that some Muslim girls change their minds later in life because of the violence they experience in the United States for that choice. My insight was only valid if it aligned with a perspective that viewed the student as a devious liar or as an oppressed girl that needed saving. She had no desire to understand the complexity of this girl's choice to wear a hat and was only interested in clearing a pathway to proceed with punishment. If I was allowed to finish my thought, I would have explained further that being a Muslim student's teacher does not automatically entitle you to that student's private decision-making process. Interactions like these demonstrate how students like this one were positioned as anti-citizens in the eyes of school staff.

Anti-citizens in my school were expected to be silent and to be happy that we were fortunate enough to have been learning (and teaching) in a liberal context. After all, we could have been subjected to more dramatic forms of bigotry. It meant being directly and indirectly asked to assimilate into a sterilized performance of the model minority. Not only were anti-citizens expected to submit to ethnic roles defined by white liberals, we were also expected to want and like these role definitions if we were ever to be accepted as good citizens in the school community. Whether it was a Muslim girl wearing a hat, Asian American educators and students compelled to say the Pledge of Allegiance during a time of peaking violence against Asian Americans, or a Palestinian teacher forced to casually discuss artifacts of Palestinian oppression proudly displayed by her principal, we could only be good citizens at my school if we accepted these alienating conditions. To inhabit that space as a good citizen meant belonging as an outsider.

It became impossible for me to continue separating my day-to-day experiences as a Palestinian American from U.S. support for the ongoing colonization of Palestine; however, in my school that is exactly what they were asking me to do. There is a demand for Palestinians in the United States to internalize imperialism and reject the ongoing resistance to settler colonialism back in occupied Palestine in order to be allowed to exist in this nation. My first major confrontation with this came when I was asked by one of the few colleagues who acknowledged and respected me as a Palestinian to come in as a guest speaker for his world history class during their unit on Palestine. This was the first, and ultimately only, time that I was asked by a fellow educator to speak as a Palestinian in my school without questioning whether or not my perspective was legitimate. The students worked on questions to ask about life in occupied Palestine, what could be done to support Palestinian liberation, and what role the United States played in the ongoing occupation. Once my own students learned that I would be teaching a lesson on Palestine for other classes, they expressed their own desire to learn more. Up until that point, I was afraid to teach about Palestine. This reignited the conviction that was instilled in me as a preservice teacher—to educate students into good citizens—a conviction that had been slowly chipped away since I started teaching. While there was a clear path in the curriculum of my class to incorporate the role of the United States in the occupation of Palestine, I was always consciously aware that Palestinians in the United States are not afforded the right to speak for themselves without a disclaimer. My guest speaking experience quickly took a turn. At the time, the teacher who had invited me was sharing a classroom space in alternating periods with a very openly Zionist and Islamophobic teacher who also taught world history. This teacher was also being groomed for an administrative position. There had been a recent wave of violence in Gaza that year, and this teacher made a point to share with close colleagues of mine that he viewed Palestinians as "tunnel-digging, rocket-throwing terrorists." Once he learned that I was going to be speaking about Palestine in a course he also taught, he proceeded to coax those teachers into giving him more information about what experiences and information I was sharing. After I had spoken in three out of four of these classes, I was feeling a new sense of visibility.

In the last session, however, I was aggressively reminded that speaking openly about Palestinian oppression was unacceptable. During the remaining five to ten minutes of my lesson, the Zionist teacher invited himself into the room and sat in the back, glaring at me, to observe everything I was saying. It was an obvious attempt at intimidation. Leaning into their curiosity, and unaware of the anxiety bubbling up in my body, the students asked several more personal questions to conclude our session. The final student raised the question, "What does it mean to be a Palestinian in the United States?" Energized by this teacher's brazen attempt to intimidate me, I found a burst of gusto within myself to push back, delivering an unapologetically forceful, Palestinian-affirming tirade that was less about answering their question and more about letting this man know that I knew why he was there and that I was unbothered by his intimidation. I was through with being a good citizen. Reminding myself of every moment of bigotry I had endured in that school, I responded to the student by explaining that, to me, being Palestinian meant actively resisting attempts to erase us. It meant wearing our resilience with pride and carrying that fight with us everywhere "no matter who is in the room or what kind of discomfort it causes them." When I finished speaking, the students applauded. I immediately ran out of the room to finally exhale in my own classroom. As much as I wanted it to be one, this was not a win. As Steven Salaita's analysis in "A Palestinian Exception to the First Amendment?" states: "The Palestinian may be granted the privilege of articulation, but only if she articulates narratives conducive to the glorification of modernity."[2] The opportunity for me to openly teach about Palestine and its struggle for liberation threatened the facade of a noble America as mediator. This teacher's attempted intimidation was a reminder that Palestinian voices, like mine, that refuse to capitulate to American historical revisionism are under calculated supervision. By speaking to students about hard truths so candidly, I had stepped out of the role of a quiet token that was created for me, and in so doing, I unmasked the eyes that had been watching me closely all along.

Prior to this event, as a new, young, nontenured teacher, I was holding onto a belief that educational structures train you to believe—things would get better once I reached the security of tenure. For that reason, I initially kept my head down and followed orders while holding my breath, waiting for a moment of power that I finally realized would never come unless I acquiesced to the tokenized role that my school demanded of me. The reality is that schools do not want the honest and authentic voices of anti-citizens to exist. Instead, they require maligned groups to offer absolution for white supremacy's legacy of violence. The platforms provided to people of the global majority in educational institutions are chess pieces. We are useful until they tell us that we are no longer useful within institutions that have been designed to facilitate social reproduction. You move as far as they allow you to within the larger purpose of protecting themselves from scrutiny. For me, that meant placing me in the box of an "Arab Muslim social-justice teacher"—as long as that social-justice teaching did not threaten the pretense that schools can be liberatory without making any fundamental changes to the way they operate and who they operate to serve.

PALESTINE AND THE LIBERAL EDUCATOR: POLICING STUDENTS' ANTI-CITIZENSHIP DISCOURSE

In my school, there was a flawed belief that younger educators were inherently progressive, and thus not in need of any diversity, equity, and inclusion or social-justice training. This belief was held not only by the supervisors but also by the educators themselves. The danger of this thinking is that it creates a false binary: those of us on the right side and those on the wrong side. When the wrong side is conceived exclusively as overt bigots loudly shouting racial slurs, committing hate crimes, and implementing travel bans, it is easy for those who engage in seemingly less problematic behaviors to assume, "Well, I am not as bad as them, so I must be on the right side." The largest perpetrators of this attitude, in my experience, have been young, white, liberal educators. Schools of education reinforce this assumption by framing their education programs as social-justice programs that are pumping out progressive young teachers

Unsettling the "Good Citizen"

to save Black and Brown students from rigid veteran teachers. What is often lost in the charge made to new and young social-studies educators to produce good citizens is the even more important responsibility to unlearn prejudices and participate more authentically in social-justice movements beyond stickers and posters. The result is an increasingly narrow civic-education curriculum that politely asks the existing structure to hold itself accountable without an examination of the fact that white-supremacist systems are doing what they were created to do.

This narrowness manifested in my school in the form of negative reactions to the inclusion of Palestine in social-justice discourse. The pushback expanded when the congressional representative of my district's community was invited to our school to speak, followed by a question-and-answer session. Students in my class asked her questions about her stance on Palestine and her approval of U.S. funding of the Israeli military that they felt did not align with her justice-oriented platform. The representative accepted the critique, vowed to do her research, and the students spoke to her privately afterward to provide her with some resources. These students' actions were a textbook example of good citizenship, but I had experienced enough criticism to know that this was not going to be received by the school community as a positive and meaningful display of democratic participation. Any claim legitimating Palestine's right to exist would inevitably be cast as a form of anti-citizenship. Any speech defending or legitimizing the statehood of Palestinians in my school was filtered through an anti-citizenship lens. Although some of these students were white, they were trafficking in anti-citizen discourse by giving license to others to view Palestine as an occupied nation.

Right after my students' exchange with their congressional representative, a young, Zionist, white social-studies teacher quickly found them in the hallway to reprimand them for their question and inform them that it was inappropriate to ask her about foreign affairs. This was an educator who had deployed her status as a white, American-born citizen with an Israeli passport to legitimate her false and self-righteous claim of Indigeneity to occupied Palestine. Her argument to students was that foreign affairs were not this representative's major focus in Congress. There were plenty of other questions about U.S. relations with foreign governments covered during the event, but the only one she viewed as a threat was the one that gave the audience a window to connect to Palestinian liberation. Their questions also threatened the presumption of authority on foreign affairs that white feminists like this teacher often hold, particularly in reference to women's experiences in Muslim-majority countries. Ignoring the fact that these were obviously students from my class, she took it upon herself to skip past me to address them directly, thereby ignoring my presence and authority as their teacher, who also happened to be the person with the most knowledge about Palestine in the school.

After the students stood by their questions, she then proceeded to coax them into sharing what made them feel compelled to ask in the first place. This was another reminder of my confinement to an orientalist image. This same teacher had approached me in the past with questions about other Arab countries and Islam. Now that she suspected I was teaching about Palestine in my class, I had clearly stepped out of the level of clearance given to me. Not only were the students scolded for their inquiry, but her choice to ignore me in the process was a reminder of how Palestinian voices in the United States are illegitimate. The students' public indictment of the United States and Israel in state-sanctioned violence against Palestinians made them targets as well: "As long as Israel is coterminous with U.S. power, it will be protected with the same vigor used to safeguard the American state."[3] This teacher justified her attack on these students by aligning her protection of Israel with her obligation to protect the United States. For students to express solidarity with Palestinians, to her, was evidence of brainwashing. Ironically, their discourse invoking Palestinian humanity was used as evidence to the contrary.

PERFORMATIVE ALLYSHIP AND THE
SCHOOL'S SUPPOSED EMBRACE OF BLACK LIVES MATTER

Being a social-justice-oriented public-school teacher produces a cyclical relationship that falsely presents itself to be linear in the direction of progress. In pushing for administration or colleagues to rethink curricula, unlearn their own prejudices, or just participate in any sort of progressive movement, there is a consistent sigh of "Yes, we hear you" and "That is what we are doing, but it takes time." Linear. Recently, in conversation about the issues I saw in our school, an administrator even went so far as to relate the process of "listening and learning" to the difficulty of a cruise ship making a 180-degree turn. As if statements, equity training, and diversity programs combined, over time, were allowing us to go in an eventual straight path in the right direction. I would argue, and did argue, that this is not an appropriate metaphor. It is a metaphor that allows the institution itself to evade responsibility because it has checked off enough boxes to appear to be part of the solution. In reality, it is checking off the boxes required to safeguard its own existence and rewarding those who serve it.

From the perspective of the social-justice educator, responding to structural violence is a cycle that begins in your own classroom. In this structure, imagine you spend day after day fostering a space of safety, honesty, and critique in your classroom that contributes to thoughtful and community-oriented students. Conversations about inequity in our school, local, and national communities ensue, leading to the conclusion that students do not feel heard, supported, or uplifted by the school. In an obvious understanding of power dynamics, educators should feel obligated, at this point, to use their own voices to bring these concerns to administrators. After being met with resistance, performative responses, and eventually a lack of fundamental shift in the experiences of students, you are depleted and return to focusing on a classroom space you falsely believe you control. Upon return, a new issue presents itself that you, again, take up with administration with, or on behalf of, your students only to be met with the same response. All the while, you are told, "Be patient. The changes are coming. We are moving in the right direction." In reality, the direction is still a circle that begins and ends with maintaining white supremacy and protecting the structure.

The response to the 2020 Movement for Black Lives in the wake of George Floyd's murder demonstrated a very obvious shift among the American public, corporations, and schools toward various kinds of allyship. At this point in my career, I reached a position where I felt a confidence to publicly and loudly push the district toward solidarity and support beyond my classroom. I and other like-minded teachers ended up in meetings with various upper-level administrators who claimed to want to handle this appropriately. We ultimately realized that demanding the bare minimum (a public statement that acknowledges the necessity of the Black Lives Matter movement) was a grueling uphill battle. These meetings were mostly spent trying to explain why a statement was important and then ultimately going back and forth about which language to use in the statement. For example, a major point of contention was over the use of the passive word "death" rather than "murder" in reference to George Floyd. After I took it upon myself to change this word in a shared document before a meeting with district leaders, my supervisor reached out to multiple teachers trying to investigate who changed it after apologizing for the change and switching it back to its original passive tone. Another argument was trying to explain why it is disingenuous to thank law enforcement in a statement of support and solidarity with a movement against police violence. Meanwhile, on a building level, we were pressing the principal on his choice to send a statement to staff denouncing the "rioting" happening in our country. He could not understand the message he was sending with this reductive choice of words. When he worked on an updated statement, we expressed the importance of highlighting that the murder of George Floyd was not an isolated incident, only to have him respond that he would not include Breonna Taylor's name because, in his opinion, her death does not "constitute as murder." These were the battles happening behind the scenes while our students were left waiting for any sort of meaningful acknowledgment. After a lot of pressure, the district finally agreed to communicate with students and involve them in the process, but days went by with nothing to show for it.

After various arguments and empty promises on the part of the administration, I met with a group of students of color who had expressed major frustrations with the district's silence. We discussed how they wanted to proceed and how I could support them. The students organized a mass email campaign to coordinate a letter to administration from students and alumni with the subject line "Black Lives Matter"—an act of disruption that was a response to their requests being ignored and an expectation that the school would take responsibility not only for its silence but also for the ways in which it operates as a microcosm of structural racial violence. Hundreds of students and alumni participated in this email blast that was sent to all administrators on the high-school and district levels. Meetings were quickly scheduled for administrators to haphazardly list out all of their various diversity, equity, and inclusion initiatives in their defense. Throughout these meetings, though, student leaders were scolded for the "aggressive attack," reminded that there were more effective (civil) ways to ask for things, and accosted for not being grateful that things here are supposedly better than other districts. One administrator even went so far as to email the parents of some of the students who participated. The ongoing question was: Why did students have to make these demands in the first place if all of these initiatives existed and were working successfully? The answer was simple and empty: It takes time.

The students' demands were clear: take accountability for your silence, make a genuine statement, and make a conscious effort to center the voices, needs, and experiences of the students you serve by teaching them what is happening and helping them participate. Instead, the school put together a virtual panel event featuring a police officer, a prosecutor, and various administrators to provide their commentary on police violence in the United States. After I expressed to the administrators planning the event that these are not the voices that should be centered, I began to be alienated altogether. Only two of the student leaders were invited, and they were told to speak from a script. The event only had room for the 150 people that received personal invitations, which were calculatingly selected by administration. Unsurprisingly, I did not receive an invitation. There is no acceptable way to be disruptive within a school's imagination of a "good citizen." The expectation is that solutions must come from those with power and authority and, if that expectation is compromised, then there are consequences for violating that structure. In response, the student leaders worked on creating their own teach-in without seeking the approval of administration, and they consulted with me to support their planning. They brought in local community organizers, a civil-rights attorney, and a university professor to speak on and respond to their questions about organizing for racial justice. This was not a solution that fit within the administration's passive image of good citizenship, so the event was ignored. Even though the students sent personal invitations to all administrators to attend, only a few made an appearance, and there was no follow-up conversation.

After responding to direct action with intimidation, discipline, tone policing, and performative accountability proved unsuccessful in controlling the students and staff, the cycle began to turn again. It was time for the institution to co-opt this student movement in order to limit it to the reach of corporate interests. The district put together antiracist curriculum-development opportunities, put out an antiracism district goal, and began the following school year by patting itself on the back for "centering students" and engaging in these conversations. These were surface-level responses that prioritized making the district appear to be leading these initiatives all along. What changed was that they got the nod to be slightly more explicit because corporate America was being slightly more explicit. Through a corporate takeover and a co-opting of social-justice movements as a marketing strategy, movements are watered down to the point that schools can acknowledge and support them without fear of any fundamental change. Movements are shrunken to be digestible to the white institution, thereby discarding the imagination of an alternative reality. Now, social-justice movements no longer are about inherently oppressive institutional structures but instead are about individuals opening their hearts and holding hands. It enables the expectation of schools to teach students to be their version of "good citizens" because the message is no longer about holding structures accountable for the violence they authorize. It is about connecting that violence to individual responsibility and thus avoids disrupting the institution itself.

The national attention to police violence in 2020 was another iteration of this cycle. Companies like Amazon, hoping to make a statement before their competitors, were very quick to make sure that customers could find their display of solidarity, from a Black Lives Matter banner on their home pages to mass emails to their customers. More than anything, we witnessed the normalization of performative gestures and statements of solidarity that worked to preemptively avoid accusations of silence and complicity. By examining when schools and districts began to make similar kinds of statements, a picture of the way in which these institutions looked toward corporate America for their cues to speak renders clearer. Working on the ground in these institutions offered me an important opportunity to test the limits and sincerity of these statements in my school.

The Denial of Palestinian Oppression to Protect the Imperial Veil

The spring of 2021 marked for many a transformation in the public discourse around Palestine in the United States both in shining a light on the experiences of Palestinians and in connecting those experiences to global solidarity movements. While this kind of language already existed for decades in organizing spaces, this was the first time we saw a temporary surface-level awakening of the general American public. Just a few weeks earlier, I could not even imagine that the word *apartheid* or a recognition of Palestinian Indigeneity would exist in everyday conversation. There was a window where it felt like Palestinians could be allowed the platform to name their own oppression for what it objectively is: an apartheid system that renders Palestinians as second- or third-class citizens on the basis of their ethnic identity and religion in order to fuel the ongoing colonial project. The takeaway was a new crowd of people that were practicing how to humanize Palestinians and tapping into the same feeling of shame for wanting to look away that had motivated them the year before. However, that is where the awakening ended. In the blog post "The Taming of Anti-Zionism in the United States," Salaita identifies the lingering question during the decline of this awakening: "What happens if we acknowledge that the U.S. colony is anathema to Palestinian liberation? We consign ourselves to economic insecurity and professional disrepute, to the remarkably difficult task of upending the world as we know it, exactly what liberation requires."[4] The need to protect the U.S. empire was already in motion, interfering with the potential consequences of this realization. The same companies and institutions that used police violence and hate crimes to revitalize their marketing campaigns were either completely silent or blaming the worldwide existence of antisemitism on Palestinian resistance to settler colonialism. Rather than make statements acknowledging the disproportionate violence against Palestinians, there were floods of statements solely focused on denouncing antisemitism. In May 2021, my graduate alma mater released a statement to address the rise in antisemitism that centered the "increasing violence between Israeli forces and Hamas in the Middle East."[5] By neglecting to mention the illegal occupation of Palestine (or even using the word *Palestine* at all) and portraying the violence as an equal conflict, statements like these lead the reader to conflate anti-Zionism with antisemitism. The statement went on to combine the murder of George Floyd and attacks against the AAPI, Indigenous people, Hindus, and Muslims together in a trivializing attempt to conclude that racism is bad while placing Palestinian oppression in opposition to that stance.

In that brief moment when it felt like Palestinians might have a legitimate voice, I reached out to my supervisor to ask what resources or support we were providing our staff and students to appropriately learn about what was happening. It was common for our department to send out a rapid response list of resources and guidance for major current events. It was also common for my supervisor to speak to me directly about the resources he intended to send out as I was still the aforementioned "social-justice diversity token." I had spent close to a year being reminded that our district produced an "unparalleled" antiracism goal and listening to boasts about how much more progressive our district was than surrounding districts. Those reminders were less about progress and more about avoiding accountability. My advocacy for the dissemination of accurate resources was rejected. I was told that in this case, it would put the district "on an island that no other district is on" and would be viewed as a "political stance." I asked him to explain "how Muslim civilians being tear gassed inside a mosque under state-sanctioned violence while being displaced from their homes is a 'political opinion.'" I received no response and later learned that he instructed teachers to avoid the words *ethnic cleansing* and *Zionism* entirely in their lessons. The same language that was used as bragging points for the en vogue public stances the district had taken against white supremacy the previous year were being walked back to avoid the potential controversy of discussing Palestinian suffering. All the work done to explain why an "all lives matter" stance is violent was undone in order to ensure that the district did not appear to be taking the supposed side of Palestinians. The boast about not catering to the feelings of white supremacists was replaced with disproportionate consideration for the feelings of Zionists in the school community.

Realizing that I was not going to inspire meaningful action from him, I shared some professional development resources with my colleagues, an action encouraged even by our evaluative tool. These were virtual events featuring leaders like Angela Davis, Rashid Khalidi, and Mohammed El-Kurd. Immediately, I was hit with a reply-all by my supervisor who added more administrators to the email thread stating:

> We cannot approach this with a narrative or agenda and should be relying on resources to present information. I'm directing that any curricular presentation on Israel and Palestine be presented to me for approval. . . . I would also ask that going forward any professional developments being shared across buildings be presented to me.

In response, a colleague and friend in the department (also an Arab Muslim woman) privately shared her notes from the events and asked our supervisor if they can be distributed to the rest of the teachers. After cutting out information, he eventually sent the notes out to the department prefaced with: "I found some of the language to be problematic and the focus was activism and not necessarily curricular." Even though she followed the newly created protocol, he discredited the information before anyone had a chance to read it. He continued this alienation by privately telling other teachers not to share their lessons with me or the other Arab teacher in our department because we were "too close to the situation." I was reduced to a biased, overly emotional, brainwashed Palestinian woman with an agenda who could not speak without permission because my resources did not fit the narrative he wanted students to take away. This narrative, he later clarified to all teachers with attached documents that did not include any Palestinian or anti-Zionist voices, was that there needs to be an acknowledgment of both sides. The implicit function of the resources provided was to prevent students from drawing conclusions that could lead to solidarity with Palestinian liberation.

Recalling the way Black and Brown students the year before refused to sit and listen to a police officer and prosecutor talk about "both sides," the wall that blocks these conversations is undeniably clear and rigid. In reality, they were presented with a one-sided discussion about youth–police relations as if state-sanctioned violence against communities of color was a squabble devoid of any power imbalance. There is no conversation more substantive than one about supposed peace talks facilitated by administrators who hold power over students and are simultaneously allocating budgets for the local police to confine them. The institution's role is to protect the argument that the road to liberation is individual (ideally, scripted) dialogue that does not lead to a conclusion that implicates the state. By this logic, I am not surprised by the surveillance of language choices describing Palestinian oppression as a form of ethnic cleansing and the insistence that any lesson I shared with students on Palestine needed to be carefully approved by an authority.

The gateway that Palestine provides is a direct resistance to the existing model of good citizenship. The policing of this gateway and "restrictions on Palestinian speech occur in part because arbiters of power are aware of Palestine's exhilarating potential"—the potential to produce real momentum in solidarity movements.[6] Providing honest resources and spaces to unpack the interconnectedness of oppression in our classrooms is not a part of this good citizenship. Confining students to political participation that starts and ends with phone calls and voting campaigns for the leaders that approve structural violence and then kneel in solidarity for victims of police violence in the United States teaches them that the solutions they seek can only come from pleading with those same leaders. It also robs students of an alternative imagination of leadership beyond elected officials—creating enough distance between them and those leaders that students do not see themselves as potential advocates for change. Alternatively, if our classrooms facilitate conversations that expose students to the police exchange programs between the United States and Israel or to the amount of funding and training both Israel and the United States have put into militarizing and destabilizing Central and South

America, for example, then that box for good citizenship becomes insultingly limiting. We should be supporting students through the process of participating in that momentum. This changes the nature of student inquiry in a way that cannot be resolved through American exceptionalist teaching standards.

When a former student organizer of mine was working on organizing a debate for an after-school club on the occupation of Palestine, he came to me for advice because he could not identify why the overarching question was not sitting right with him. I had not taught his class about Palestine yet, but since we had already discussed the ongoing American exploitation of Central America, his anti-imperialist lens was already engaging with Palestine in the same way. The club adviser expected him to pose a typical power-deficient question about which side, Palestine or Israel, was "right." We talked about why that question did not feel right to him, and I offered him my copy of Angela Y. Davis's *Freedom Is a Constant Struggle* to support him in thinking through the implication of the question. He returned with an entirely restructured debate plan around the question "What is the responsibility of the United States in resisting the continued illegal occupation of Palestine?"—a question that rejects the placement of the colonizer and colonized as two equal and legitimate sides and rejects the image of a benevolent colonizer. A question that also opens up an entirely new avenue to explore the ongoing settler colonialism in the United States, as well as its imperial arms, legs, and teeth in the Americas, Asia, and Africa.

Decolonizing Our Classrooms

Educators have a responsibility to resist the existing goal of students and teachers to be "good citizens." As educators, we are expected to model and teach our students to only participate with imperialism and American exceptionalism at the center. We are expected to reinforce the very limited notion that progress can only come from within the imagination of the existing structure. Actual resistance is decolonizing and disruptive. Steven Salaita uses the term *decolonization* in his book *Inter/Nationalism: Decolonizing Native America and Palestine* "not simply to signify the process of expunging a foreign occupier from one's ancestral land, but also to identify the extirpation of a foreign occupier from one's economy, education system, and self image."[7] How do we participate in this process?

It is crucial, first and foremost, to acknowledge decolonization as a literal and physical movement rather than a purely theoretical one. While working through the ways we, as individuals, have internalized colonial structures, the process of decolonizing spaces requires community support, action, and collective relearning. When applied to our education systems, this means working through the ways our schools exist to maintain colonialism and justify colonization historically. The power structures, curricula, disciplinary practices, etc., all operate to duplicate the kind of control that colonialism needs to maintain itself. This means that upholding a seemingly apolitical classroom is inherently colonial—a lack of resistance is authorization.

Identifying the limitations that were placed on me as a Palestinian educator helps identify the subversion that decolonization necessitates. I propose a reexamination of the way educators are expected to keep their students at an arm's length while also herding them to conform to supposed civility in their activism. "The first order of business is the acknowledgment that all peoples of America and Palestine must, of geopolitical necessity, be liberated together, and that our scholarship should be an asset toward that goal, not a mere recapitulation of state power."[8] There is an obvious divide-and-conquer mentality imposed in schools that places educators in opposition to students: teach them, but do not teach them everything; support them, but do not support them too much; center their voices, but only the ones that do not challenge too much. Resisting this division requires educators not only to relinquish the power they hold over students but also to ask themselves who that power was serving in the first place. What if that power was redistributed across our classrooms and we cultivated spaces that were horizontally supportive to each other rather than vertically gatekeeping who can move up the ladder to speak? If moving up the ladder requires us to give up the parts of ourselves that think radically different from the structure, why are we told to aspire to be at the top? Traditional views of "good citizenship"

Unsettling the "Good Citizen"   219

expect our students to look to those who hold positional superiority and politely ask them for changes that would require them to relinquish power. Decolonization rejects positional superiority and individual glorification. Instead, it mobilizes and prioritizes the interconnected voices of those who have been most harmed by the colonial structure in solidarity for true collective liberation.

Notes

1. Edward Said, *Orientalism* (New York: Pantheon Books, 1978), 283.

2. Steven Salaita, "A Palestinian Exception to the First Amendment? The Pain and Pleasure of Palestine in the Public Sphere," in *With Stones in Our Hands: Writings on Muslims, Racism, and Empire,* ed. Sohail Daulatzai and Junaid Akram Rana (Minneapolis: University of Minnesota Press, 2018), 4.

3. Salaita, "Palestinian Exception to the First Amendment?," 11.

4. Steven Salaita, "The Taming of Anti-Zionism in the United States," *Steve Salaita* (blog), August 4, 2021, https://stevesalaita.com/the-taming-of-anti-zionism-in-the-united-states/.

5. Rutgers University New Brunswick Provost, email message to author, May 26, 2021.

6. Salaita, "Palestinian Exception to the First Amendment?," 13.

7. Steven Salaita, *Inter/Nationalism: Decolonizing Native America and Palestine* (Minneapolis: University of Minnesota Press, 2016), xiii.

8. Salaita, *Inter/Nationalism,* xix.

CHAPTER 10

Enacting Identities of
Resistance in Suburban Schools

*Latinx Youth and the Possibilities
of Anti-citizenship*

GABRIEL RODRIGUEZ

> I guess me and my friends hate people who put a bad name out there for
> Latinos. Why are you doing this? Don't be stupid; you're making us look
> bad. . . . This is why they don't like us here, because of all the problems
> you guys cause.
>
> —JOAQUÍN (pseudonym)

The study of identity formation is a messy and tension-rich endeavor requiring an understanding grounded in recognizing it as a socially constructed and fluid process. Moreover, to render identity formation without sensitivity to its interplay with history, context, and larger sociopolitical factors depoliticizes a process that is deeply political. For Latinx youth, this is no exception, particularly during a time when important conversations are taking place about panethnic labels such as "*Latinidad*" and coming to grips with their historical complicity in white supremacy and anti-Blackness.[1] In this chapter, I do not delve into the important nuances of this debate but rather consider how these issues informed Latinx youth enactments of identity at a predominately white, equity-oriented, and well-resourced high school outside of Chicago, Illinois.

I focus on the identities of Latinx students at Shields High School (SHS) to consider how their enactments of identity highlighted not only the ways they wished to be affirmed but also the tensions they wrestled with among themselves. This chapter contributes to this book project's foci by examining the ways Latinx youth wrestled with anti-citizenship. More specifically, I center Latinx youth experiences to explore how they embraced and resisted anti-citizenship through their enactments of identity. Joaquín's perspective shared in the epigraph serves as an entry point to consider how Latinx youth performed their identities in a school where whiteness shaped how they made sense of themselves. I argue that, while Latinx youth carved out moments to perform identities meaningful to them, ultimately, they needed support in making sense of the larger structures around them that at times positioned them against one another. Given this schooling context, this chapter delves into the relationship between identity and anti-citizenship. More specifically, I argue that Latinx identity performances need to be understood as acts of anti-citizenship in the ways they contest whiteness and white supremacy. Further, while it is vital to understand enactments of identity as acts of resistance or anti-citizenship, this chapter also highlights the ways Latinx youth avoid notions of anti-citizenship by reifying whiteness through respectability politics.

This chapter also highlights a schooling context that is representative of the demographic changes occurring in suburban communities across the United States. Most Latinxs in the United States live in suburban communities, yet much of what scholars know about their experiences is through critical research in urban schools.[2] Latinx youth and other youth of color who attend majority-white suburban schools navigate environments that make it difficult for them to embrace their cultural and linguistic identities.[3] These studies collectively highlight the navigational strategies Latinx youth and other youth of color employ to adapt and survive in predominantly white schools. While these studies showcase Latinx youth's and other youth of color's navigational and resistance capital, they also highlight how they are silenced and pushed to the margins of their respective schools. It is essential to continue to learn from Latinx youth in schools that, on the surface, seem ideal but refuse to recognize the complexity of their social worlds and their impact on students' lives in school.

Research Framework

Performing the Political: Understanding Anti-citizens' Enactments of Identity

To ground my analysis of the complicated ways in which Latinx youth navigated anti-citizenship within Shields High School, I build upon the work of performativity theory, which understands identities as acts of production that occur through the social interactions people have—enactments that are coconstructed, negotiated, and at times in conflict with how others see one another.[4] As Mary Bucholtz argues, people do not have unconstrained agency to construct their desired identities in ways that are meaningful to them.[5] Instead, it is important to consider Sherry B. Ortner's premise that identities are byproducts of "structurally embedded agency" and "intention filled structures."[6] My analysis of how Latinx youth enact and embody their cultural and linguistic identities in the context of a predominantly white suburban high school relies on José Esteban Muñoz's conception of "disidentification," which he describes as "survival strategies" that "the minority subject practices in order to negotiate a phobic majoritarian public sphere that continuously elides or punishes the existence of subjects who do not conform to the phantasm of normative citizenship."[7]

Understanding identity performances through a disidentification framework allows for a richer analysis that sits with the hybridity and dexterity Latinx youth employ in order to survive, thrive, and resist. This approach highlights the tensions of anti-citizenship that Latinx youth wrestle with daily. More specifically, it works toward a more nuanced and honest conversation on how youth resist or practice anti-citizenship. Further, I analyze how participants enact competing notions of authenticity.

In writing about authenticity regarding second-generation Indian American youth, Sunaina Marr Maira argues that distinctions and hierarchies exist among young people. She writes:

> Authenticity is an ideology shaped by complex historical and political processes within any subculture or community and is a difficult creature with which to do battle, as the sometimes contradictory discourses and performances of ethnic purity among second-generation youth suggest.[8]

224 GABRIEL RODRIGUEZ

Authenticity took on added significance for the youth of this study, given their outsider status; for some youth, authenticity took shape as resistance or anti-citizenship, while for others, it spoke to conformity as an act of survival.

Youth Participant and School Snapshot

The nineteen youth of the study were purposefully recruited based on the questions that informed the larger study this chapter draws from.[9] Of the nineteen student participants, ten were female, nine were male, and all possessed different identities and affiliations (e.g., social cliques). I recruited for varying identities and perspectives to capture as many complexities of Latinx experiences at SHS, as this community is not a monolith.

Located in the predominantly white and middle- and upper-middle-class suburban community of La Vista, SHS also served students from neighboring Northwood. Unlike La Vista, Northwood is mainly Latinx and working class. Over the course of the fieldwork, the student body at SHS was just above two thousand students. Most of the students at SHS were white (71 percent), with the second-largest bloc of students being Latinx (22 percent). SHS benefited from a positive reputation in the community and was considered one of the strongest high schools in Illinois, given its consistent track record at maintaining a college-going culture, its affluent tax base, and its numerous opportunities (e.g., after-school activities, Advanced Placement coursework). The school also espoused a commitment to equity, which not only was reflected in school documents but also manifested in school-wide initiatives (e.g., college access programs).

Data Collection

Through a critical ethnographic approach, I learned from youth at SHS over the course of two school years (2014–2016). I engaged in participant observations with students by shadowing them in and out of the classroom (e.g., hallways, cafeteria).[10] For two years, I was at SHS three to five days of the week before, during, and after school. Each subject of the study participated in one audio-recorded, semistructured interview at SHS for ninety minutes. In addition to these formal interviews,

I conducted informal interviews regularly with youth, which helped build rapport, offered clarification, and pointed me to new things to consider or ask. Finally, artifacts and documents (e.g., student artwork) were collected to help augment and provide a holistic understanding of the everyday lives of Latinx youth at SHS.

Note on Positionality

My critical ethnographic approach requires an examination of myself vis-à-vis the project and the Latinx youth of the study. While I was not from the community I learned from, I too grew up in a suburban community in the Chicagoland region. Coupled with my Mexican American identity, I used these aspects of my upbringing and identity to connect with and build relationships with the youth of the study. My experiences growing up in a majority-white suburb brought multiple moments of marginalization that silenced me and made me question my cultural and linguistic identities, which helped shape this research project and relationship building. Despite some insider status and commonalities I shared with many student participants, there were always ways in which I functioned as an outsider.[11]

FINDINGS

The findings examine the multiple ways Latinx youth at SHS enacted their identities, with a particular focus on how whiteness shaped their self-presentation styles and larger tensions of identity performances within the Latinx community. These findings are significant because they underscore the constraints Latinx youth face as anti-citizens and how they make sense of and struggle to exist in ways that are meaningful to them against a school and society that demand ritual assimilation into whiteness as a precondition of "belonging." *Belonging* appears in quotes to suggest that any kind of belonging that is offered to Latinx youth—even youths that submit to assimilation—is always precarious, as youths remain indefinitely vulnerable to the project of whiteness that has historically redefined the conditions of belonging and insider status at its whim to accomplish political and economic goals.

Mapping the Contours of Contested Latinx Identities

SHS hosted an annual arts festival that featured student work alongside performances, speeches, and workshops by different artists and local celebrities. SHS dedicated a whole week to its arts festival, with school days blocked off for students and staff to attend and enjoy the sessions offered. On one particular day, I headed toward the exit of the school's auditorium when I saw Joaquín and Arturo seated on the other side. They had just taken their seats, and I walked over to join them for the next session.

As I took my seat next to Arturo, Joaquín received playful criticism from his friends for wanting to sit on the other side of the auditorium, to sit next to Myriam, who he wanted to ask to prom. After withstanding the verbal onslaught of jokes, he departed. During this time, students continued to come in and take their seats. A different group of Latino students led by Marcos entered the auditorium and cracked jokes with one another as they came in. Upon hearing them joke around and take their seats a few rows behind us, Leo, with a tone of disgust, slowly said, "Oh my God." Shortly thereafter, Liliana, a Latina student, walked in with a group of white female friends. She saw me and excitedly remarked, "Gabe!" In turn, Arturo quietly and slowly said to himself, "Just keep walking." In doing so, Arturo signaled that he did not want Liliana to sit by him. Liliana did not appear to notice and proceeded to take a seat near the front of the auditorium. The dance troupe walked onto the stage, and students quieted down as they began their performance.

During the dance performance, Arturo and his friends intermittently talked to one another in hushed voices. Behind us, the group of Latino students who came in cracking jokes continued to do so by making fun of the dancers on stage. The guys I sat with grumbled, and a group of white female students seated in front of us showed their displeasure by turning back and throwing dirty looks at the group of Latino students seated behind Arturo and his friends. Ms. Lennox, one of the school's college counselors, asked this group of students to quiet down and remain respectful. Arturo turned to me and said, "If [they] don't want to be here, then don't." He then briefly sympathized by saying that the dance

Enacting Identities of Resistance in Suburban Schools   227

performance was boring. As the remaining modern dance companies performed their sets, I could not stop thinking about the fast-moving and complex interplay between these three sets of Latinx students.

However, you have Arturo, who made it clear that Liliana was not welcomed because of her friendships and associations with white youth. For some Latinx youth, like Arturo, Liliana was perceived as someone who was disconnected from the school's Latinx community. You then have Arturo and his friends who were not happy with the Latino students seated behind them. Arturo and his friends were critical of these young men, as they felt they gave them and the larger Latinx student body a bad name by engaging in disrespectful behavior and because of their school-based reputation as troublemakers, without considering ways SHS contributed to their marginalization. These three cliques brushed up against each other in a contentious manner. For Arturo and his friends, they performed an authentic enactment of how Latinx youth should act at SHS; while in their eyes, someone like Liliana was "too good" for other Latinx youth and Latinx peers like the chatty group behind Arturo perpetuated negative stereotypes of Latinos that played into negative perceptions white youth and staff already held. What Arturo and his friends perceived as disruptive behavior should be interpreted as "deviance as resistance."[12] This group of Latino students recognized that this performance was not for them. The performance put on by the modern dance company did not reflect anything related to Latinx culture; instead, it reflected Eurocentric art that did not speak to the lives of Latinx youth. While Arturo also did not enjoy this performance, he opted to comply and not voice criticism and, in so doing, conformed and did not engage in anti-citizenship.

Performing Whiteness?

Based on my conversations with Latinx youth, a lot was at stake for Latinx youth who hung out with white students. For Liliana, it was apparent that some of her Latinx peers labeled her as someone who was not sympathetic to the Latinx community. She indeed was someone who was comfortable being around white youth. In shadowing her, I noticed that she often sat next to white students, some of whom were friends. For instance, Liliana typically ate her lunch in the school's college resource

228   GABRIEL RODRIGUEZ

center, which was a space primarily used by white, academically oriented juniors and seniors. In my interview with her, Liliana spoke about the perceptions she felt some Latinx students had about her. She shared:

> There was this idea that I was better than myself just because I went to Woodland [Middle School]. Hispanics were mean, and so I avoided them on all terms. The expectations that you were going to get judged or bullied by Hispanics versus white, I found it Hispanic versus Hispanic.

Unlike many of the participants of this study, Liliana went to a middle school in a predominantly white and more affluent part of La Vista. Unlike her other classmates who went to slightly more diverse middle schools, Liliana felt more comfortable around white students. As she put it, "I think I have a bias just because I went to Woodland. So, I know most of them [referring to white students]." Liliana spoke about how she had close friendships with other Latinx youth but that those friendships dissipated because of different priorities, which positioned her further apart from many other Latinx students at SHS. What was at stake for her and other students who did not socialize with Latinx youth were repercussions for how they were seen. During interviews, several students spoke about what they thought were the implications of hanging out primarily with white youth. For instance, Jacobo spoke about the push–pull effect Latinx people may experience:

> I guess we can choose what we want to do. Acculturation or assimilation. I think a good number of Latinos choose to assimilate. I don't want to say it's bad; certain people were born and raised here. Perhaps the idea about being Mexican and their traditions they don't know about, but the other people who weren't born here, that I have a problem. You shouldn't have to forget about who you are and your identity in the past, but certainly, for Latinos in general, it's about assimilation, it's about fitting in, it's about not being Latino.

As an immigrant student who came to the United States from Central America as a child, Jacobo expressed understanding and sympathy for

Enacting Identities of Resistance in Suburban Schools   229

the issues second-generation Latinx youth felt. He was more willing to entertain the idea of why some second-generation youth would want to assimilate. But for immigrant youth like himself, Jacobo had a different viewpoint. In my interview with Humberto, he shared another aspect Latinx youth grappled with:

> GABRIEL: What do you think when a Latino student mainly hangs out with white students?
>
> HUMBERTO: Yeah [*laughs*]. Whitewashed, I would call it. I do have—I don't want to call him a friend, a classmate, I guess. We don't really hang out. He hangs out with a bunch of, what's it called, a bunch of white people, and basically, I feel like he lost his accent too. He has nothing. When he tries to talk, he sounds like someone who is trying to learn for the very first time.
>
> GABRIEL: Any ideas why he hangs out with white kids?
>
> HUMBERTO: Maybe he just feels more comfortable with them. Because I feel more comfortable with Latino students, maybe he feels more comfortable having white friends or being with white students.

For Humberto, the student he talked about had no connection to his cultural identity, and therefore, in his view, this student had "nothing." His commentary highlighted the pressures that some students like Liliana felt. It was clear that Latinx students had different interpretations of what it meant to enact authentic Latinx identities. Latinx students were interpreting different peer enactments based on their understanding of what was meaningful and, in turn, at times judged others through this lens. Humberto's perspective raised a critical point of not only what was at stake but the costs of acceptance and inclusion at this majority-white high school. In my conversations with Joaquín and Michelle, they offered different elements that helped unpack some of the polarizing views some Latinx youth held.

> GABRIEL: What goes through your head when you see Latinx students mainly hang out with white students?

230 GABRIEL RODRIGUEZ

JOAQUÍN: I think maybe they're smart, maybe they don't like hanging out with this [referring to Latinx students] crowd. I don't really think bad of them; it's their decision.

In talking with Michelle, I asked her about the tensions, if any, that existed among Latinx students. We had the following exchange:

MICHELLE: I think that a lot of times, Latinx students will look at people that aren't like them as whitewashed or something, and they'll see that as bad and won't talk to those people. I think you have to act a certain way to actually be considered Latino.

GABRIEL: Do you feel you fall into the group of being an acceptable Latina, or do you feel like you have to fight that battle?

MICHELLE: I feel like sometimes I have to fight it. Sometimes I feel like, oh, like, with, I don't know, Jackie and Elizabeth and some of our friends, sometimes I do feel like I have to act a certain way. I have to not kind of care so much about school and kind of, like, I don't know, act tough in a way that's not really me sometimes, but that's not really, I'm not like them, and so yeah, it is hard. I think they think of me sometimes like, "She's not Mexican enough." For me now that I'm leaving, and I know where I'm going, and there's a long future ahead of me, I don't really mind it, I'm not going to make a big deal out of it, I'm not going to change who I am.

What was apparent with the youth participants was that there were gendered differences in how they interpreted youth who were closer to white students. The gendered differences should not be lost on educators in the building, particularly in how students were tracked academically. The likelihood of Latina students tracked into honors or AP classes was higher than for Latino students at SHS. In doing so, it put them in contact with more white students. Male youth were likely to find respite with their ethno-racial community and feel solidarity among one another. Ultimately, we are left to still think about what acting white means. As Abigail put it, "I hate when people say, 'You're acting white.' What does that mean? That's weird. I feel like you do act differently. I think everyone tries to

Enacting Identities of Resistance in Suburban Schools   231

be the same, but you don't want to be different, but you are different." Abigail and Michelle were more willing to confront notions of acting white because for them that was not their goal. Their enrollment in honors and AP coursework was an investment not in whiteness but in their academics.

I argue that Latinx youth are not acting white but instead are trying to survive their contexts. Latinx students who had more contact with white students have developed skills to put up with white students and the micro- and macroaggressions they put them through. Students navigating predominately white spaces are highly aware of the racial boundaries and use them to their advantage to get by.[13] In critiquing research on oppositional culture regarding Black youth, Amanda E. Lewis and John B. Diamond argue that "the oppositional culture argument has it wrong. If anything, instead of perceived discrimination undermining black students' commitment to school, just the opposite occurs: black students are buffered by their pro-achievement orientations in the face of often vast social inequalities."[14] Similarly, Latinx youth's academic orientations fuel them in the face of the pressures they face in their mainly white classrooms. Another issue Latinx youth contended with was a desire to be labeled as a "stereotypical" Latinx student.

Performing the Stereotype

Students in Immigrant Perspectives, an English senior elective, had finished taking a quiz and socialized with one another while Ms. Cuomo got ready for the next portion of the class. A Latino student walked in late, which prompted Arturo, Joaquín, and Jay to slowly clap and give him a hard time for being late. Ms. Cuomo had students take out a piece of paper to work on a writing exercise for a few minutes. She asked the class not to worry about grammar or organization. She wanted them to write as freely as they possibly could. All the students wrote, taking brief breaks to think about what they wanted to write about. While Arturo and Jay dove into their writing, Joaquín did not write. A few minutes had passed, and Joaquín's friends had already written half a page. At this point, I was curious as to what Joaquín was doing. I initially thought he was brainstorming, but then Jay turned to him and asked, "Why aren't you writing?" Joaquín shrugged his shoulders. He then took his notebook and lifted it, and had his friends look at it as he pointed to the empty page with a smile on his face. A few seconds later, Ms. Cuomo brought the class back together, and as she spoke about the class agenda, Joaquín began to write. He wrote feverishly as he hunched over his notebook and had written a page and a half by the end.

This moment was fascinating to observe. I had seen Joaquín engage in this class before. He joked around with his friends, but rarely did he ever disengage in such a way. Joaquín appeared proud of the fact that he did not initially write anything. He enacted a performance that had been ascribed to many Latinx youth at SHS, one that maintained that the Latinx student body, on average, did not care or try. Yet, Joaquín did care and, in fact, proceeded to write more than any of the students around him. This student was someone who downplayed his intelligence. He did not want the attention; whenever called upon, he would deflect and joke around by asking or telling his teachers to call on someone else. At other times, he would say he did not know the answer, even when he did. When I interviewed Joaquín, we spoke about how Latinx students are perceived at SHS through a question I asked about the problems he believed existed at SHS. He shared:

> I guess me and my friends hate people who put a bad name out there for Latinos. Why are you doing this? Don't be stupid; you're making us look bad. They like dissing class. Like, why? This is why they don't like us here, because of all the problems you guys cause.

In his response, Joaquín spoke about how he and his friends hate when people, as he said, "put a bad name out there for Latinos." Because some white students had a negative perception of Latinx youth, for Latinx students to joke around, not do homework, and talk back to their teachers, among other actions, hurt Latinx youth at SHS. Yet, on the surface, one may wonder why Joaquín performed the way he did in his Immigrant Perspectives class. In analyzing that moment, I argue Joaquín walked a fine line between the stereotype he argues diminished the standing of Latinx students at SHS and performing notions of coolness and intelligence. In

Enacting Identities of Resistance in Suburban Schools

speaking with Jacobo, he shared other aspects that help complicate some of the things Joaquín noted:

> To fit in with Latinos, sometimes we discriminate our own. Part of the problem when I arrived was my accent. I talked funny, and so I definitely changed my vocabulary. I started swearing a lot in Mexican Spanish, and I did certain things to fit in. In high school, I also did certain things, the way I dressed, the people I tried to talk to that was a problem, that was a problem in general with me, and I think that's why I was doing so bad in school, because I was trying to fit in and trying to assimilate.

Earlier in his high-school career, Jacobo struggled to fit in. He felt he tried too hard to fit in by acting out and, because of his Honduran identity, he felt the need to try to appeal to the majority-Mexican student body within the Latinx community at SHS. But there are costs to these types of performances, as I have argued with the vignette in the opening of this chapter between Arturo, Lilliana, and Marcos. In the end, what does it mean to perform authentic Latinx identities?

Performing Authenticity

I spoke more explicitly with the youth of the study about what their identities meant to them. Overlap existed with the importance of being comfortable around people who looked like them. Participants spoke about the importance of connecting or reconnecting with their culture. For Xóchitl, she can be her authentic self in spaces with people who look like her. She said, "You're so comfortable with who you're sitting with that everybody makes you feel comfortable. Being with all Latinos, it's so comfortable; you can be yourself, and you don't have to pretend to be someone you're not." Xóchitl's comment raised the question: What about being around other Latinx youth and the spaces they had carved out made them feel comfortable?

At SHS, the Physical Education Department had a class devoted to what they called "PE leaders." These students helped mentor first-year students during their gym class by instilling the importance of leadership. During this class, students prepared and delivered motivational speeches.

234 GABRIEL RODRIGUEZ

The assignment asked them to share what they wanted their first-year students to know about SHS. Abigail decided to direct her address to the Latinx student body. On the day she delivered her speech to her peers, Abigail looked nervous; she did not want to give the speech. She sat next to me on this day of class. Her nervousness took on added significance because school administrators and teachers were invited to watch and provide feedback. Finally, Abigail's turn came. She stood and walked to the front of the room. She put her notes down on the table in front of her and delivered the following:

> Welcome. Today is your first day of high school. High school is different from middle school; you need to know how to play the game. You need to know who your MVPs are. Everything that you do will impact you. You are one step away from the real world. One of the challenges is being a minority. Personally, there were days when I didn't want to go to class, but you can do this! You are strong because we are Latino. If it's one thing I leave you with is that *todos somos* Saxons.

In her remarks, Abigail was honest about the difficult journey Latinx had before them. She spoke her truth and did not shy away from the difficulties she experienced. Moreover, Abigail's decision to conclude her speech in Spanish and not to translate highlighted the importance she had toward preserving her language by not downplaying it. This took on added significance as she performed this aspect of her identity in front of a predominately white class, which was not dissimilar to the other academic spaces Abigail traversed. Abigail's speech spoke to the risk she took in being vulnerable and honoring aspects important to her identity. For her, this was meaningful and authentic. This performance and others like it took shape in multiple ways. For instance, in the case of Hannah, it took shape through a tote bag she used.

In addition to their backpacks, many of the white female students at SHS carried Lululemon tote bags to haul around small items, such as snacks or school supplies. I noticed that Hannah also had a small tote bag, but it was not from the popular yoga-apparel store. Her bag was a replica of a coffee bag. This identity performance was an act of resistance,

Enacting Identities of Resistance in Suburban Schools 235

a refusal to acquiesce to the norm Hannah witnessed. Hannah observed Lululemon bags, and perhaps liked the idea of carrying one around, but this served as an opportunity to display an aspect of her Latina identity.

DISCUSSION: UNDERSTANDING THE INTERPLAY BETWEEN ANTI-CITIZENSHIP AND IDENTITY

The findings of this chapter highlight the ways Latinx youth wrestled with anti-citizenship through their identity enactments. Whiteness positioned Latinx youth as anti-citizens. The power of whiteness and white supremacy shaped how Latinx youth performed their identities. It shaped their enactments of identity by what they played up or downplayed and also by how they policed each other through the politics of respectability. This process not only underscores the struggles of embracing the anti-citizenship status whiteness conferred onto the bodies of Latinx youth. In the context of SHS, anti-citizenship is connected to being a bad student. Latinx youth recognized what was at stake and what they felt they needed to do to be tracked into the opportunities SHS offered. That meant downplaying aspects of their identity, an unwillingness to rock the boat because they did not want to be perceived as troublemakers and as ungrateful.

Moreover, the internal dynamics of the Latinx student community at SHS highlights another level of precarity in their lives. This is not to excuse investments in respectability politics and the ways they policed one another, as Latinx youth need to be challenged in culturally affirming ways to consider the possibilities of what they bring to the table. Further, when youth did resist, it charted a different set of possibilities to enact different types of identities meaningful to students and challenges to respectability politics and whiteness at large. These efforts point to the need for more outlets for Latinx youth to learn more about themselves and how to come together as a community to confront the violence whiteness enacted upon them and other youth of color at SHS.

The Latinx youth of the study were deeply prideful of their cultural and linguistic identities. Yet, the context they inhabited and traversed prompted serious challenges to themselves and the collective Latinx student body. These challenges caused serious internal dilemmas that forced Latinx youth to question their pride and, in turn, affected how they presented themselves to the outside world. These performances were not static; they were fluid. Their enactments of identity changed depending on where they were and who Latinx youth interacted with. In so doing, this highlights the resiliency Latinx youth possess and the awareness they carry of a schooling environment that often did not understand them. The racialized boundaries at SHS led to a culture of silence and erasure.[15] Latinx youth played with aspects of whiteness to survive and navigate a context that struggled to understand their cultural and linguistic worlds. Yet, this process created tension among Latinx youth searching for acceptance and needed opportunities to process notions of being a good Latinx student in order to understand the structural issues that led them to blame themselves or others in their community rather than holding white youth, educators, and the school at large accountable for not pushing back on whiteness more actively.

Schools need to consider how prevailing deficit-based structures and discourses negatively affect students' lives. Paul C. Gorski argues for the importance of teachers to possess a structural understanding of inequity and injustice.[16] This orientation facilitates an understanding that considers the possibilities of an asset-based approach that seeks to enact culturally and linguistically relevant and sustaining approaches in schools.[17] Moreover, the experiences and perspectives of Latinx youth at SHS highlight the struggles equity-oriented schools have in fulfilling their espoused commitments. As scholars argue, good intentions and equity initiatives often still frame Latinx youth and other youth of color as the problem.[18] This reframing allows educators and school administrators to ask different questions that shift accountability to themselves and the schools they work in. It also demands that equity initiatives not lose sight of whiteness and white youth and the work required to foster antiracist commitments and meaningful solidarity. This type of focus can offer a path that takes the pressure off Latinx youth to seek conformity and acceptance through respectability politics. Some of the youth of this study judged and policed one another, and these tensions are a direct result of white supremacy. It is critically important to understand Latinx youth identity performances as forms of resistance. In doing so, educators and administrators can work alongside them to construct schools that redefine what inclusion and success look like.

Notes

1. I use *Latinx* throughout the article to refer to the student body and larger community. I do so to be gender inclusive but will use *Latino* and *Latina* when specifically referencing student participants.

G. Cristina Mora, Reuben Perez, and Nicholas Vargas, "Who Identifies as 'Latinx'? The Generational Politics of Ethnoracial Labels," *Social Forces* 100, no. 3 (2021): 1,170–94; Richard T. Rodríguez, "X Marks the Spot," *Cultural Dynamics* 29, no. 3 (2017): 202–13; Jonathan Rosa, *Looking like a Language, Sounding like a Race: Raciolinguistic Ideologies and Learning of Latinidad* (Cambridge: Oxford University Press, 2019); Salvador Vidal-Ortiz and Juliana Martínez, "Latinx Thoughts: Latinidad with an X," *Latino Studies* 16, no. 3 (2018): 384–95.

2. William H. Frey, *Diversity Explosion: How New Racial Demographics Are Remaking America* (Washington, D.C.: Brookings Institution Press, 2018). On urban school research, see, for example, Gilberto Q. Conchas, *Streetsmart Schoolsmart: Urban Poverty and the Education of Adolescent Boys* (New York: Teachers College Press, 2012); Nilda Flores-Gonzalez, *School Kids/Street Kids: Identity Development in Latino Students* (New York: Teachers College Press, 2002); Angela Valenzuela, *Subtractive Schooling: U.S.-Mexican Youth and the Politics of Caring* (New York: State University of New York Press, 1999).

3. Gilberto Q. Conchas, Leticia Oseguera, and James Diego Vigil, "Acculturation and School Success: Understanding the Variability of Mexican American Youth Adaptation across Urban and Suburban Contexts," *Urban Review* 44 (2012): 401–22; Thandeka K.Chapman, "Is Integration a Dream Deferred? Students of Color in Majority White Suburban Schools," *Journal of Negro Education* 83, no. 60 (2014): 311–26; Simone Ispa-Landa, "Gender, Race, and Justifications for Group Exclusion: Urban Black Students Bussed to Affluent Suburban Schools," *Sociology of Education* 86, no. 3 (2013): 218–33; Simone Ispa-Landa and Jordan Conwell, "'Once You Go to a White School, You Kind of Adapt': Black Adolescents and the Racial Classification of Schools," *Sociology of Education* 88, no. 1 (2015): 1–19; Maria Eugenia Matute-Bianchi, "Ethnic Identities and Patterns of School Success and Failure among Mexican-Descent and Japanese-American Students in a California High School: An Ethnographic Analysis," *American Journal of Education* 95, no. 1 (1986): 233–55; Gabriel Rodriguez, "Suburban Schools as Sites of Inspection: Understanding Latinx Youth's Sense of Belonging in a Suburban High School," *Equity & Excellence in Education* 53, no. 1–2 (2020): 14–29.

4. Julie Bettie, *Women without Class: Girls, Race, and Identity* (Berkeley: University of California Press, 2014); Judith Butler, *Gender Trouble: Feminism and the Subversion of Identity* (London: Routledge, 1990); José Esteban Muñoz, *Disidentifications: Queers of Color and the Performance of Politics* (Minneapolis: University of Minnesota Press, 1999); Mary Bucholtz, *White Kids: Language, Race, and Styles of Youth Identity* (Cambridge: Cambridge University Press, 2011); Stuart Hall, "Cultural Identity and Diaspora," in *Identity: Community, Culture, Difference*, ed. Jonathan Rutherford, 222–37 (London: Lawrence Wishart, 1990).

5. Bucholtz, *White Kids*.

6. Sherry B. Ortner, *Making Gender: The Politics and Erotics of Culture* (Boston: Beacon Press, 1996), 12.

7. Muñoz, *Disidentifications*, 4.

8. Sunaina Marr Maira, *Desis in the House: Indian American Youth Culture in New York City* (Philadelphia: Temple University Press, 2002), 136.

9. Robert. C. Bogdan and Sari Knope Biklen, *Qualitative Research for Education: An Introduction to Theory and Methods* (Boston: Allyn & Bacon, 2003).

10. Victor Rios, *Punished: Policing the Lives of Black and Latino Boys* (New York: New York University Press, 2011).

11. Sofia Villenas, "The Colonizer/Colonized Chicana Ethnographer: Identity, Marginalization, and Co-optation in the Field," *Harvard Educational Review* 66, no. 4 (1996): 711–32.

12. Cathy J. Cohen, "Deviance as Resistance: A New Research Agenda for the Study of Black Politics," *Du Bois Review: Social Science Research on Race* 1, no. 1 (2004): 27–45.

13. Gabriel Rodriguez, "Suburban Schools as Sites of Inspection: Understanding Latinx Youth's Sense of Belonging in a Suburban High School," *Equity & Excellence in Education* 53, no. 1–2 (2020): 14–29.

14. Amanda E. Lewis and John B. Diamond, *Despite the Best Intentions: How Racial Inequality Thrives in Good Schools* (New York: Oxford University Press, 2017), 44.

15. Rodriguez, "Suburban Schools as Sites of Inspection."

16. Paul C. Gorski, "Poverty and the Ideological Imperative: A Call to Unhook from Deficit and Grit Ideology and to Strive for Structural Ideology in Teacher Education," *Journal of Education for Teaching* 42, no. 4 (2016): 378–86.

17. Gloria Ladson-Billings, "Toward a Theory of Culturally Relevant Pedagogy," *American Educational Research Journal* 32, no. 3 (1995): 465–91; Django Paris, "Culturally Sustaining Pedagogy: A Needed Change in Stance, Terminology, and Practice," *Educational Researcher* 41, no. 3 (2012): 93–97; Django Paris and Samy Alim, "What Are We Seeking to Sustain through Culturally Sustaining Pedagogy? A Loving Critique Forward," *Harvard Educational Review* 84, no. 1 (2014): 85–100.

18. Lewis and Diamond, *Despite the Best Intentions*; Dinorah Sánchez Loza, "Dear 'Good' Schools: White Supremacy and Political Education in Predominantly White and Affluent Suburban Schools," *Theory into Practice* (2021): 380–91; Savannah Shange, *Progressive Dystopia: Abolition, Antiblackness, and Schooling in San Francisco* (Durham, N.C.: Duke University Press, 2019); Sabina E. Vaught, *Racism, Public Schooling, and the Entrenchment of White Supremacy: A Critical Race Ethnography* (New York: State University of New York Press, 2011).

Contributors

KARLYN ADAMS-WIGGINS is associate professor of applied developmental psychology at Portland State University.

ARIANA DENISE BRAZIER is a Black, queer feminist and smiley, sad mom-girl. She is a play-driven community organizer and educator who is motivated to raise a joyous, free Black child. She documents how Black child play functions as a grassroots method of community-based storytelling, teaching, and organizing.

JULIO CAMMAROTA is professor of education at the University of Arizona. He is the author of *Sueños Americanos: Barrio Youth Negotiating Social and Cultural Identities* and editor of *Liberatory Practices for Learning: Dismantling Social Inequality and Individualism with Ancient Wisdom.*

KEVIN L. CLAY is assistant professor of Black studies in education at Rutgers, the State University of New Jersey.

MICHAEL DAVIS is a doctoral candidate at the School of Education at the University of Wisconsin–Madison.

DAMARIS C. DUNN is a doctoral candidate in the Department of Educational Theory and Practice at the Mary Frances Early College of Education at the University of Georgia. Her research focuses on the labor(ing) of K–12 Black female teachers, including their creative and inventive capacities. She is a former social studies teacher and youth development professional.

DIANA GAMEZ is a PhD student in the Department of Anthropology at the University of California, Irvine.

RACHEL F. GÓMEZ is assistant professor in the Department of Teaching and Learning and faculty with the Institute for Inclusion, Inquiry, and Innovation (iCubed) at Virginia Commonwealth University.

LUMA HASAN is a Palestinian activist, New Jersey public schools social studies educator, and cofounder of Teach for Liberation. She has led and facilitated student-centered youth participatory action research programs throughout Central New Jersey.

KEVIN LAWRENCE HENRY JR. is assistant professor of educational leadership and policy analysis at the University of Wisconsin–Madison.

GABRIEL RODRIGUEZ is assistant professor at Iowa State University in the School of Education.

CHRISTOPHER R. ROGERS received a PhD from the University of Pennsylvania Graduate School of Education. He is the coeditor of *How We Stay Free: Notes on a Black Uprising*. He serves on the National Steering Committee for BLM@School, which advocates for racial justice practices and policies in K–12 public education.

DAMIEN M. SOJOYNER is associate professor of anthropology at the University of California, Irvine. He is the author of *First Strike: Educational Enclosures in Black Los Angeles* (Minnesota, 2016), *Joy and Pain: A Story of Black Life and Liberation in Five Albums*, and *Against the Carceral Archive: The Art of Black Liberatory Practice*.

Index

Abigail (student), 230–31, 234
abolition, 89, 128; Black youth and, 135–36; change and, 71–72; of school, 144, 149, 151, 157, 159–60; teachers and, 70–71
Abrego, Leisy, 130n3
AC. *See* Assata's Children
academics, 35, 145, 192; Black girls and, 56, 93–96, 102–4; Latinx youth and, 231, 235
accounts, of students, 37–39, 54–62, 92–104, 228–34
activism, 77–78; Chicano youth and, 186–88; civil disobedience and, 189, 192; civility and, 11–12, 16, 211, 218; discipline and, 210–11; organizing practices and, 168–69, 192; teachers and, 197
administrators, 37, 210; curriculum and, 208–09, 212, 215, 218
adultification, 46; of Black girls, 70, 85; criminality and, 100; unaccompanied minors and, 118–19
Afropessimism, 16–17, 86–87, 133; anti-citizenship and, 138–39; Blackness and, 137, 142
afterlife, of slavery, 28–29, 67–72, 76, 79–80

agency, 10, 13, 46, 177; familiar zones and, 50; political, 8–9, 11; students and, 203; survival and, 154–55
Allen, Robert L., 11–12
allyship, 189; performative, 208–13
Americanization, citizenship and, 181–83. *See also* assimilation
anonymity, in research, 64n7, 90, 143–44
anti-Blackness: charter schools and, 38; discipline and, 68; in El Salvador, 109–10, 114–15, 124; Latinx youth and, 221; racism compared to, 133–34; schooling and, 134–36, 142, 145–53, 156; teachers and, 57; in U.S., 70; white supremacy and, 30–32, 139
antiblack racism, 15–16, 85, 87–88, 92; coloniality and, 86; contradictions and, 101–2; gender and, 98; individualism and, 89, 127; justice and, 104
anti-citizen: Black students as, 27–28, 40–41; Humanity and, 153–159; poetics of, 166; in schools, 136–42, 155–56; the state and, 9, 48–49
anti-citizenship, 7–14, 46–47, 53, 87–88; Afropessimism and, 138–39; binaries and, 110, 113–14, 125; of

244   Index

Black girls, 69–72; Black youth and, 48–49, 86; Chicano people and, 176–77, 188, 191–92; familiar zones and, 63; gender and, 97; "good citizens" and, 198, 203, 206–7; identity and, 235; Latinx youth and, 222–25; play and, 61–62; praxis of, 165, 167–69; resistance and, 4, 15, 105, 192n4; Slave and, 154; students and, 206–8
Ariah (student), 55–57, 60
Arizona (AZ), Tucson, 188–90
art, 72, 74–75; diaspora and, 111, 125–26
Arturo (student), 226–27, 231
Assata's Children (AC), 143–45, 157–58
assimilation, 17, 123; Chicano people and, 182–83, 191; language and, 233–34; in Los Angeles, 114, 116–17; Muslim women and, 202–3; whiteness and, 228–29
authenticity, 69; identity and, 199–201, 223–24, 229–30; performance of, 233–35
authority, 49, 58–60; Black students and, 39, 54–57; of teachers, 54–55, 208
Ayanna (student), 136, 143–58
AZ. *See* Arizona

Baker, Ella, 71–72
Bambara, Toni Cade, 163–64, 166
behaviors, 27, 52, 95–96, 157; anticitizenship, 7–8, 13; deviance and, 140, 227; familiar zones and, 50
binaries, 129n2, 151–52, 206; anticitizenship and, 110, 113–14, 125; citizenship and, 129
Black communities, 12–13, 165–66
BlackCrit, 69
Black excellence, 12–13, 136, 144, 147, 152
Black Ghetto, 14–15, 46, 51

Black girls, 68–69; academics and, 56, 93–96, 102–4; adultification of, 70, 85; development of, 86, 92, 94, 96, 102, 105; invisibility and, 96; needs of, 71–72; play and, 14–15, 45; queer, 78–79; racial/colonial order and, 92–98, 104–5; respectability politics and, 50, 56, 97–98
Black joy, 15; collectivity and, 73–74; radical, 67–69, 72–75, 79–80
Black liberation, 112–14, 168; Slaveness and, 134
Black Lives Matter movement, 90, 208–13
Blackness, 93, 96, 102, 115, 119; Afropessimism and, 137, 142; citizenship and, 112–13, 120–21, 126–27, 141–42, 153; erasure of, 135; Humanity and, 135–37; invisibility and, 87–88, 138; in Los Angeles, 110–12; neoliberalism and, 75; normativity and, 140–41; queerness and, 145; Salvadoran migrants and, 128–29; Slaveness and, 134, 160n1; violence and, 137, 150
Black respectability, 97, 100. *See also* respectability politics
Black specificity, 149–50, 154–56, 159, 160n1
Black students: as anti-citizens, 27–28, 40–41; authority and, 39, 54–57; fear and, 59–60, 93
Black studies, 17, 72–74
Black teachers, in New Orleans, 34, 38
Black women, in Los Angeles, 126–27
Black youth, 1, 26–27; abolition and, 135–36; anti-citizenship and, 48–49, 86; coloniality and, 16; criminalization of, 85, 116; death of, 133–34, 152–53, 160; history and, 65n20, 77–78, 148–49; identity and, 46–47, 49, 54, 59; in New Orleans, 35;

Index   245

resistance and, 14, 134–35, 137, 139–41, 156–57; in schools, 142–53; suffering of, 133, 139; surveillance of, 85

Blaze Rods Elementary School, 46, 50, 54–62, 64n7

blues, 31; resistance and, 73–75, 167

Brooks, Joanna, 38–39

Brown v. Board of Education, 34, 159, 184–85

Bruce, La Marr Jurelle, 30

Bryant, Ma'Khia, 67–68, 98

bureaucracy, play and, 49–51, 57

CA. *See* California

CAFTA-DR. *See* Dominican Republic-Central America FTA

California (CA), laws of, 117–19. *See also* Los Angeles

Cannon, Katie G., 72–73

capital, 89, 222; cultural, 58; social, 60–62

capitalism: coloniality and, 15–16, 86, 88; hip-hop and, 75–76; play and, 62–63; racial/colonial order and, 105

carceral state, 67, 74–75, 79; Los Angeles and, 116; neoliberalism and, 38; schools and, 70–72; social practices and, 99–100

Cardi (student), 136, 143–59

Carruthers, Charlene, 78–79

Cartwright, Samuel, 29–30

Carver Collegiate school, 36–38

Carver Preparatory school, 36–38

Cavazos, Lauro, 184

change, 2–3, 206, 217; abolition and, 71–72; anti-citizenship and, 48–49; education and, 177–78; futures and, 15, 126–29, 164; new worlds and, 67, 163–70; otherwise worlds and, 27–28, 32, 36–38, 40–41, 166;

performative, 209, 211–12; radicalism and, 72, 129; school and, 158–59, 237; solutions and, 13, 62, 86, 104–5; survival and, 154–55, 166–67; transformation and, 94, 165, 176; world-making and, 75–80, 113, 213

charter schools, 34; in New Orleans, 36–41; segregation and, 32–33

chattel slavery, 25–26, 155

Chester, PA, 165–67

Chicano Blowouts, 177–78, 186–87

Chicano people: anti-citizenship and, 176–77, 188, 191–92; criminalization of, 179; identity and, 175; Mexican American and, 192n1; movements of, 17, 177, 186–87, 189–90; race and, 185–86

Chicano studies, 189–90; resistance and, 186–88

Chicano women, 179, 182–83

Chicano youth: activism and, 186–88; curriculum and, 177; protest and, 189–90, 192; resistance and, 175, 177–78, 181–91; schooling and, 181–83; as students, 186–87; transformation and, 176

childhood, normativity and, 45, 104

children, 65n22; familiar zones of, 50–51; power and, 45, 52–53, 56

choice, individualism and, 102–4

citizens, 9–10; civility and, 29, 75, 88–89, 113; fitness of, 175–76, 183–84, 190–91; "queering?," 110, 120–22, 125, 127, 129; violence and, 109, 126–27

citizenship, 1–4, 192n2; Americanization and, 181–83; binaries and, 129; Blackness and, 112–13, 120–21, 126–27, 141–42, 153; contradictions of, 122; individualism and, 51; liberalism and, 109; "Mexican Problem" and, 178–81; normativity and, 121,

Index

127, 129, 223; race and, 15–16; resistance and, 217–18; Salvadoran migrants and, 114–21; schooling and, 5–6, 181–82; students and, 118, 120, 124, 126; U.S., 48, 175–78
civic engagement, 55, 192; Black liberation and, 112–14; change and, 2–3; "good citizens" and, 10–12; violence and, 113
civics, hip-hop and, 77
civil disobedience, 189, 192
civility, 166; activism and, 11–12, 16, 211, 218; citizens and, 29, 75, 88–89, 113; Humanity and, 137, 142, 145, 160
Civil Rights Act, 123
Civil War, U.S., 29
C. J. (student), 54, 57–58
Clark, Victor S., 180
classifications, of race, 89
Clay, Kevin L., 75
Cohen, Cathy J., 139–40, 143
collectivity, 13, 15–16; anti-citizenship and, 10; Black joy and, 73–74; colonialism and, 109–10; play and, 60–62; self-governance and, 164, 166
Colón, Kristiana Rae, 169
colonialism, 202; collectivity and, 109–10; language and, 179, 182–83, 214–15; Palestine and, 204, 213–14, 217–18
coloniality: capitalism and, 15–16, 86, 88; enslavement and, 88–89
colonias, migration and, 180, 193n15
colonization, curriculum and, 186–87
community, 15–16, 53, 167; Black, 12–13, 165–66; interiority and, 47; isolation and, 61; Latinx youth and, 227; resistance and, 121; Salvadoran migrants and, 122–23, 125; the state and, 63; suburban, 109, 198, 222–25

compliance, 198; resistance and, 227; surveillance and, 93
Cone, James H., 73–74
conflict resolution, 52
consequences, 40, 94, 127; play and, 52
contexts: out-of-school, 96–102; research and, 91–92
contradictions: antiblack racism and, 101–2; of citizenship, 122; for students, 55, 88
cooperative learning, 45–48, 58
co-opted movements, 10, 212
counternarratives, 26, 38, 163, 177
Covid-19 pandemic, 200
criminality, 100, 119
criminalization: of Black youth, 85, 116; of Chicano people, 179; citizenship and, 120–21; gender and, 97–98; in Los Angeles, 111, 118–19, 124; out-of-school contexts and, 98–102; poverty and, 98–99
critical engagement: liberation and, 63; play and, 53, 59–60, 62
cultural capital, 58
culture, play and, 53–54, 58, 61–63. *See also* local culture
curriculum: administrators and, 208–9, 212, 215, 218; anti-Blackness and, 147–48; Chicano youth and, 177; colonization and, 186–87; Get Free, 76–79; teachers and, 202, 204, 207
customs of care, 53; play and, 58, 62; in poverty, 51

Dalton, Roque, 122
death, 67–68, 98, 166; of Black youth, 133–34, 152–53, 160; murder compared to, 210; social, 46, 137–39, 145, 169
decolonization, of schools, 217–19

Index

democracy, 4, 123; emancipation and, 2–3; radical, 112, 127–28; schooling and, 5–6, 39–40
destruction: of institutions, 75; schooling and, 16–17; of World, 134, 143, 153–54, 160
development, of Black girls, 86, 92; antiblack racism and, 102; punishment and, 96, 105; transformation and, 94
deviance, 143; behaviors and, 140, 227; survival and, 140–41; teachers and, 203
Diamond, John B., 231
diaspora: art and, 111, 125–26; Blackness and, 115; futures and, 126–29
disasters, 27; disparities and, 30–31
discipline: activism and, 210–11; Black girls and, 68, 70–71; poverty and, 51; in schools, 28–29, 55; students and, 200; teachers and, 145–47, 207–8
disconnection, with teachers, 104
disparities, disasters and, 30–31
disruption: neoliberalism and, 14; play and, 47–48, 62; in schools, 8–9; youth organizers and, 210–11
diversity, in schools, 38, 152, 198–202, 206, 214
dominant narratives, 29, 31, 34–35, 215–16
Dominican Republic-Central America FTA (CAFTA-DR), 115
Douglass, Frederick, 25–26
drapetomania, 27–30, 36
Dumas, Michael J., 69–70, 72
dysaethesia aethiopica, 28–30, 36

economics: migration and, 178–80; solidarity and, 110–11
education, 5; change and, 177–78; hiphop, 76–77; in New Orleans, 27,

31–34, 36; policies of, 11, 31–33, 37, 175, 177–78, 181–82, 184; white supremacy and, 28–29, 178, 184–88, 209, 214–15. *See also* schools
educational justice, 41
Ellis, Pearl Idelia, 183
Ellison, Ralph, 167
El Paso, TX, Houchen Settlement, 182–83
El Salvador, 123; anti-Blackness in, 109–10, 114–15, 124; slavery and, 116; U.S. and, 114–20, 127–28; violence in, 128
emancipation, 28–30, 188; democracy and, 2–3
embodiment: Black girls and, 68, 71; play and, 47, 49, 52–53, 60–63
enslaved people: coloniality and, 88–89; games and, 65n20; resistance and, 27, 29; U.S. and, 25–26
erasure, 160n1, 205; of Blackness, 135; survival and, 222, 236–37. *See also* invisibility
ethics, 52, 60, 64n17, 87, 144–45
ethnographic research: in Fun Middle School, 54–62, 64n1, 64n7; in La Vista, 221–22, 224–35; in New Orleans, 37–41; in TX, 90–104
excellence, Black, 12–13, 136, 144, 147, 152
exchange, of knowledge, 57–60, 77
exploitation, of labor, 116, 119, 124–25

fairness, for students, 55–57
familiar zones, 46, 49, 52, 64n17; anticitizenship and, 63; of children, 50–51; knowledge and, 58; play and, 53, 60
Fanon, Frantz, 72, 87
fantasy, liberation and, 69, 72–73, 80
fear: Black students and, 59–60, 93; race and, 116–17, 179, 190

248　　　　　　　　　　　Index

Federal Housing Administration
　(FHA), 1–3
federal policies, 1–3, 17, 117
FHA. *See* Federal Housing
　Administration
fitness, of citizens, 175–76, 183–84,
　190–91
Floyd, George, 209–10, 214
Foley, Douglas E., 8
Fourteenth Amendment, 68, 185–86,
　190
freedom, 9–10, 35; destruction and,
　17; Douglass on, 25–26; hip-hop
　and, 165–67; individual, 48–49;
　play and, 63; resistance and, 40,
　168–69; schools and, 156; students
　and, 29–30; survival and, 169–70;
　U.S. and, 116; violence and, 111;
　World and, 138
fugitive praxis, 67, 74
fugitivity: resistance and, 141; respon-
　sibility and, 169; schooling and,
　142–44; survival and, 157, 159
fungibility, of Slave, 137–39
Fun Middle School, 46; ethnographic
　research in, 54–62, 64n1, 64n7
futures, 15, 164; diaspora and, 126–29.
　See also change

GA. *See* Georgia
Galeano, Eduardo, 164
games, 61; enslaved people and, 65n20
gang membership: Blackness and,
　128–29; in Los Angeles, 116–20, 124
Garba, Tapji, 138
Gaunt, Kyra Danielle, 65n25
gender: criminalization and, 97–98;
　racial/colonial order and, 96, 98;
　violence and, 119; whiteness and,
　230–31
generational learning, 53, 57–58, 62
Georgia (GA), 46, 57–58

gestalt, social, 9–10, 15–16, 20n32
Get Free curriculum (Love), 76–79
Gillen, Jay, 6
Glenn, Evelyn Nakano, 4, 6
Gonzalez, Gilbert G., 180
"good citizens," 7; anti-citizenship
　and, 198, 203, 206–7; Black
　communities and, 12–13; civic
　engagement and, 10–12; students
　as, 207, 212, 216–19; teachers and,
　198, 203–5, 211–12
Gordon, Avery F., 169–70
Gordon, Lewis R., 87, 98
Grant, Carl A., 35
Grigsby, Juli, 126–27

Hannah (student), 234–35
Hartman, Saidiya, 28–29, 67, 168
hip-hop: local culture and, 165–67;
　world-making and, 75–79
history, 7, 204; Black youth and,
　65n20, 77–78, 148–49; Chicano
　people and, 177, 186–87; El Salvador
　and, 118–20
Homeland Security Act, U.S., 118
Hooks, Mary, 167–68
hope, 2, 13, 136, 143, 159
Houchen Settlement, El Paso,
　182–83
Housing and Urban Development
　(HUD), 1–3
Humanity, 87, 160n1; anti-citizens
　and, 153–59; Blackness and, 135–37;
　civility and, 137, 142, 145, 160
Humberto (student), 229
Hurricane Katrina. *See* post-Katrina
　New Orleans
Hurston, Zora Neale, 72–73

ideas, surveillance of, 93–94
identity: authenticity and, 199–201,
　223–24, 229–30; of Black youth,

46–47, 49, 54, 59; Chicano people and, 175; Latinx youth and, 221–22, 226–27; liberation and, 176–77; performance of, 223–25, 236–37; play and, 52–54; in research, 91–92, 136, 145; resistance and, 235–36; surveillance and, 92–96

Illinois (IL), La Vista, 221–22, 224–35

imagination, 3, 157–58, 164, 212, 216–17

Immigration Reform and Control Act (IRCA), 117, 120

imperialism, of U.S., 17, 178, 183–84, 204, 213–17

incarceration, schools and, 36–37, 70–71. *See also* carceral state

inclusion, predatory, 1–3

Indigeneity, 115–17, 121, 177, 207, 213

individual freedom, 48–49

individualism: antiblack racism and, 89, 127; choice and, 102–4; citizenship and, 51; neoliberalism and, 26–27, 40, 88, 105; schools and, 61

institutions, 212–13; destruction of, 75; responsibilities of, 209

interiority: community and, 47; Hurston and, 73

intimidation, teachers and, 205, 212

invisibility: Black girls and, 96; Blackness and, 87–88, 138; Palestine and, 214; in schools, 148; in U.S., 201

IRCA. *See* Immigration Reform and Control Act

isolation, community and, 61

Israel, 200; Palestine and, 197, 217; U.S. and, 207–8, 216–17

Jacobo (student), 228–29, 232–33

Jade (student), 90, 93–94

James, Joy, 71–72

joaning, 56, 65n25

Joaquín (student), 222, 226, 229–33

joy, 68; Black, 15, 67, 72–74, 79–80; hip-hop and, 78; play and, 61–63; teachers and, 69

Julio (student), 54–59

justice: antiblack racism and, 104; educational, 41; social, 147, 152, 206–9, 212

Kenzo (student), 90, 95, 101–3

Khaila (student), 89–90, 94–101

killings, police and, 135–36

knowledge, 34–35, 163; exchange of, 57–60, 77; liberation and, 114

LA. *See* Louisiana

labor: Blackness and, 87, 128; exploitation of, 116, 119, 124–25; Mexican immigrants and, 177–81, 193n15

language: assimilation and, 233–34; colonialism and, 179, 182–83, 214–15; surveillance of, 214–16

Latinos, Salvadoran migrants as, 117–18

Latinx youth, 18, 95–96, 237n1; academics and, 231, 235; anticitizenship and, 222–25; identity and, 221–22, 226–27; respectability politics and, 222, 235–36; in SHS, 228–35; solidarity and, 230–31

La Vista, IL, ethnographic research in, 221–22, 224–35

laws, of CA, 117–19

learning, 51; cooperative and, 45–48, 58; generational, 53, 57–58, 62

legitimacy, 7, 87, 164; citizenship and, 48

Lewis, Amanda E., 231

liberalism: citizenship and, 109; school and, 147

liberation, 14–15, 47–48; Black, 112–14, 134, 168; change and, 206; co-opted, 10, 212; critical engagement and, 63;

fantasy and, 69, 72–73, 80; identity and, 176–77; oppression and, 133; Palestine and, 18, 218–19; suffering and, 167–68; transformation and, 165

Liliana (student), 226–29

local culture, 32; hip-hop and, 165–67; in Los Angeles, 111, 123–25; play and, 60, 62, 77; teachers, 38

Lorde, Audre, 73, 79, 170

Los Angeles, CA, 184–85; assimilation in, 114, 116–17; Blackness in, 110–12; Black women in, 126–27; Chicano students in, 186–87; criminalization in, 111, 118–19, 124; gang membership in, 116–20, 124; Salvadoran migrants in, 109–10, 115–16, 121–25; Watts uprising in, 111–12

loss of opportunity, as punishment, 95–96

Louisiana (LA). *See* New Orleans

Louisiana Recovery School District (RSD), 33–34

Love, Bettina, Get Free curriculum of, 76–79

Maira, Sunaina Marr, 223

Marshall, T. H., 4, 6

MAS. *See* Mexican American Studies

Master, Slave and, 133, 154, 160n1

Matless, David, 7

Matsuda, Mari, 26

McKittrick, Katherine, 76

MEChA. *See* Movimiento Estudiantil Chicano de Aztlán

Mendez v. Westminster, 177–78, 184–86

mestizaje, 115, 124, 128

Mexican Americans. *See* Chicano people

Mexican American Studies (MAS), 189–90

Mexican-American War, 176, 192n2

Mexican immigrants, labor and, 177–81, 193n15

"Mexican Problem," 175–76, 190–92; citizenship and, 178–81

Mexican schools, 181–82; resistance and, 184–86

Mexico, U.S. and, 175–76, 178–80, 190–91

Michelle (student), 229–31

migrants: "crisis" of, 130n3; othering of, 116–17; Temporary Protected Status of, 120, 125. *See also* Salvadoran migrants

migration, 115; colonias and, 180, 193n15; economics and, 178–80

Mills, Charles W., 3

Mis-education of the Negro, The (Woodson), 5–6

Morel, Domingo, 10–11

Morris, Monique W., 68

movements: Black Lives Matter, 90, 208–13; Chicano, 17, 177, 186–87, 189–90; co-opted, 10, 212

Movimiento Estudiantil Chicano de Aztlán (MEChA), 187–88

multiculturalism, in U.S., 69, 123, 192, 199

Muñoz, José Esteban, 223

murder, 63, 68, 139, 147, 209, 214; death compared to, 210

Muslim women, 199, 208, 215; assimilation and, 202–3

Myers, Scott A., 8–9

NAACP Legal Defense and Educational Fund, 36

NAFTA. *See* North American Free Trade Agreement

narratives, 15, 27; counternarratives and, 26, 38, 163, 177; dominant, 29, 31, 34–35, 215–16; hip-hop and, 166 needs: of Black girls, 71–72; play and, 50, 65n22

neoliberalism: Blackness and, 75; disruption and, 14; individualism and, 26–27, 40, 88, 105; school reform and, 26–28, 30, 35, 38, 40–41; the state and, 33; subjectivity of, 102–4

New Orleans, LA: Black youth in, 35; charter schools in, 36–41; education in, 27, 31–34, 36; ethnographic research in, 37–41; post-Katrina, 26–27, 31–35, 38

new worlds, change and, 67, 163–70

normativity: Blackness and, 140–41; childhood and, 45, 104; citizenship and, 121, 127, 129, 223

North American Free Trade Agreement (NAFTA), 115

Obama, Barack, 130n3

obedience, authority and, 56–57

Ocho Jinks (student), 57–58

oppression, 12–13, 31–32, 73, 165; citizens and, 9–10; liberation and, 133; Palestinian, 203, 205, 213–14, 216; resistance to, 77, 187–88, 191; schools and, 177–78, 183–84

organizers, youth, 135, 143–44, 159, 210–11, 217

organizing practices, 163; activism and, 168–69, 192; of Salvadoran migrants, 121–26

Ortneer, Sherry B., 223

othering, of migrants, 116–17

otherwise worlds, 27–28, 32, 36–38, 40–41, 166. See also change

out-of-school contexts, 96–97; criminalization and, 98–102

PA. See Pennsylvania

Palestine: colonialism and, 204, 213–14, 217–18; Israel and, 197, 217; liberation and, 18, 218–19; schools and, 200–201, 204–5, 207–8, 216–17; U.S. and, 213–14

Palestinian people: oppression and, 203, 205, 213–14, 216; suffering and, 214–15; in U.S., 204–5

pandemic. See Covid-19 pandemic

Patterson, Orlando, 137

Pennsylvania (PA), Chester, 165–67

People of Color (POC), 160n1; in schools, 150–52, 155–56

People of Humanity (POH), 160n1

performance, 203; of allyship, 208–13; of authenticity, 233–35; of identity, 223–25, 236–37; play and, 47, 51–53; of stereotypes, 231–33; of whiteness, 227–31

performance scores, of schools, 32–33

performative change, 209, 211–12

plantation, schools as, 28–29, 134–35, 137, 149–50

play, 46, 65n20; Black girls and, 14–15, 45; bureaucracy and, 49–51, 57; critical engagement and, 53, 59–60, 62; culture and, 53–54, 58, 61–63; disruption and, 47–48, 62; embodiment and, 47, 49, 52–53, 60–63; joaning and, 56, 65n25; local culture and, 60, 62, 77; needs and, 50, 65n22; performance and, 47, 51–53

POC. See People of Color

poetics, anti-citizen, 166

POH. See People of Humanity

police, 11, 46, 57–60; Black youth and, 27; killings and, 135–36; violence of, 211–12

policies, 7, 49; education, 11, 31–33, 37, 175, 177–78, 181–82, 184; federal, 1–3, 17, 117; play and, 46; U.S., 114–15, 117–18

political agency, 8–9, 11

politics, 52, 221

252   Index

positionality, 13, 127, 177; in research, 90–92, 225
Possessing the Secret of Joy (Walker), 74
possibilities, for change, 113
post-Katrina New Orleans, 26–27, 31–35, 38
poverty, 1, 8, 46, 51; criminalization and, 98–99
power, 13, 38; children and, 45, 52–53, 56; survival and, 169–70; teachers and, 206, 218
praxis, 188; of anti-citizenship, 165, 167–69; fugitive, 67, 74; play as, 47–48
predatory inclusion, 1–3
privatization, of schools, 32, 39
protest: Chicano youth and, 189–90, 192; students and, 37–38, 40–41
punishment, 9, 55, 100; assimilation and, 202–3; development of Black girls and, 96, 105; resistance and, 139–40, 148–49; teachers and, 36–37, 70–71, 93, 95–97

"queering the citizen?," 110, 120–22, 125, 127, 129
queerness, Blackness and, 78–79, 145

race, 15–16, 89, 115; Chicano people and, 185–86; fear and, 116–17, 179, 190; neoliberalism and, 26–27
racial/colonial order, 86–89, 100, 102; Black girls and, 92–98, 104–5
racism, 28–30; anti-Blackness compared to, 133–34; structural, 13, 31–32, 75, 88. *See also* antiblack racism
radical Black joy, 68–69, 72–73, 75, 79–80; as fugitive praxis, 67, 74
radical democracy, 112, 127–28
radicalism, 11–12; change and, 72, 129

Rap City Flow (student), 90, 92–93, 103–4
Reagan, Ronald, 16, 117
research, 64n1; anonymity in, 64n7, 90, 143–44; identity in, 91–92, 136, 145; positionality in, 90–92, 225. *See also* ethnographic research
resistance, 47, 77, 87, 121, 227; anti-citizenship and, 4, 15, 105, 192n4; Black youth and, 14, 134–35, 137, 139–41, 156–57; blues and, 73–75, 167; Chicano youth and, 175, 177–78, 181–91; citizenship and, 217–18; enslaved people and, 27, 29; freedom and, 40, 168–69; identity and, 235–36; joy and, 72–74, 79–80; punishment and, 139–40, 148–49; school and, 5–6, 142–44
respectability politics, 11, 113, 139–40; Black girls and, 50, 56, 97–98; Latinx youth and, 222, 235–36; in schools, 136, 152
responsibilities, 12–13, 169, 209
Rethink NOLA, 36, 38–41
revolution, 11, 170; hip-hop and, 76
rights, 65n22, 68; in education, 177–78; schools and, 55
risk, 52, 63; Salvadoran migrants and, 120
Robeson, Paul, 164
Robinson, Cedric J., 129n2
Rodney, Walter, 168
Rose, Tricia, 75
ross, kihana miraya, 69–70, 72, 133
RSD. *See* Louisiana Recovery School District

safety, in schools, 38, 62, 157, 199, 209
Said, Edward, 201
Salaita, Steven, 205, 213, 217–18
Salvadoran migrants, 114, 119–20, 126; Blackness and, 128–29; as Latinos,

117–18; in Los Angeles, 109–10, 115–16, 121–25

schooling, 4, 16–17, 49, 143–44; anti-Blackness and, 134–36, 142, 145–53, 156; Chicano youth and, 181–83; democracy and, 5–6, 39–40; Latinx youth and, 236

schools, 8–9, 11, 17, 56–57, 60–61; abolition of, 144, 149, 151, 157, 159–60; anti-citizen in, 136–42, 155–56; behaviors in, 27, 157; Black youth in, 142–53; carceral state and, 70–72; change and, 158–59, 237; charter, 32–34, 36–41; decolonization of, 217–19; discipline in, 28–29, 55; diversity in, 38, 152, 198–202, 206, 214; incarceration and, 36–37, 70–71; liberalism and, 147; Mexican, 181–82, 184–86; oppression and, 177–78, 183–84; Palestine and, 200–201, 204–5, 207–8, 216–17; performance scores of, 32–33; as plantation, 28–29, 134–35, 137, 149–50; POC in, 150–52, 155–56; privatization of, 32, 39; reform of, 26–28, 30, 35, 38, 40–41; resistance and, 5–6, 142–44; safety in, 38, 62, 157, 199, 209; social justice in, 147, 152, 206–9, 212; solidarity and, 209–10; suburban, 222–25; survival in, 136, 149, 153; suspension in, 36–37, 145–47; tokenism in, 18, 198–200, 205–6, 214; violence and, 127, 136

SEA. *See* Southeast Asian students

segregation, 181; charter schools and, 32–33; in Los Angeles, 184–86

self-governance, collectivity and, 164, 166

Shields High School (SHS), 221–26, 228–35

Silver, Lauren J., 49–50

SJEP. *See* Social Justice Education Project

Slave, 137–39; Master and, 133, 154, 160n1

Slaveness, Blackness and, 134, 160n1

slavery: afterlife of, 28–29, 67–72, 76, 79–80; chattel, 25–26, 155; El Salvador and, 116

social capital, 60–62

social death, 46, 137–39, 145, 169

social gestalt, 9–10, 15–16, 20n32

social justice, in schools, 147, 152, 206–9, 212

Social Justice Education Project (SJEP), 188

social media, 125

social practices, 92, 98–100, 109

Sojoyner, Damien M., 11, 141

solidarity, 88, 122, 164; economics and, 110–11; Latinx youth and, 230–31; schools and, 209–10

solutions, change and, 13, 62, 86, 104–5

Sorentino, Sara-Maria, 138

Southeast Asian students (SEA), 151

specificity, Black, 149–50, 154–56, 159, 160n1

Spillers, Hortense, 34–35, 163–64

state, the: anti-citizen and, 9, 48–49; community and, 63; neoliberalism and, 33; schools and, 198; violence of, 16, 112–13, 216. *See also* carceral state

stereotypes, performance of, 231–33

structural issues, 16, 39, 126, 165, 236

structural racism and, 13, 31–32, 75, 88

structural violence, 123, 151, 209, 211, 216

struggle, 10, 17, 168, 235–36; citizenship and, 6

students, 29–30, 86, 151, 200, 203; accounts of, 37–39, 54–62, 92–104,

228–34; anti-citizenship and, 206–8; Chicano, 186–87; citizenship and, 118, 120, 124, 126; contradictions for, 55, 88; as "good citizens," 207, 212, 216–19; protest and, 37–38, 40–41; risks for, 52, 63

suburban communities, 109, 198, 222–25

suffering: of Black youth, 133, 139; joy and, 74; liberation and, 167–68; Palestinian, 214–15

surveillance, 36, 49; of Black youth, 85; identity and, 92–96; of language, 214–16

survival: change and, 154–55, 166–67; deviance and, 140–41; erasure and, 222, 236–37; freedom and, 169–70; fugitivity and, 157, 159; in schools, 136, 149, 153; whiteness and, 231

suspension, in schools, 36–37, 145–47

Tashima, A. Wallace, 190

El-Tayeb, Fatima, 121

Taylor, Breonna, 98, 210

Taylor, Keeanga-Yamahtta, 1–2

teachers, 14, 198, 202–4, 211, 236; activism and, 197; anti-Blackness and, 57; authority of, 54–55, 208; Black, 34, 38; discipline and, 145–47, 207–8; disconnection with, 104; fairness and, 55–56; identity and, 199–201; intimidation and, 205, 212; joy and, 69; power and, 206, 218; punishment and, 36–37, 70–71, 93, 95–97; surveillance and, 92–94; youth organizers and, 217

Teach for America, 34, 38

Temporary Protected Status, of migrants, 120, 125

Teo, Thomas, 88

Texas (TX), 86; El Paso, 182–83; ethnographic research in, 90–104

tokenism, in schools, 18, 198–200, 205–6, 214

transformation, 94, 176; liberation and, 165

Treaty of Guadalupe Hidalgo, 175–78, 185–86, 190, 192n2

Trump, Donald, 148, 183–84, 200

Tucson, AZ, Chicano Ethnic Studies in, 188–90

TX. *See* Texas

U.N. *See* United Nations

unaccompanied minors, adultification and, 118–19

Unicorn (student), 90, 93, 96–97

United Nations (U.N.), Convention on the Rights of the Child, 65n22

United States (U.S.), 31, 70, 89, 201; citizenship and, 48, 175–78; Civil Rights Act of, 123; Civil War, 29; El Salvador and, 114–20, 127–28; enslaved people and, 25–26; Homeland Security Act of, 118; imperialism of, 17, 178, 183–84, 204, 213–17; Israel and, 207–8, 216–17; Mexico and, 175–76, 178–80, 190–91; multiculturalism in, 69, 123, 192, 199; Palestine and, 213–14; Palestinian people in, 204–5

violence, 64n17, 111, 136–37, 150; Black youth and, 46; citizens and, 109, 126–27; in El Salvador, 128; gendered, 119; in Los Angeles, 110, 122; of police, 211–12; of the state, 16, 112–13, 216; structural, 123, 151, 209, 211, 216

Walker, Alice, Possessing the Secret of Joy, 74

Warren, Calvin, 135

Watkins, William H., 6

Index

Watts uprising, Los Angeles, 111–12
whiteness, 227; assimilation and, 228–29; gender and, 230–31
white supremacy, 10, 73–74; anti-Blackness and, 30–32, 139; education and, 28–29, 178, 184–88, 209, 214–15
Williams, Patricia, 69
Willis, Paul, 6, 8
women: Black, 126–27; Chicano, 179, 182–83; Muslim, 199, 202–3, 208, 215
Woods, Clyde, 31
Woodson, Carter G., 68; *The Miseducation of the Negro*, 5–6
World, 160n1; destruction of, 134, 143, 153–54, 160; freedom and, 138

world-making, 80, 113, 213; hip-hop and, 75–79. *See also* change
Wun, Connie, 68, 127

Xóchitl (student), 233

youth of color, 1, 3–6, 14. *See also* Black youth; Chicano youth; Latinx youth
youth organizers, 135, 143–44, 159; disruption and, 210–11; teachers and, 217

Zimmerman, Arely M., 122
Zuri (student), 55–57

Printed and bound by CPI Group (UK) Ltd, Croydon, CR0 4YY
09/05/2024

14500141-0002